Summer 1942: with the Afrika Korps less than a hundred miles from the Nile Delta, Erwin Rommel had succeeded in converting a 'side show' of the Second World War into a major offensive for the Axis powers. The British had been thrown back across the frontiers of Egypt until, at El Alamein, Rommel's army posed a serious threat to Cairo, Alexandria, and to the British communications with the Far East. And, in the distance, there lay the rich oilfields of the Middle East.

The charisma of the 'Desert Fox'—his romantic image, his dash and verve—has built up the legend of a heroic man of action and a military genius. His death in the final phases of the war, a martyr to Nazism, further enhanced a reputation that, after the war, grew still more—that of a soldier above politics, an emblematic figure of German chivalry and courage. Kenneth Macksey's new study of Rommel's battles and campaigns brings the cool eye of an expert in tank warfare to bear on the military exploits of this legend, and examines critically his achievements and failures.

An opportunist with a well-developed sense for the smell of victory, Rommel was worshipped by his troops. He could inspire them to great efforts, while his tactical flair—amounting even to brilliance on occasion—was well suited to seizing the initiative from British North African forces that were weakly and indecisively led. His offensive during the spring of 1941 caught the British completely off balance, and his advance in January 1942 to Benghazi and Gazala was, by any standards, a brilliant feat of arms. But the opportunist (off the battlefield as well as in action) was also an arrogantly ambitious man, and a ruthless glory seeker. Therein lay the seeds of his ultimate failure.

Rommel: Battles and Campaigns provides a perceptive and incisive analysis of his military operations from the First World War, when he performed outstandingly as a Company and Battalion commander in Rumania, Italy and France, through his North African campaigns, to his command in Normandy and the fatal (though false) implication in the 20 July bomb plot against Hitler. Lavishly illustrated, with maps and photographs, it provides a fresh—and frank—perspective on one of the great legends of military history.

Ethel K. Smith Library

Wingate University
Wingate, North Carolina 28174

Rommel

Battles and Campaigns

KENNETH MACKSEY

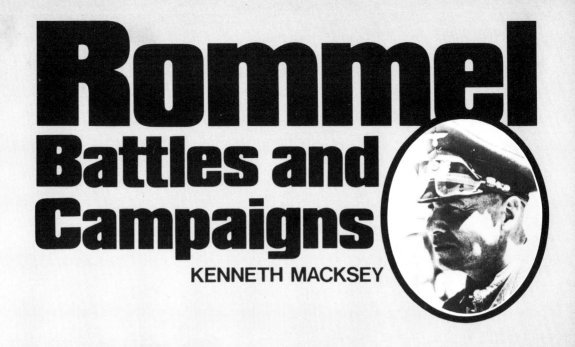

Mayflower Books
New York

Library of Congress Cataloging in Publication Data:
Macksey, Kenneth
Rommel: battles and campaigns.
1. Rommel, Erwin, 1891–1944. 2. Marshals – Germany –
Biography. 3. Germany. Heer – Biography. 4. World
War, 1939–1945 – Campaigns. I. Title.
U55.R6C47   940.54'23'0924 [B]   78–31786
ISBN 0–8317–7477–0

FIRST AMERICAN EDITION

Half-title illustration:
Rommel as Generalfeldmarschall. (Bundesarchiv)
Title page illustration:
*A Pz Kpfw III leads a column forward in preparation
for the Gazala offensive. (Bundesarchiv)*

Designed and edited by David Gibbons.
Picture research by John MacClancy.
Maps by Michael Haine. Diagrams by Anthony A. Evans.
Set, printed and bound in Great Britain by
Cox & Wyman Ltd,
London, Fakenham and Reading.

Contents

Introduction

This is the story of the campaigns and battles of Erwin Rommel – of those he fought against the enemies of his country and of those he fought to win the promotion that would enable him to lead troops and armies in combat. For Rommel was not among those of Germany's leaders who were born with silver spoons in their mouths. Whatever advances he made were won by struggle, often against established people and their systems: from the cradle to the grave, he was in conflict. In that competitive environment, pitted against a variety of hostile elements, he developed into a fighting animal who, once the tocsin had sounded, scarcely understood what it was to relax.

Rommel has been the subject of more books than almost any other Second World War general, a saturation which has enhanced his reputation, but which, at the same time, has frequently obscured his failings. As a pre-eminent member of the Third Reich's élite, whom Josef Goebbels and his Propaganda Ministry exploited to the utmost degree, he came to serve Germany as well after 1945 as he did during the war years themselves. While it well suited Goebbels' aims to exploit Rommel's battle-winning habits and charismatic personality to lift the nation's morale, it was also to post-war Germany's political advantage, in restoring her self-respect, that the memory of this 'beau sabreur' should be enhanced and closely associated with chivalry – and, above all, anti-Nazi ideals. In consequence, much that has been written about Rommel since 1945 falls short of the truth, with the result that even his qualities as a military commander have become exaggerated, distorted and misunderstood.

In changing societies, there is a continuing need to investigate prominent personalities (especially those who set standards of behaviour) and, if necessary, to adjust their position in the public eye. Does Rommel deserve his reputation? It could well be argued that there were some within the German military hierarchy of the Second World War who might justly have been accorded equal status with Rommel. So it is appropriate to examine more closely Rommel's own account of his First World War battles in *Infanterie Greift an*, and his published *Papers* concerning the Second World War, and to compare them with the written records and much else that has been revealed over the years by a host of close colleagues, mentors and detractors.

At the back of this book is a Bibliography from which I drew much of my material. Additionally, I am indebted to the following people, institutions and libraries for making available to me, with their usual helpfulness and generosity, items that hitherto have not seen the light of day, as well as to those who contributed fresh personal evidence: the US National Archives, the Library of the British Ministry of Defence, Hauptstaatsarchiv, Stuttgart; General der Kavallerie Siegfried Westphal; Manfred Rommel; Dr. Rainer Kesselring; Dr. Karl Ulrich Schroeder; H. von Luck; and Vice-Admiral Friedrich Ruge.

Finally, I wish to express my thanks to Reinhold Drepper for his indefatigable work in translating German sources; to Felicity Northover for typing the manuscript; and to my wife for her usual unfailing encouragement and for reading the proofs.

Kenneth Macksey, Beaminster, 1979

The Education of a Tactician

The realization of a man's ambition is possible only within the limitations imposed by his physiology and psychology. If, in addition to exploiting their natural endowments to the full, illustrious leaders could but detect, evaluate and subjugate their frailties, how much more contented and effective they might be, and how different the course of history. Consider the biographical details of the 'Great Captains': how many of them managed to check the onward rush of their careers before becoming overstretched by sheer exhaustion or by attempting feats beyond their capacity? In particular, recall to mind the men of action who sought fame at the cannon's mouth, and ask how many of them considered in any depth the consequences of their search for glory. Few among the brave will publicly admit to failings or to constraints that have, at times of crisis, held them back. It is extremely rare for a courageous, ambitious hero to restrain himself when the target of his ambition is in sight and, seemingly – temptingly – within reach. Frequently in the past, even the strongest of characters have been urged on by impetuous aspiration to overreach themselves, and have been dashed to pieces on the hard rocks of destiny.

Yet at least one famous twentieth-century soldier, eager at an early stage of his career to acquire laurels, was tentatively aware of his defects, and prepared to reveal them to a wider public. In writing about his early experience of combat, Erwin Rommel, warrior in one war and martyred commander in the next, did more than merely explain the tactical philosophy that would later form the cornerstone of his methods as a higher commander: he also exposed both his inner motivations of strength and his weaknesses in physique and character that would bring him triumph and tragedy. Published in 1937, *Infanterie Greift an* ('Infantry Attacks') is an anthology of his lectures while an Instructor

at the Infantry School, Dresden. They provide a revelation of modern tactical methods, and an insight into the (at times, irrational) driving force of an aggressively cunning, fighting animal. In a highly personal manner, it paints a very flattering picture of its author and gives a foretaste of the propaganda campaign that was to win for him the public adulation of a knightly victor in battle. At the same time, it illuminates the flaws that led to his failures at the hands both of his intellectual superiors and of his enemies in North Africa and Normandy. *Infanterie Greift an* warrants far closer examination than it has been given by Rommel's successive biographers.

Take, for a start, Rommel's frank admission of a severe physical disability even before he first heard a shot fired in anger. Even as his sub-unit, the 7th Company of the 124th Infantry (6th Württemberger) Regiment, was crossing the frontier during the invasion of Luxembourg and Belgium in August 1914, he was suffering from an acute stomach complaint. That is not so very unusual with fighting men and, as the rumble of guns comes closer, nothing for any man to be ashamed of. But with Rommel it was sometimes a chronic disability and one to which, characteristically, he would not yield, "... for I did not want to be regarded as a shirker". It may be, as Desmond Young says, that the trouble was caused by food poisoning. At the same time, it cannot be overlooked that the same defect was frequently to plague him on subsequent occasions when the strain was intense and the battlefield environment of low sanitation and poor diet overcame his resistance, undermined his will and distracted his concentration. If, at the age of 22, after only a few days' strenuous combat, his physical state was in collapse and he felt compelled to write: "the terrible condition of my stomach had sapped the last ounce of my strength. I must have been unconscious for some time", it is reasonable to take critical note of similar admissions from his own pen when he held the destiny of something more than a platoon in his hands.

Nevertheless, Rommel's performance in battle in the days to come was to indicate with precision the essential features of this natural soldier's capabilities. Rashness and impetuosity may have been the primary impression he gave his superiors as well as his subordinates when, on 21 August at Bleid in Belgium, he found his advanced guard of three men face to face with a score of Frenchmen. His instant reaction was not to call up the rest of his platoon, but to jump into the open, firing on the enemy, killing some, but then coming under hot fire from the rest. Even so, with surprise made forfeit, he dashed headlong among an enemy who was far from shaken, and was lucky to escape as he did. This inconclusive action illustrates his own immaturity as well as that of the enemy. The inability of the French to hit these foolhardy Germans and the brash folly of Rommel for taking such a risk were the activities of green soldiers who are soon killed or who, through subsequent caution, survive. But Rommel was ever to be the same, regularly putting boldness before prudence, and frequently committing dangerous errors as a result. Later at Bleid, he assembled his platoon for an unsupported but most carefully and guilefully prepared assault upon the village. This succeeded in the most praiseworthy manner, but he let his men get out of control and incur quite unnecessary casualties, exposing his exhilarated followers to fire from French flanking positions covering the exits from burning houses. When noting the lessons of this encounter he was to write: "An attack on a village is usually accompanied by heavy casualties and should be avoided whenever possible. Pin down the enemy by means of fire or blind him with smoke and hit him outside the village or town." Twenty-six years later in France, in somewhat similar circumstances, it would be seen to what extent he remembered this.

Again and again in the days to come, he drove himself beyond the point of endurance. His narrative presents a tale of miraculous good fortune in the utmost peril, as his regiment joined the advance on Verdun. "Bullets struck around me, throwing dirt in my face. The man on my left cried out and rolled on the ground in pain . . . I crawled to him but he was past help." For future use, he was to conclude that "it is advisable to have a number of machine-guns well forward. It will be necessary to fire them on the move in case of chance encounters or while engaged in the assault." This was a philosophy he would adapt admirably to mobile, tank warfare in 1940. But repeatedly he was to press too far ahead and find himself well out of touch with support. Intensely excited by the thrill of battle, it was he who had to play every part: Rommel who had to wend his way back to get the rest of his company or battalion to catch up; dashing off on horseback to make contact with laggardly flank units; and, all too often, Rommel whose men found themselves so far ahead of the kitchens that they were without food or supplies. This is not to decry a man of quite outstanding gallantry; but bravery has its limits, and high casualties are not always justifiable, no matter how deeply felt a commander's compassion for those who fall. He admits, for example, that a heavy price was paid on 7 September 1914 when, prematurely "believing that enemy resistance was over, we abandoned our assault formation in depth and brought the reserves and machine-guns up to the front line . . . The enemy opened up on us with well-aimed rifle fire at 150 yards."

He was next to learn the agonies of defeat, and to experience the enervating consequences of retreat. In mid-September, while pulling back from the almost-completed encirclement of Verdun, and after the German Army on the Marne had been out-manoeuvred, he discovered what it was like to heave desperately at the wheels of artillery stuck in the muddy tracks of the Argonne, and to march with little food for twelve hours at a stretch on the way to an undisclosed destination. "Exhausted men were beginning to drop out with increasing frequency", he wrote. "At every halt the men ... were sound asleep ... every one of them had to be shaken awake. We marched, halted and marched again. I was constantly going to sleep and falling from my horse ... My stomach was in a terrible condition both day and night. I lost consciousness frequently."

Eventually, Rommel was to take one risk too many. With his rifle jammed and the enemy but twenty paces distant, "the bayonet was my only hope ... Even with odds of three to one against me I had complete confidence in the weapon and my ability." But the French shot straighter this time, and he was lucky to escape with a wound in his upper left leg, leaving him to be rescued by his men before he bled to death. A few days later, glowing with pride, he received the Iron Cross, Second Class, the first of many decorations to come. This was his initiation into the cult of Glory, and he unconstrainedly wrote it down for all to read in 1937, when his star was in the ascendant in Nazi Germany.

"A very promising young officer"

How did it come about that this young Württemberger found himself so exalted by war? Not, it may be assumed, through any deep family tradition or heredity in the military sphere, for the Rommels of Heidenheim, where Erwin was born on 15 November 1891, were schoolmasters for two generations before him, mathematicians both. Erwin's later boyhood was spent in the tranquil calm of the Realgymnasium at Aalen, where his father was headmaster from 1898 until his death in 1913. True, Rommel senior had once served a short spell in the artillery, but that had nothing much to do with his son's sudden resolve to join the Army as an officer cadet (Fähnenjunker) in 1910. In fact, the Army was Erwin's second choice, for his original desire to be an engineer had been firmly discouraged by his father. One might ask why a mathematician should deter his second son from so laudable and profitable a pursuit as engineering and then, within a few weeks, willingly allow the youth to join up as a simple infantryman? This is but one

of several bewildering questions posed whenever Erwin Rommel's academic qualifications come under consideration, the first recorded instance of his entry into an 'intellectual' sphere being blocked. Unhappy experiences such as these were to inject the thwarted aspirant with a discernible grudge against authority, a diffidence when dealing with 'enlightened' individuals (as Desmond Young points out when he refers to Rommel's pronounced scholastic inability becoming evident when he found his classmates moving ahead of him). However, not only did Professor Erwin Rommel undoubtedly hold a sceptical opinion of his second son's academic ability, he also knew him to be ill disciplined. The boy had sometimes played truant, and only in his late teens did he rouse himself to scrape through important exams. In other words, he needed a firm hand from above. One of the less expensive regiments of the Army, the father seems to have concluded, would be a suitable home for this rather pale lad, who at least generated frenetic energy in fencing, mountaineering and athletics, and whose frugal management of a small allowance threatened no fear of high living or insolvency. A commission in the none-too-fashionable 6th Württembergers might accomplish what Professor Rommel had failed to achieve at home and in school.

And, as soon became evident, the Army, suited Rommel. It stirred his sense of dedication to service, and this, allied to an instinctive knack for dealing with the rank and file, made him a fine trainer of men. To the Army, too, he owed his meeting with Lucie Maria Mollin while he was attending his initial course at the War Academy in Danzig in 1911. The encouragement given by this forceful daughter of a Prussian landowner was to be vital. Without her patient yet thorough urging, he could well have failed his examinations, and might never have struggled to a place in the Regiment upon which to build his reputation. As it was, the impression he made upon his superiors was that of a good troop officer, one who might one day reach the rank of major if he was lucky, but whose chances of entering the coveted ranks of the General Staff were remote. Luck, however, which so frequently was to smile upon him at crucial moments, did so to good effect in 1914. The war provided him with the chance to demonstrate his most pronounced attribute, a natural, practical ability as a leader of men in battle. Rommel's commanding officer, Colonel Stein, was sure of this when he wrote his report in 1913, praising his "strong character, great will-power and zeal". "He worked", went on Stein, "with great energy and achieved much as an athlete ... as well as in the rôle of platoon and patrol leader" – an opinion reinforced, no doubt, by the occasion when, by sheer speed of movement, Rommel outmanoeuvred during an exercise the best company commander in the Regiment. In conclusion, he noted that Rommel was "a very promising young officer. A highly regarded comrade who lives within his means."

The boost that the award of the Iron Cross, Second Class, gave to Rommel's career was important, but it is appropriate to remark that very few of the German officers of distinction who later came to write their memoirs bothered to record their own receipt of this lowly medal. Neither Heinz Guderian nor Albert Kesselring, paragons of the Army whose qualities Rommel would have good reason to appreciate in the years to come, mentioned their receipt of the Iron Cross, First Class. For Rommel, however, fame had applied its spur; fierce ambition now imparted a relentless driving force which lasted for the rest of the war – indeed, for the remainder of his career.

The Iron Cross, First Class, was given to Rommel for his part as company commander in a raid on the French in the Charlotte valley of the Argonne on 29 January 1915. This was an operation of the sort that was commonplace in the trench warfare that now embraced the entire Western Front after the initial German invasion of 1914 had been frustrated. However, Rommel's performance on this occasion was by no means commonplace. The part his 9th Company was to play on the flank of the main attack seems to have been supplementary to the original scheme, but, according to Rommel, the Battalion Adjutant arrived to say that the main attack was going well and would Rommel "care to join in the fun" – just the sort of invitation he could never refuse. At first, things did not go too well, and the leading platoon commander and his men, faced by an obstacle, went to ground and declined to advance farther. Having discovered a safer way round to the flank, Rommel curtly informed the junior officer that he could either take that route or be shot on the spot ... and the reluctant troops may well have been surprised, a short while later, to find themselves alive and one mile deep into the enemy position. But by then, though in possession of a strong French fortification, they were in greater trouble still, for Rommel's enthusiasm and the sight of an enemy in confusion obliterated caution, short

of ammunition though he was. Growing bolder, he led the Company yet farther into enemy territory, well ahead of the rest of the Battalion (which had not the faintest idea where he was going) and straight into a trap as French reserves closed in. By now, he was completely out of ammunition and encumbered by five wounded men. Surrender might have been excusable, but not to Rommel. Abandoning the wounded, he executed a swift about-turn and led the survivors through a narrow unguarded corridor, pell-mell for safety, in a charge that might more accurately be described as headlong flight. Both the débâcle and his description of it in *Infanterie Greift an* are highly revealing c the essential Rommel, with his ruthles determination, thorough understanding c the vital need to maintain momentum – a well as his beastliness to junior officers. H paints the picture in vivid colours to his ow advantage, omitting any suggestion of erro on his part in leading his Company into suc trouble. Indeed, as an observation on thi adventure he wrote: "It was unfortunate tha neither the Battalion nor the Regiment wa able to exploit the 9th Company's success." A later generation of superior officers woul become wary of Rommel's trait of blamin others for his own indiscretions, and of hi

self-centred tendency to warp overall strategy by a local success.

Throughout the rest of 1915 and the first half of 1916, he remained engaged in the nagging trench warfare of the Western Front. Not once did his eagerness for a fight flag, despite innumerable narrow shaves. In fact, there is ample evidence that, despite suffering from fear, he managed to subjugate it to his will. It is possible that he was one of that rare breed whom danger and fear stimulate, since it was mainly when in danger that his inspiration waxed strongest. Out of the line, in repose, he was kindly. In battle, a characteristic of insensitivity for others became pronounced, together with supreme confidence in his own destiny, based possibly upon an innate belief in his own indestructibility.

With the Alpine Corps

His chances of survival were enhanced when his Regiment was sent to the Vosges, a move that saved him from the artillery maelstrom engulfing Verdun and the Somme in 1916 (where an individual infantryman's skill was of little account). It was further to his advantage when he was transferred to the Württemberg Mountain Regiment in October 1915, and given an intensive course in mountain warfare. This was to pave the way to his career as an outstanding combat leader, for in such a specialist assault force, his flair for mobility and initiative would be developed to the full. With them, he took post in the Vosges mountains and engaged in raids, mostly by night, on the French occupying this 'quiet' sector of the Western Front. Under ideal conditions, methodically and in his own time, he was here able to develop techniques of stealth and guile with the maximum resort to intensive fire support – an ideal preparation for the wars of movement to come.

Towards the end of November 1916, a few weeks after his unit had been transferred to the Rumanian Front, he took a short leave to marry "Lu", as he called her in his daily letters. Their five years' courtship had developed into a love-match of the most enduring quality, but, despite this, one is left with the feeling, after reading the published sources, that she was to take second place to the Army and his career. Patriotism urged him on, but the evidence of his pen and the comments of his closest colleagues portray an individualist absorbed in his profession to the exclusion of practically everything else. War was almost the sole subject of his reading; he cared not for the other arts and, in the company of his social equals, would often lapse into a deep silence, seemingly lost for conversation. Conviviality and relaxation he found much easier among the rank and file, with whom he would mix and jest in the rough Swabian dialect. Indeed, it was his sympathy for the men, rather than for his brother officers (with a few exceptions), that set him apart. The number of words he expends on descriptions of the suffering of the wounded and the praise he gives to non-commissioned ranks, to the virtual exclusion of his junior officers, indicate a clear bias. Of those officers, he demanded nothing more than he asked of himself: and, while many

Below:
A river-crossing operation by the German Army in Rumania, 1916. (Bundesarchiv)

Left:
*Men of the
Alpine Corps
standing beside a
monument to
their achieve-
ment in capturing
the Red Tower
Pass in Rumania,
1916. (Bundes-
archiv)*

another newly-married man might have taken fewer risks, Rommel, in the words of one friend, "was just the same, just as tough, just as regardless of danger, *just as pre-occupied with winning the war in his particular sector*". The italics are mine, since that phrase does seem to underline Rommel's self-centred approach to war-making, his preoccupation with events on his own front regardless of the overall demands of those set above him or positioned to a flank. True, as his closest comrade, Hermann Aldinger, was to say, "If Rommel was on your flank you knew you had nothing to worry about ..." and, less convincingly, "In those days he believed that every order must be carried out exactly ...". But already, in fact, he was fostering within himself a habit of insubordination which, in certain circumstances, would generate mistrust.

His wedding took place in Danzig, during an interval in the overtures to the German offensive aimed at driving the Rumanian Army out of its own country and at checking the Russians, who had come to the side of their allies in the aftermath of the Brusilov Offensive. Rommel was to find his Company opposed by an enemy already dispirited by setbacks and only too willing to give way before a determined charge – especially if it were heavily supported by artillery fire and concentrated machine-gunning at 200-yards range. The battle groups of the élite Alpine unit now had the character of storm troops, which, like the commandos of the next war, could be employed to spearhead special missions against key objectives.

Returning from leave in December, he was almost at once on the march again, part of the Alpine Corps driving back a reinforced enemy into the Magura Odobesti range during a session of winter fighting at altitudes up to 3,300 feet, where the temperature in January fell as low as minus 10°C. At times, he would lead small patrols deep between the enemy positions, utilizing the folds of steep and wooded slopes, and laying telephone cables to observation posts well in the Rumanian rear. On these occasions, he and three or four companions might spend days on end lying in isolation in the freezing cold. At other times, his men would descend like ghosts upon astonished Rumanians, putting them to rout. Systematically, he recorded the lessons of each action for future reference. "Reconnaissance must be active while the troops are resting," he noted – which meant that, for the officers (and, above all, for himself), there was to be no rest. "It is important

to move towards the enemy with weapons at the ready (safety catches off, submachine-guns ready for shooting), for he who fires first wins because he can deliver the heaviest fire." This would become routine procedure in later days, but in early 1917 it was by no means common.

In August 1917, as a mere Oberleutnant, his reputation was such that his advice was frequently sought by all manner of senior officers on the most profitable tactics to be adopted in a variety of situations. They recognized his skill in appreciation of ground and his gift for sensing the timing of a stroke and how best to catch the enemy at a complete disadvantage. As a result, they were prepared to let him lead anything up to four companies among the most complicated terrain, well knowing that his sense of direction was unerring. They also learnt that he could perform miracles of endurance.

For a spell in May 1917, Rommel and his battle groups were sent back to France, to their old stamping ground in the Vosges. But in August, they were once more on the Rumanian Front, in reserve, as part of the élite Alpine Corps that was to play a prominent part in the culminating offensive. Before them loomed steep heights more than 3,000 feet high, with slopes swept by skilfully deployed fire. Once the attack had started, Rommel's group was committed: employing the technique of advanced scouting by a small party carrying a telephone to report weaknesses in the enemy line (the radios of the day being far too big and fragile for such work), Rommel led his men through the gaps. Making full use of each fold in the ground, he seemed to sense as much as detect the enemy's presence even in the dark. He was now embarked on a battle that was to last eleven days with but the slightest respite, sustained by short, snatched hours of sleep made restless, on his own frank admission, by tingling nerves. To make this exhausting and nerve-wracking experience worse, he received a nasty wound in the forearm on the second day. But his spirit and resolve, according to his own story, was unbending. Refusing for three days to relinquish command on account of his wound, he persisted in leading his men from the front, in seemingly endless attacks, defences and counter-attacks. Though his nerves were stretched and his body weary, his ingenuity was inexhaustible. Each move was planned with care, within the framework of the drill to which his men had become accustomed by meticulous training.

Right:
*A machine-gun
post high in the
mountains.
(Bundesarchiv)*

On the day that Rommel received his wound, Mount Cosna fell, and this was the prelude to a bitter struggle in which the Rumanians, whose resistance was exemplary and ardour in counterattack courageous, threw in everything. In his book, Rommel spares them the derision he heaps upon the French (and was later to heap on the Italians). But, at the same time, he denies them praise even when recording their successes.

For a few hours he retired to have his wound dressed, "completely exhausted"; but he was soon back for an intensive phase of defensive fighting that gave him slightly more time for repose, even though at one time he was placed in command of no fewer than 16 companies – more than the strength of the entire regiment, a fact he proudly points out in *Infanterie Greift an*. This was a superb example of the German procedure of combining separate units or sub-units into ad hoc

battle groups under the command of the best man on the spot. He remarks that, although exhausted, "we were in fine spirits" and, in his reflections about the episode as a whole (while mourning the 60 dead and 500 wounded among his young troops), he recalls it as his greatest achievement to date, looking back on those "days as a commander of such troops with intense pride and joy".

Caporetto to the Piave

More splendid triumphs were to come. In early October, recovered from his wound, he was able to rejoin his Battalion in Carinthia, ready for employment on the Italian Front, where a combined German and Austro-Hungarian offensive was projected in order to at last smash the Italians on the Isonzo. Here, the infantry infiltration tactics that the Germans had initiated so auspiciously in 1917 and demonstrated with verve against the

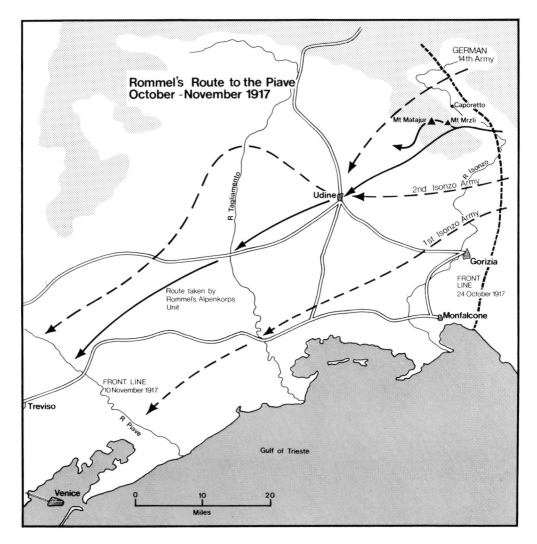

**Rommel's Route to the Piave
October - November 1917**

GERMAN
14th Army

Caporetto

Mt Matajur ▲ ▲ Mt Mrzli

R Isonzo

2nd Isonzo Army

Udine

1st Isonzo Army

R Tagliamento

Gorizia

FRONT
LINE
24 October 1917

Route taken by
Rommel's Alpenkorps
Unit

Monfalcone

FRONT LINE
10 November 1917

Treviso

R Piave

Gulf of Trieste

Venice

0   10   20
Miles

Russians at Riga and against the Rumanians at Mount Cosna, provided a key, linked to the revived technique of a short, concentrated bombardment, which would unlock the mountain front barring the way into Italy.

In *Infanterie Greift an*, Rommel catches the mood of excitement as the assault force secretly assembled east of the River Isonzo, and describes the long night marches and the careful concealment of men and guns in daylight – which in no way deluded the Italians as to the danger that threatened. But, as well as the thrill of impending action, he also mentions the underlying weakness of the German Army in the way "these night marches made great demands on the poorly fed troops". Already, the Allied naval blockade, which Germany could not break, was producing malnutrition among the Central Powers: prolonged physical efforts, as yet but slightly assisted by mechanization, were proving

beyond the troops' fighting stamina. And, since the demands placed on the Alpine Corps, with Rommel among its stars, required near-impossibilities of endurance by its picked men, it was scarcely likely that formations of lower grade could long maintain intensive campaigning.

Fortunately for the Germans, the Italians were at once routed, stunned by an initial assault delivered in poor visibility and driving rain on a wide front on 24 October, and ripped apart by a fifteen-mile-wide rent torn in their lines. The catastrophic collapse of Italian morale, the wholesale surrenders and the massed departure of more than a quarter of a million men in abject flight may be ascribed to a variety of reasons ranging from war-weariness to inept leadership. But nothing could have been more demoralizing than to find the enemy swiftly and aggressively infiltrating in strength and depth

among their defences. Taken by surprise in flank and then in rear, even the staunchest troops have been known to give way. Rommel's impressions during the first few hectic days were marked by the realization that his rapid advance towards the main objective of Mount Matajur (upon which, it was said, the Pour le Mérite, Prussia's equivalent to the Victoria Cross and the Congressional Medal of Honor, hung for the first to reach it) was made easier because, at the outset, the enemy was broken. His claim that one Württemberg Mountain Trooper was worth twenty Italians could have been applied to practically any other German or Austrian unit involved. None of this, however, diminishes the praise due to Rommel for leading his troops so dextrously across the most difficult peak country, progressively undermining enemy resistance as he advanced into the hills. In a single sentence he sums up his battle philosophy prior to the final assault on Mount Mrzli, the penultimate peak before Matajur: "I had the impression that I must not stand still or we were lost." In other words, movement was protection – a precept that all the great German armoured commanders of the next war were to understand and practise.

According to Rommel, the 1,500 Italians defending Mount Mrzli surrendered at call to him on the 26th after three days' ceaseless combat, and this opened wide the way to Matajur. Here, his contribution was certainly immense. Scarcely halting to gather prisoners, but putting them in the charge of three men, he pressed on in the hope that following troops would make all secure. With but 100 men, supported by the six heavy machine-guns at his disposal – and not the slightest chance of help from elsewhere – Rommel briefly considered, and as quickly rejected, the notion of obeying orders forbidding farther advance, for that would allow the flanking 12th Division to capture Matajur. Employing intensive machine-gun cover, he attacked and, at once, the Italians began to give way; crossing a crest, they saw on the road below them the entire 2nd Regiment of the Italian Salerno Brigade formed up and placidly laying down its arms – all 35 officers and 1,200 men of it. Pressing forward again, and leaving only the scantiest guard for so many prisoners, Rommel at last found himself within striking distance of Matajur, little knowing that an advanced guard of the German 12th Division was also approaching from the other side. Indeed, so intent were the Italians on this Division that they did not notice Rommel until he was among them.

The mountain peak was now Rommel's. But, to his intense rage, the supreme credit for this achievement was accorded to others! For

Above right:
*The field
headquarters of
General von
Below,
commander of
Fourteenth Army
on the Isonzo
Front. Note the
communications
centre in the
foreground.
(Bundesarchiv)*

the capture of Mrzli a Pour le Mérite was given to a Bavarian Lieutenant, Ferdinand Schörner, while the same coveted decoration was received by a Silesian Lieutenant named Walther Schneiber who had actually captured another peak altogether. Rommel's indignation would take years to assuage. The record of his protests includes what amounted to a demand that he should receive the Pour le Mérite as his just reward, plus a determined (and, eventually, successful) campaign after the war to persuade the Official Historian to amend the record by crediting him with the lion's share of the praise.

The Mrzli-Matajur action was but the preliminary to a succession of exhausting episodes in chasing the Italians to the River Piave. Pursuit was a facet of warfare in which Rommel was to become a master, and the essence of it he learnt here in Italy. Time and again, he was to discover the merit of keeping a demoralized enemy on the move by swift, head-on attacks, rather than allowing him time to recover by deploying widely to the flanks. Shock and surprise reduced the risks to himself and kept his opponent in a state of nervous tension. He became accustomed to taking evasive action when ambushed by Italian rearguards, depended upon captured supplies to sustain his own advance, and gave little consideration to his own logistic

support. Frequently, he found himself almost out of ammunition, a supply of which was always crucial to him in this war, since his expenditure in attack was colossal, his experience telling him that intensive machine-gun fire was, in itself, a splendid psychological means of persuading the Italians to abandon their positions prior to attacking them. To sustain mobility, petrol would be the vital commodity during the next war, but in the First World War it was muscle power that counted: on horseback or on a bicycle, he urged his men forward at a terrific rate, driving them almost to the point of collapse.

The crossing of the River Piave at Dogna on 9 November provides a fine example of Rommel's bold infiltration of small parties across an obstacle. Arriving on the west bank, under fire and short of ammunition, he began coolly collecting the prisoners who had emerged in droves from nearby Longarone. However, not satisfied with establishing a tenuous foothold, he decided to attack Longarone itself that night, having rejected the more prudent course of waiting for an enemy, vastly his superior in numbers, to attack him as the only way of escape from a trap. A passive method, according to his own account, "was not according to my taste". But this time he had overstretched himself. The Italians fired back with asperity, and his own arrangements, too hastily made, fell apart. Ruefully, he commented as his advance stopped dead: "Machine-gun fire at eighty yards, without a chance of taking cover, is enough to drive one crazy." This time, the Italians were on top, and Rommel was on the run with unpleasant losses; the Italians gathered themselves for a charge which totally overwhelmed the Germans, and Rommel himself was bowled over, but managed to escape in the confusion and darkness. The rest of his party were captured. Inevitably, at daybreak, when strong German reinforcements arrived from the east, the Italians in Longarone found further resistance impossible. But it is arguable that Rommel might have achieved the same result at negligible cost, had he desisted from his unnecessary charge.

By now, the pursuit had lost its momentum, as men and supplies became exhausted. The December battles reverted once more to affairs of attrition with their accompanying heavy casualties, as the Italians regained confidence and began to apply counter-pressure. For Rommel, it was the last advance of the war. On 18 December, together with his commander, Major Sprösser, he at last received by post the Pour le Mérite and, on 7 January 1918, they were both sent on leave to

Below:
Tired German infantry near the end of their advance into Italy while Italian prisoners are taken to the rear in lorries. (Bundesarchiv)

Right:
Proudly wearing his Pour le Mérite, Rommel (seated right) poses with the staff during his only spell away from regimental duty during the First World War. (Image Press)

recuperate and enjoy the public adulation reserved for the Fatherland's chosen heroes.

This, for Rommel, was the last of the fighting he was to experience in the First World War. "... to my great sorrow," he wrote, "I was not to return to the Mountain troops. I was attached to a higher headquarters [LXIV (Württemberg) Corps] and later to the staff of a Bavarian Landwehr regiment as assistant staff officer." It was a phase of his career in which, quite obviously, he took no delight: one in which, on the testimony of a fellow staff officer at the time, Karl Strölin, he was unhappy, and one that was barren of laurels. The front held by LXIV Corps throughout the last year of the war stood to the east of the Vosges, covering Alsace. While the rest of the Western Front was in turmoil, the armies moving greater distances and with greater mobility than at any time since 1914, LXIV Corps remained stationary, in trenches that had changed but little in alignment since the beginning of the war. From the Corps headquarters at Colmar, Rommel could only sniff the Front from afar and, as an Escort Officer (Ordonanz-Offizier) and, latterly, third grade staff officer to the Chief of Operations, quite clearly, could make little impression. There is nothing to be found among his records to suggest that his superiors regarded him as worthy of advancement in the intellectual sphere, although, on 25 October 1918, his name appeared for the first time on the monthly list as an officer fit to command a battalion. However, there was no General Staff recommendation. When the war ended, he was returned almost at once to regimental duty, where the best natural leaders of men were desperately required.

2

The Limbo of Peacetime

During the years following the end of the First World War, the entire political fabric of Germany was torn to shreds, and it became evident that the very best men available would be required if the task of reconstruction was to be achieved. Mutinies throughout the armed forces would have to be suppressed and a new Army built upon the ruins of the old. Despite the impediments of the Peace Treaty (the so-called Versailles Diktat), which prohibited possession of modern offensive weapons such as heavy artillery, tanks, gas and military aircraft, ingenious ways had to be found to solve a multiplicity of problems in a hostile political environment. So the most careful selection was undertaken from among those of the old officer corps who wished to remain to fill 4,000 vacancies in the 100,000-man Army.

Why, therefore, was Hauptmann Erwin Rommel returned to regimental duty on 21 December 1918 when, almost to a man, the officers who were to win the finest reputations in the ensuing years were retained in responsible staff positions to help lay the foundations of the new order? Siegfried Westphal, a future chief of staff to Rommel, observed: "After the war nearly all the front line officers with the Pour le Mérite without previous leadership training were transferred to the General Staff. But not Rommel—and I have never found out why." We may hazard a guess, however. Apart from the lack of a recommendation for General Staff training, Rommel was not the kind of staff officer Hans von Seeckt, the Chief of the Reichswehr, chose for the new force he was building. True, von Seeckt intended that its officers should work more closely than before with the ranks, closing the mutual gap in understanding that had opened prior to 1918, and this was a rôle Rommel had always played. But the men von Seeckt gathered closely around him in the Truppenamt (which per-

formed the function of General Staff after the Treaty of Versailles had banned the Great General Staff as an official organization) were to be men who combined their military talent with a cultured outlook and intellectual flair—qualities with which he, himself, was well equipped.

Rommel did not fit into this category. Never an intellectual, he had, by his conduct over the actions at Caporetto and in demanding the Pour le Mérite, offended deeply. To many brother officers, his behaviour was rated uncomradely and beneath contempt: such a man could not be trusted to behave with the discretion and trustworthiness to be expected of the team constituting the German Army's brain and nervous system. So he was denied a nomination to the War Academy (before it, too, was abolished by the Treaty of Versailles). This was not just because he was a tyro compared with the élite von Seeckt recruited (men of the calibre of Ritter von Haack, Wilhelm Heye, Werner von Blomberg, Kurt von Hammerstein-Equord, Walter von Reichenau, Ludwig Beck, Franz Halder, Albert Kesselring, Heinz Guderian and Werner von Fritsch). Nor was it because he was a Württemberger rather than a Prussian, as was von Seeckt: von Haack, Kesselring and Halder, for example were Bavarians, so one can scarcely infer that Rommel was excluded on tribal grounds. Simply, he did not satisfy the stringent requirements of the selection. As Westphal points out, this had an adverse psychological affect on Rommel: "I knew he, Rommel, had reservations about the General Staff Club ... and had experienced many rebuffs, particularly with regard to the War Academy, which had made him bitter ..."

Apart from this serious setback to his eager hopes of a sparkling career, Rommel managed to avoid the other pitfalls of the immediate post-war period without harming his reputation. Proudly wearing uniform and his

Pour le Mérite, he scornfully faced – and later, by sheer force of personality, out-faced – rebellious soldiers and sailors who hurled insults, and sometimes inflicted harm upon officers whom, a few months before, they had been ready to follow into battle. When authority was at a discount, it was leaders such as Rommel, with the common touch, who almost alone were capable of imposing a modicum of order – while yet avoiding contamination by the political stains of Spartacist communism or the right-wing reaction associated with the Freikorps, which was being improvised to fill the defence gap left by the defection of the old Army. Rommel was lucky. He was never faced with having to order German to fire upon German, or to find himself involved in raising Freikorps units. By the good fortune of his posting to regimental duty, where he had merely to execute the orders of the hard-pressed General Staff (some of whom inadvertently became tarred with the brushes of the extremist parties), he was spared involvement with subversive activities, and was fortunate enough to avoid the major confrontations forced upon the Army in putting down the successive putschen (uprisings) between 1918 and 1923. In the manner of the vast majority of Germans, he yearned for a strong, stable government that would restore the nation to a respected place in the world. If a new Bismarck arose, loyal to the Army, he would follow him without question.

For almost two decades, Rommel's career moved along conventional and unspectacular lines. In 1921, there was a disruption of his prospects when his old Regiment, the 124th, was disbanded and he was transferred to the 13th Infantry Regiment. He remained a Hauptmann and Company Commander until posted on 1 October 1929 as an Instructor at the Infantry School, Dresden, where he was to spend four happy years immersed in his work

and assembling the lectures that were to form the basis of Infanterie Greift an. There, with his family, he was snugly remote from the turmoil of political and economic troubles afflicting Germany. With Lu and their only son, Manfred (born on Christmas Eve 1928), he was able to enjoy family life, which meant much to him, and the study of his profession, which meant even more. Indeed, Rommel appears to have been obsessed by the study of the military art to the exclusion of almost everything else: of appreciating the fine arts, elegant conversation, good food and the social intercourse of the garrison (let alone contacts with civilians) he seems to have been deficient. Instead, he chose the Spartan life, perhaps because he was intent upon living within his means, or maybe because he felt ill-at-ease with men of 'intellectual' standing. It is hardly likely, then, that he would have seen too much in after-duty hours of the local artillery regiment's commander, with whom he would have had much to do ten years later; for Albert Kesselring was a cultivated, classical scholar, who appreciated the good things of life – quite apart from being one of the most outstanding and polished products of the Great General Staff.

The Nazi connection
Rommel, in fact, was beginning to look elsewhere for advancement. To Lu, he once remarked that the Nazis, who in 1932 were making their successful bid for power, seemed "a set of scallywags"; but in 1934 he met Hitler in person. Like so many junior officers, Rommel at once formed a good impression, recognizing in this man the Bismarck who would restore the Army to its predestined place in society. For Rommel, Hitler's arrival in power was a turning point rather more crucial, perhaps, than for most other German officers of destiny.

Left:
Rommel's first
contact with
Adolf Hitler at
Goslar in 1934.
Wearing a steel
helmet, he
marches (out of
step) at the left of
the picture.
(Bundesarchiv)

In 1933, with the rank of major, he had taken command of one of Germany's best infantry units, the 3rd Battalion of the 17th Infantry Regiment (Goslar Jägers), the same regiment to which Heinz Guderian, the man at that moment engaged in creating the German Panzerwaffe (Tank Arm), had once belonged. Jägers were taught to think and move more quickly than ordinary infantry, but Rommel was at pains to show them that even a 'heavy infantryman' at the advanced age of 42 was their match in speed and endurance up and down the slopes of the Harz Mountains. He was equally determined to defend their status. In 1935, when detailed to provide an escort for Hitler on a visit to Goslar, he was instructed to allow an SS bodyguard to take post in front of his men; he declined to be superseded – and was successful in convincing Heinrich Himmler (the SS leader) as well as Josef Goebbels (Head of the Propaganda Ministry) as to the propriety of his stand. Undoubtedly, the encounter was decisive in the impression it made on Goebbels, an impression of Rommel being a "big shot" that is subsequently recurrent in the surviving fragments of Goebbels' diaries. Probably, it was Goebbels who persuaded Himmler to give way, because he recognized in this highly-decorated major, of youthful bearing, the type of Germanic hero his propagandists were sponsoring to improve the public estimation of the Army. For, at that moment, it was Hitler's expressed policy to woo the Army, as the traditionally stabilizing political force in Germany, to his side (even though he privately held divergent views and long-term pernicious intentions).

This, Rommel's second confrontation with Hitler, a few hours after the interview with Himmler and Goebbels, was brief: a formal exchange of salutes, a handshake and the Führer's compliments upon the turnout of the Goslar Jägers. But a lasting, mutual impression had been made, and a rôle was now sought for Rommel that would involve him, as an Army officer, with one of the Nazi Party organizations (an unlikely suggestion to have been made had not Rommel given Goebbels some indication of willingness).

The proposal, that Rommel be given command of the Nazi Party's paramilitary SA, to apply the discipline desired by von Reichenau – or to "smarten them up", as Rommel put it – lapsed, however; it was a job jealously reserved for a Party loyalist. So a compromise was produced. With splendid irony, Rommel was appointed as an Instructor at the War Academy, which was due to

reopen in Potsdam on 15 October, as yet another step in Hitler's renunciation of the Treaty of Versailles. Following his announcement, in March, of the rearmament of Germany and his intention to build tanks, submarines and warplanes, Hitler had revived the General Staff, apparently in its old glory. Yet it was not his intention to allow the new General Staff quite the same authority as it had previously enjoyed: no longer was it to be the arbiter of so many vital decisions. This generation's staff officer was to be but a 'leader's assistant' with lowlier functions, despite the aspirations of the 'old guard' who saw no reason for change. There was thus symbolism as well as irony in the appointment of Rommel (who had never attended the War Academy) to teach the latest staff aspirants, and an implied announcement that selection to Potsdam in the future would be governed rather less by élitist principles. These things apart, Rommel's appointment also had a string attached, for still it was apparently somebody's aim to get him thoroughly involved with the Party, a desire that was to be made manifest on several occasions in the future. With the SA job denied him, it was now suggested that, while a member of the War Academy staff, he should train the quasi-military Hitler Jugend, a Party-orientated organization of the Reich Youth Leader, Baldur von Schirach. This too was foredoomed to failure, not because the job did not appeal to Rommel, nor because he could not have excelled in its execution. It was simply that von Schirach's aristocratic, cultured demeanour and upbringing were anathema to Rommel, quite beside his stated objection to von Schirach's policy of concentrating overmuch upon the military training of 13- to 18-year-olds to the exclusion of their broader education.

These setbacks in no way put an end to Goebbels' patronage and, in 1937, he arranged to have *Infanterie Greift an* suitably edited and published. That same year, the edited version of Heinz Guderian's lectures, *Achtung! Panzer!* ('Look out! Tank!') also appeared as propaganda for the tanks. Rommel's book went into many editions and earned him a great deal of money, the amount of which he was careful to conceal (even, it seems, from Lu). Both books were intended to act as Army propaganda, and both authors were selected by Goebbels as model officers having the modern outlook, to whom future German soldiers should look for examples to emulate. Guderian, however, was cast in a very different mould from Rommel, in that he was a Prussian, a thoughtful, polished, if tempestuous, product of the General Staff, a superb staff officer as well as a calculating leader.

It was now becoming quite clear to the upper hierarchy of Germany's political and military leaders that Hitler was embarked upon a course leading to war. Men of Rommel's proclivities, to whom war was not wholly repugnant and who would not try to impede the Führer's will, would soon be at a premium, especially in an Army deficient in well-grounded staff officers, and Rommel's dedication to his work was exemplary, fully justifying his appointment in November 1938 as Commandant of the Austrian War Academy at Wiener Neustadt, where junior officers were taught minor tactics. Here, he would be in his element, enthusing young and uninitiated leaders with his own brand of combat philosophy.

But already fate and the Führer had resolved that the work at Wiener Neustadt should be part-time. In September 1936, Rommel had made a strong impression on Hitler when attached to his escort at the Nazi Party's Nuremberg Rally (an appointment indicative of Goebbels' support). In October 1938, he commanded Hitler's personal escort for the march into the Sudetenland, and clearly won approval for his execution of this task, for, in March 1939, he performed the duty again during the occupation of the remainder of Czechoslovakia. In August, this culminated in his formal appointment to Führerhauptquartier, Unterstab (Hitler's headquarters staff); in his promotion to Generalmajor; and, along with all other Pour le Mérite holders, the award of two years' extra seniority to enable him to catch up – just as if he had, all along, been a member of the General Staff.

The signals ahead were clearly set at green, though his work for Hitler tried his patience considerably. As well as escorting the Führer throughout his visits to the Front during the ensuing Polish campaign, he had also to regulate the arrangements and movements of the political and military dignitaries who insisted upon accompanying their leader to war, and who jostled for privileges at his elbow in order to advance their own interests. These Party 'hacks' Rommel claimed to despise, and there were many occasions when his composure was severely strained. But, while it is true that he was not (as was sometimes said) a Nazi, there is ample evidence that his association with the Party hierarchy was by no means reluctant. As time

Above right:
Albert Kesselring reports to Hitler during the Polish campaign, as Rommel stands in the background.
(Image Press)
Below right:
Hitler is greeted by the troops during the Polish campaign. Rommel is to the fore, with Wilhelm Keitel behind him; Martin Bormann and Walter von Reichenau are on the Führer's left.
(Bundesarchiv)

went by, he would be prepared to help them if they sponsored him. In Poland, not only was he given close insight into the workings of mechanized armies closely supported by air power, which the masters of the General Staff had created so well, but he was brought into close association with the Supreme Commander whose favour was practically irresistible within the Wehrmacht. Having seen for himself that the winning blows had been struck by armoured forces, and that tanks had relegated artillery and infantry to lesser rôles (while the Luftwaffe had failed quite as often as it had succeeded), he realized instantly where he should address his career. When asked by Hitler what he would like to do next, Rommel had no hesitation in requesting command of a Panzer division. Once more he scented battle: ambition and thirst for glory urged him onward.

3

With the Ghost Division

The Panzer Division that Rommel took over on 15 February 1940, though new in number and form, was by no means totally inexperienced in war. In the Polish campaign, under the name of '2nd Light Division', it had been among the invading forces, but, like three similar mechanized formations raised from the old horsed cavalry units, it had been a failure. A single battalion of 90 light tanks to support 4 motorized infantry battalions was found incompatible with the mode of mobile warfare practised by the six existing Panzer divisions that Guderian and the Panzerwaffe had developed and demonstrated with such startling effect, for these contained anything up to 320 tanks each. However, absorbing new tanks from the German and Czech factories, each 'light division' had by now been converted into a Panzer division by giving it two additional tank battalions (including the latest medium machines), thereby increasing its tank strength to 218. Rommel's 7th Panzer Division, in fact, was different from the others in that its infantry content of two lorried regiments instead of one incorporated five battalions plus an independent motorcycle battalion.

Preparations for war

When Rommel took command, the Division lay at Bad Godesberg, its equipment suffering in the open from exposure to a perishingly cold winter, and its rôle in the forthcoming invasion of the West yet to be revealed. As part of Hermann Hoth's XV Corps, it was to provide the main striking power of Günther Kluge's Fourth Army, which would operate on the northern flank of Gerd von Rundstedt's Army Group A, and spearhead the northern axis of the ambitious drive the Germans intended to launch through the Ardennes on 10 May, seizing bridgeheads over the River Meuse. While Hoth's XV Corps made for Dinant, the two elements of Ewald von Kleist's Panzer Group, Guderian's XIX Corps (three Panzer divisions strong) and Reinhardt's XLI Corps (with two Panzer divisions) would head for Sedan and Monthermé respectively; then, if all three Corps achieved initial success, they would strike west with the coast of the English Channel as their objective.

Such daringly deep penetrations were second nature to Rommel: they embraced, in modern form, the battle techniques he had practised as an infantryman during the First World War, and which he had expounded ever since as a teacher. Tanks merely offered a quicker and more reliable way of advancing, while their thin armour (no German tank's protection exceeding 30mm, compared with twice that thickness on many French and British tanks) merely gave an improved chance of survival against artillery and machine-gun fire.

With so little time before the campaign, and with training in any case limited by a chronic shortage of fuel and ammunition, Rommel did not have much chance to get to know his men and machines before the invasion began. Nor could it be hoped that his staff would comprehend his style. No tactical training manuals in armoured warfare existed, but a standardized Panzer doctrine, such as it was, had been disseminated mainly by Heinz Guderian when he was Inspector of Panzer Forces before the war and, thereafter, improved by random discussions during the months of the 'phoney' winter war. Certain immutable principles had at least been established and drummed into every German armoured commander and staff officer: the necessity of reconnaissance, speed, concentration and reliable fuel replenishment. Reconnaissance would expose weak spots in the enemy defences, which could be exploited. Speed would help to surprise the enemy and, thereafter, prevent him from

The Panzers advance, with a Pz Kpfw 38(t) leading a Pz Kpfw IV. (Image Press)

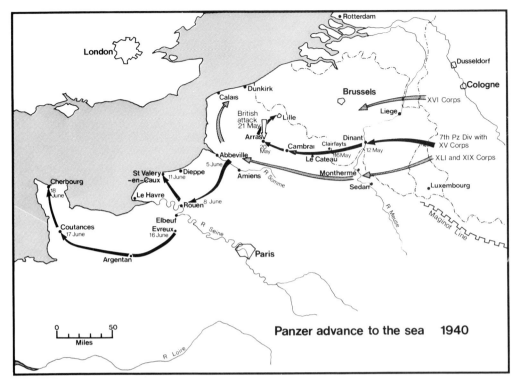

Panzer advance to the sea 1940

The Panzer advance to the sea, 10–20 May 1940. The 5th and 7th Panzer Divisions of XV Corps make the initial crossing of the River Meuse on 13 May, followed 12 hours later by XLI and XIX Corps. The French begin to withdraw opposite XV Corps on 14 May, as their 1st DCR advances to its destruction. XLI Corps strikes westward, soon accompanied on the flank by XIX Corps, which is also heavily engaged in fighting off determined counterattacks on its southern flank, prior to being reinforced by infantry divisions. Panzer Group Kleist races westward, only occasionally hampered by desultory French attacks from the south, and lining its corridor with infantry divisions following more slowly behind. The 7th Panzer Division breaches the Maginot Line extension at Clairfayts on 16 May, and thrusts deep into the enemy rear. By the evening of 20 May, with the 5th Panzer Division echeloned to right rear, it has reached the outskirts of Arras, where it runs into stiff British defences and has its axis cut in rear by the French. Meanwhile, XLI and XIX Corps have moved even faster, Guderian's XIX Corps reaching Abbeville on the evening of 20 May to complete the drive to the sea. The second phase begins on 5 June: the 7th Panzer Division races from the Somme, brushing aside resistance, and arrives at Cherbourg just too late to prevent remnants of the British 1st Armoured Division escaping.

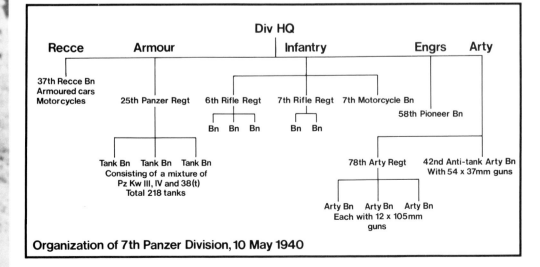

Organization of 7th Panzer Division, 10 May 1940

counterattacking in sufficient time at the right place—pace, in effect, would enhance security and safety. Concentration, by the employment of mass on a narrow front, would also purchase a measure of safety by distracting and overwhelming the enemy. And, perhaps above all, only an unchecked supply of fuel and ammunition would make these things possible. Such principles Rommel understood and had no need to digest—with the distinct exception of the last. He would use his tanks, armoured cars, lorries and motorcycles as he had previously used horses, bicycles and men on foot; he would utilize the wireless as once he had utilized a mobile telephone set; and, apart from the superior facilities provided by 1940s technology, he could operate as he had done in 1917, carefully rehearsing critical operations (such as the crossing of the Meuse) that could be foreseen. But, when battle began, he would dismiss logistics almost as an irrelevance.

Across the Meuse

The approach to the River Meuse, beginning at dawn on 10 May, must have awoken his memories of the march of 124th Regiment in 1914, taking him, as it did, through the enclosed terrain of the Ardennes. This time, he was in the lead from the outset, and immediately encountered opposition from the Belgian outposts, which were soon to be reinforced by the French 4th DLC (Division Légère de Cavalerie) as it arrived. Obstacles protected by enemy fire hampered progress, but were rapidly overcome by Rommel, drawing instantly upon his deeply-rooted intuition and applied in person from the forefront of battle. "I have found again and again", he wrote in his comments on these skirmishes, "that in encounter actions, the day goes to the side that is the first to plaster its opponents with fire. The man who lies low and awaits developments usually comes off second best." This admirably sums up so much of his approach to life, let alone against an enemy; and, against the light mechanized cavalry and infantry forces opposed to him at this moment, the technique worked like a charm. On schedule (while the rest of XV Corps and Panzer Group Kleist closed up to the Meuse), Rommel's armoured cars and motorcyclists arrived at Dinant on the afternoon of the 12th. That evening, the motorcyclists infiltrated across the river, just as his mountaineers had crossed the Piave in 1917. By the following morning, the Division was tucked in among the steep ravines leading down to that fast-

flowing river; artillery registered on targets across the water; dismounted, motorized infantry and assault pioneers steeling themselves for the main crossing; tank battalions carrying out the maintenance work before being ferried over to continue the advance on ground more suited to their capability. On the right flank, the 5th Panzer Division had kept pace. As night fell, both divisions put the final touches to the preconceived plan for a crossing at 0300 hours next day.

The plan, however, was not to be: for the 7th Panzer Division was to beat its neighbour across the Meuse by nearly twelve hours—and at the cost of but twenty-four lives. By an enormous stroke of luck, Rommel had hit the boundary between two French Corps, a weak and sensitive point in any defence. Instinctively, he seized his opportunity and exploited it with a verve that few tacticians possess. His opponents, Generals Bouffet and Martin, were antagonists of pusillanimous calibre commanding units that were already badly shaken by bombing and the German onrush. But the French were not the only people to be disturbed. So, too, was Hoth, Rommel's own Corps commander, who had forbidden him to cross independently and who now told him to halt and detach troops to help the 5th Panzer Division (whose bridging material he had coolly filched) coming up on the right flank. This Rommel refused to do, and he was supported by the Army commander, Kluge, who saw the possibilities of immediate exploitation.

By nightfall on the 13th, Rommel was in possession of a useful, if precarious, bridgehead on the west bank, secured in part by anti-tank guns, with eight-ton pontoons and rafts under construction at its base. But here was revealed a fault in his original orders: the eight-ton pontoon was incapable of supporting the heavier tanks. The resulting delay, while sixteen-ton pontoons were built, meant that only fifteen tanks were floated across during the night, but the rate of build-up increased with daylight and, at 0800 hours on the 14th, with thirty tanks of the 25th Panzer Regiment assembled, he directed the assault upon the key village of Onaye, an operation that had been carefully rehearsed in exercises at Bad Godesberg. Rommel now ran into trouble. As heavy enemy artillery fire came down, and his tank driver swerved into a depression, Rommel was wounded in the cheek. For a short while he was a fugitive, out of touch with his Division. Onaye remained in French hands that evening, but the 5th Panzer Division was at last across on the

Above:
An artist's sketch
of the assault
crossing of the
River Meuse. In
its original form,
it was based on
Guderian as the
commander
concerned, but it
was published in
a Dutch-language
book as if it were
Rommel. (Image
Press)

right, and the rest of the 7th was beginning to arrive in strength, virtually unchallenged by any serious French counterattacks – despite Rommel's exaggerated claims to the contrary. Perhaps it was his very proximity to the heart of the action that led him to overestimate, on this and several future occasions, the magnitude of the enemy threat. But perhaps it was something else: an outright determination to portray his activities to the maximum possible advantage before Hitler. At any rate, Lieutenant Hausberg, who had been one of Rommel's students at Wiener Neustadt, had the task each evening of taking an aircraft and presenting to the Führer a map depicting the day's advances by the 7th Panzer Division, extravagant objectives for the morrow, and showing the flanking formation well in rear, signified by a question-mark. Hausberg's embarrassing duty, which had been settled at a very high level prior to the invasion, brought him a fair measure of derision from those in the know; it also irritated officers of the other formations in the Corps, who justifiably felt slighted.

To make matters easier for the Germans, the French stood motionless while XV Corps built up its strength on the west bank during the 13th. They did not begin to react with their own armoured divisions until after midday on the 14th, when the threat at Dinant, Monthermé and Sedan gradually, but forcibly, came to their notice. If this delayed reaction was another stroke of luck for Rom-

mel, so too was the inept manner in which the 1st DCR (Division Cuirassée Rapide) approached from Charleroi on the 14th and 15th, in its attempt to counter the penetration achieved by XV Corps. For the 1st DCR, a recently-founded armoured formation like the 7th Panzer Division, was deficient in its communication equipment, lacking in its traffic-control organization and inadequately supplied by its fuel echelons; furthermore, its men were given to outbreaks of ungovernable panic on the random occasions when they were bombed by the Luftwaffe. Its line of march now bisected the advancing prongs of Hoth's two armoured spearheads, enabling both Divisions to share the killing. On the afternoon of the 15th, the Germans caught a thoroughly disorganized, immobile 1st DCR in open ground, where it was engaged in a delayed refuelling. The German tanks, free to manoeuvre, hit the French heavy tanks in flank. By the end of the day, only 50 out of the original 160 French tanks remained serviceable, many having surrendered intact; by the next morning, they were down to 17, the rest having been abandoned in flight and from shortage of petrol; and, the following night, these demoralized survivors were mopped-up by the 7th Panzer Division as it burst into the town of Avesnes. Only 3 escaped.

Breaching the Maginot Line

The sudden arrival of Rommel's division in Avesnes was itself the product of the Panzer units' overall success. The breakthrough, which had opened a fifty-mile gap in the French defences, had utterly disrupted their Army. The wholesale destruction of three-quarters of their best mobile armoured forces, within a period of seventy-two hours, demolished any hope of their recovery. Apart from a few semi-mobile infantry divisions, backed up by scattered tank detachments, the French were rendered defenceless. Their Maginot Line proper, which terminated at Longwy, had been outflanked, and the thin line of pill-boxes, which extended its coverage westward along the frontier with Belgium, put up but the barest resistance – as Rommel demonstrated on the night of the 16th in the advance that carried him to Avesnes, to complete the rout of the 1st DCR.

Rommel's personal account of the breaching of the Maginot Line extension at Sivry and Clairfayts is among his best writing, and explains to perfection his methods of conducting a pursuit. The fortifications were to be reconnoitred in daylight; the Rifle Regiments supported by tanks and artillery were then to seize the fortifications, whereupon the 25th Panzer Regiment would burst through towards Avesnes. "I rode ... in the regimental commander's command tank ... When a report came in from a reconnaissance troop that the road through Clairfayts had been mined, we bore off to the south and moved in open order across fields and hedges in a semi-circle round the village ... Suddenly we saw the angular outlines of a French fortification about 100 yards ahead ... In a few moments the leading tanks came under heavy anti-tank gunfire from the left ... and two of our tanks were knocked out." The battle became general over a wide front, as the Germans explored and tackled the complexity of ditches and hedgehogs guarded by the pill-boxes. At nightfall, the enemy was still very much in evidence, although gaps had been cleared in the obstacles and several French guns had been destroyed by a Panzerkampfwagen IV [the German close-support tank with a short 75mm gun firing high-explosive shells]. Rommel took his place immediately behind the leading tank company as its engines were revved-up and its machine-guns began spraying the surrounding countryside.

"The way to the west was now open. The moon was up ... The tanks now rolled in a long column through the line of fortifications and towards the first houses, which had been set alight by our fire. In the moonlight we could see the men of the 7th Motorcycle Battalion moving forward on foot beside us ... Our artillery was dropping heavy harassing fire on villages and the road far ahead ... Gradually the speed increased. Before long we were 500 – 1,000 – 2,000 – 3,000 yards into the fortified zone. Engines roared, tank tracks clanked and clattered ... Troops lay bivouaced beside the road, military vehicles stood parked in farmyards ... Civilians and French troops, their faces distorted with terror, lay huddled in the ditches ... the flat countryside lay spread out around us under the cold light of the moon. We were through the Maginot Line! It was hardly conceivable!"

For the ensuing forty-eight hours, Rommel drove his men hard, not for one moment letting the pace slacken, urging them beyond the point of exhaustion and frequently pushing the tank regiment so far ahead that the infantry regiments were left miles behind while the tanks themselves ran out of petrol. Whereas the other Panzer divisions advanced on a relatively broad front, Rommel's thrust a narrow pencil line of red crayon across the

map, with himself either in action at the tip or racing backwards and forwards like a dervish, berating the units that failed to keep up. Several times he was within an ace of being captured, and hardly ever was the 7th Panzer Division complete master of the country it had traversed. French soldiers roamed about as they pleased, surrendering when convenient and then escaping as they chose, a constant menace to this handful of impudent Germans in their midst. Although Rommel often pushed his luck beyond the limits of prudence, the results proved him correct in taking such risks. The French nation's morale had collapsed – the Polish Army would never have allowed itself to be bullied like this in 1939. Never again would he fight so innocuous a foe, whose soldiers were presented with innumerable opportunities to end his career there and then, but who supinely threw in the sponge. Rommel was lucky to get away with it.

Certainly, Major Otto Heidkämper, his principal staff officer and chief of operations was seriously alarmed by Rommel's unorthodox methods and the risks he took with the Division. Not for the first time, on 18 May, Heidkämper, at Divisional headquarters, was unable satisfactorily to arrange replenishment of the tanks, which as usual were in the far distance and cut off. And, since contact with Rommel (who was closely engaged in battle) was also broken, he turned, a worried man, to Corps headquarters for help – to the immense rage of his commander who subsequently wrote: "This young General Staff Officer, scared that something might happen to him and the staff, stayed some twenty miles behind the Front and, of course, lost contact with the fighting troops ... Instead of rushing everything up forward he went to Corps headquarters, upset the people there and behaved as if the command of the division were no longer secure ... I'll have to make a thorough study of the documents so as to put the boy in his place." Apart from its manifestation of his attitude to the staff, this is the first recorded instance of discord between a General Staff officer and Rommel. It may not have been the first, and it certainly would not be the last. Although it is easy to understand Rommel's anger, one must have sympathy too with Heidkämper, who was a brilliant officer, one day to become a lieutenant-general. Lacking clear instructions from Rommel, he had had good reasons for being anxious about the command's security. And here Rommel displays a significant misconception of how the staff

should work. A headquarters cannot function calmly and efficiently if it is dashing from place to place and coming constantly under fire: uniform procedures are essential, and the commander must behave in a rational manner if misunderstandings are to be avoided. Rommel's cavalier notion of 'rushing' soft-skinned lorries forward was risky. In due course, peace would be restored between commander and chief of operations, but those at Corps headquarters were also decidedly, and justifiably, alarmed.

General Hoth came forward in person on the afternoon of the 19th, anxious to call a halt, since in his opinion the Division was exhausted and too far separated from the 5th Panzer Division for comfort. By then, the 7th Panzer Division stood with its head at Cambrai, in the process of bringing up supplies, resting its men and taking time for essential vehicle maintenance. Retorting that "the troops have been twenty hours in the same place", Rommel managed to dissuade his superior and, before dawn next day, they were off again, traversing the site of the first great tank battle of the First World War. At noon, they were in sight of Arras, where the

British stood firm. Rommel's infantry were again slow to follow and, as the day progressed, French troops cut the 7th Panzer Division's axis to the east. Turning back to hasten the infantry forward, Rommel was nearly captured. Once more, the advance had to be halted to allow the Division to consolidate its gains and concentrate south of Arras. That night came the news that Guderian had reached the English Channel. At the same time came fresh orders. The Division was to wheel north on Lille, accompanied by the SS 'Totenkopf' Motorized Infantry Division (as it arrived) and followed, in due course, by the 5th Panzer Division, which was still some distance to the east of Cambrai, mopping-up the mass of the bypassed enemy in stiff fighting.

Setback at Arras

Rommel's conduct of the action that now began to the south of Arras is a classic example of improvident generalship. Ignoring reports of enemy tanks concentrating to the north, he hardly deigned to leave outposts covering his threatened right flank, but

travelled himself, as usual, with the 25th Panzer Regiment – far ahead of the vulnerable infantry in their lorries. His towed 37mm anti-tank artillery (which was already known to be inadequate against the armour of the best French and British tanks) lay back to guard the infantry on its line of march; his 105mm field artillery was deployed well in rear purely to provide long-range indirect fire support on call, while the attached Luftwaffe 88mm dual-purpose guns were located still farther in rear, fulfilling their anti-aircraft rôle. (None of this artillery was, as is some-times claimed, positioned specifically as an anti-tank screen.) Quite by chance, the German advance started at precisely the same moment as the British 50th Division, with the 1st Tank Brigade, began to destroy Rommel's 6th Rifle Regiment at Agnez. Yet not a word of this disaster reached Rommel: it was by luck that he arrived back in time to see the impending destruction of the 7th Rifle Regiment, his return to the assembly area prompted purely by the desire to hasten them forward. His arrival at Vailly coincided with the assault by the right-hand British column

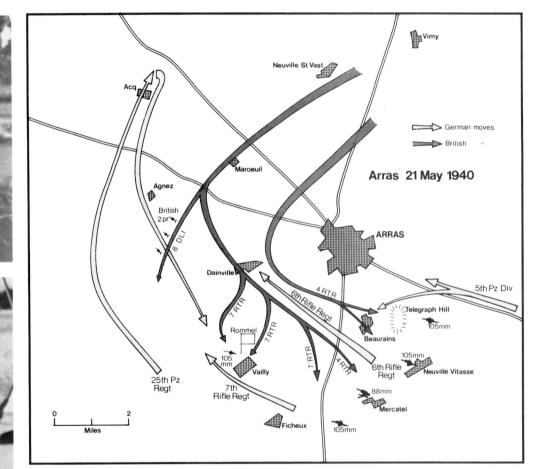

On the morning of 21 May, 74 British heavy tanks with infantry in two columns, guarded on their right flank by 70 French tanks of the Cavalry Corps, begin to pivot upon Arras with the intention of then moving eastward. They are completing their wheel as the 7th Panzer Division, with SS 'Totenkopf' Motorized Division on its left, is beginning a reciprocal wheel aimed on Lille via Acq. Since the 25th Panzer Regiment is sent far in advance of the rest of the Division, the Rifle Regiments receive the brunt of the British attack, their 37mm anti-tank guns proving quite inadequate to penetrate the British tanks' armour. The 6th Rifle Regiment is overrun, and the 7th avoids the same fate only because the British right column loses direction and falls behind schedule. As it is, Rommel is compelled to abandon the advance and call back the 25th Panzer Regiment, inadvertently causing it heavy losses on a line of British anti-tank guns near Agnez. The British, meanwhile, have also been stopped by the combined efforts of the 7th Panzer Division's 105mm field artillery and 88mm dual-purpose guns at Mercatel and Telegraph Hill. The subsequent arrival of the 5th Panzer Division, post-haste from Cambrai, completes the British repulse and, next day, XV Corps can recommence its wheel to the north.

The three types of tank in the 7th Panzer Division, shown in a photograph taken by Rommel. Left, Pz Kpfw IV: weight 20 tons, armour (max) 30mm, gun 75mm, speed 25mph, crew 5. Centre, Pz Kpfw III: weight 19 tons, armour (max) 30mm, gun 37mm, speed 25mph, crew 5. Right (top), Pz Kpfw 38(t): weight 10 tons, armour (max) 25mm, gun 37mm, speed 26mph, crew 4. (Image Press)

(which itself happened to be in a state of some confusion). According to Rommel, some nearby field-gunners were in flight, the rest lying low. But he too was out of touch, and his sole constructive contribution to this battle was, with his ADC, managing to get a few light (20mm) anti-aircraft guns into action in time to help repulse the already-failing British advance at Vailly. But here, as elsewhere, the real credit for the defeat of the British belonged to the crews of the 105mm and 88mm guns that just happened to be standing in the way of the triumphant British left column as it debouched into open country at Beaurains. It was they who defeated the British tanks, but even they were lucky, since the British utterly failed to co-ordinate their artillery fire and use it to neutralize the exposed German guns.

Later that evening, it was Rommel's failure to arrange sound reconnaissance that led to the heavy losses sustained by the 25th Panzer Regiment after he had recalled it to the rescue (the first and only retrograde movement by any part of the Division during the campaign). For it ran, quite unexpectedly, into an anti-tank-gun ambush laid by the British at Agnez, and here lost the majority of the thirty German tanks knocked out that day. On this one day, Rommel lost 388 men—four times more than had been suffered by the Division during the previous fighting. It was as the result of his experiences in the heat of this action that Rommel actually contributed to the British success. For, in assuming that "hundreds of enemy tanks" and "five divisions" were against him (when only 140 tanks were involved), he greatly exaggerated the strength of the Allied forces, and radiated panic in his wireless calls for help. The 5th Panzer Division raced to the aid of what its War Diary describes as "the hard pressed 7th Panzer Division", and ripples of alarm spread along the channels of command to the Führer himself. There is little doubt that, when Hitler later told Rommel "we were very anxious about you", he was referring to this moment. Hesitancy already had the High Command in its grip. Rommel's reports reinforced its anxiety that the Panzer force might have overreached itself. Through a compound of mis-appreciations, the certainty of seizing Dunkirk almost unopposed was forfeited—and with it the opportunity to encircle and annihilate the best British and French formations.

For Rommel, his Division, the Panzer force and the rest of the German Army, however, the failure to wipe out the British at Dunkirk

seemed merely a minor disappointment at the conclusion of a month of incredible triumphs. When Hitler called Rommel to see him on 3 June, while the 7th Panzer Division recuperated and prepared for the next phase of the campaign, he was, as Rommel told Lu "radiant", and "I had to accompany him afterwards. I was the only division commander who did." They all knew that France was prostrate and the British unlikely to come back for many years. That Rommel was held in high favour had been made plain eight days previously, when one of his own officers, Lieutenant Karl-August Hanke "acting on behalf of the Führer, ceremonially decorated me with the Knight's Cross and gave me the Führer's regards". It may seem strange that so junior an officer should perform this duty, but Hanke was no ordinary junior officer. Not only had he demonstrated, according to Rommel, exceptional bravery and initiative in action, but he was one of Goebbels' favourite officials from the Propaganda Ministry, sent quite obviously to keep an eye on one of his master's protégés and to act as a special Nazi Party link with Berlin. He had brought with him as officers to the 7th Panzer Division several Nazi members of the Reichstag, including Kraus, the Chief of the Nazi Motor Corps (NSKK), and his financial adviser, Koebele, who later succeeded Julius Streicher as Gauleiter of Franken. And there was another man called Karl Holz, who had to remain a sergeant because he had twenty-four 'previous convictions'–twenty-two of them 'political' and two criminal! But Hanke (who, at the end of the war, would be Hitler's nomination as head of the SS in place of the infamous Heinrich Himmler), was the most important of this liaison team, and to him Rommel extended the greatest favour, awarding him the Iron Cross (without consulting his battalion commander) even though he carried out his duties no more courageously than anybody else. A few days later (again without consultation), he recommended him for the Knight's Cross–but this application was withdrawn because Hanke refused to take command of a tank company, telling Rommel that he scarcely knew how to lead a troop let alone a company, and that he was not prepared to risk the soldiers' lives. This snub may well have angered Rommel, for Manfred Rommel inserts a lengthy footnote in *The Rommel Papers* to explain how unpopular Hanke was with the other officers of the Division, and mentions an incident in the Mess when Hanke boasted that he had, as an official, the power to remove Rommel from

command. This, so Manfred says, led Rommel to report the matter to Hitler's Army adjutant, Rudolf Schmundt, with the result that Hanke was posted away (and, much later, found his way to be Gauleiter of Breslau, where he achieved a certain notoriety). Be that as it may, it is unquestionable that Rommel, in furthering his ambition, saw no impediment to using any means to curry favour within the Nazi Party; subsequent suggestions that he was a Nazi, hotly denied as they are and technically correct though they may be, were by no means groundless

Below:
Rommel flies over his tanks in his Storch immediately prior to the start of the final offensive in France. (Image Press)

The pursuit south

The next task for Hoth's XV Corps looked, and was, a good deal less difficult than the initial drive across the Meuse. For a start, the enemy were cripplingly deficient of mobile forces, and this time there was only a canal to cross from a well-established bridgehead south of the River Somme, east of Abbeville. The fact that the French had at last adopted a defence in depth based upon a sort of 'chequer-board system' did not in the least deter Hoth's men (even though it had disastrous consequences for von Kleist's armour to

the left when it attacked southward from Amiens). On 5 June, with smooth precision behind artillery concentrations, the 6th Rifle Regiment seized a bridgehead, while the Pioneers set to work clearing obstacles from the short bridges that had not been demolished by the French. Rommel walked forward just behind his infantry, to be joined a few hours later by the leading tanks of the 25th Panzer Regiment.

It was now that the French put up their best performance ever against Rommel. Fortified villages were costly and time-consuming to

reduce: although the tanks bypassed this opposition with ease through the fields on either side, they dared not proceed too far until the villages and woods had been secured and, meanwhile, they came under intense gunfire from many directions. It was here that the improvised grouping of tanks with infantry was beneficial. Each time, the French were overcome by a mixture of direct and indirect fire, followed up by an all-arms assault to close quarters. Hard though Rommel makes this battle sound in his *Papers*, the penetration achieved by nightfall was more than five miles, and the tanks were still rolling forward. Prisoners gave themselves up by the hundred. The enemy guns fell silent.

The Germans were now entering open country, their momentum on one occasion checked only by an order prohibiting further advance until the Luftwaffe had bombed a fortified village that stood in the way. Here and there, French tanks put in an appearance. Often the French artillery made good practice against 88mm guns pushed too far ahead for their own safety. On the left flank, the 5th Panzer Division was keeping pace, cutting a wide swathe deep into the enemy rear. From now on, there was scarcely a question of strategic risk: the worst that could befall the Germans was that of aggravating casualties from sporadic ambushes. The subsequent story of the 7th Panzer Division's rapid advance mirrors that of the other German armoured formations and some of the infantry ones too. It becomes a catalogue enumerating prisoners captured and a log of distances covered each day, a succession of rivers crossed, villages, towns and cities conquered.

The Advance to Elbeuf

Date	From	To	Distance	Principal Events
5 June	R. Somme	Montagne	8 miles	Breaching of main French defence with heavy fighting.
6 June	Montagne	Caulières	14 miles	Breakout across country.
7 June	Caulières	Sigy-en-Bray	30 miles	Pursuit and incursion into French base areas.
8 June	Sigy-en-Bray	Elbeuf	45 miles	Abortive attempt to seize Seine bridges intact.

Throughout these hectic days, the 7th Panzer Division wrought havoc upon the Allied lines of communication. The route between Paris and Le Havre was cut, vast munitions dumps captured, and enemy units pinned, in pockets, to the coast. Having failed in an attempted coup de main of the Seine bridges (which were blown in his troops' faces) at Elbeuf, just south of Rouen, Hoth switched the Division on the 10th to round up several French divisions and a single British division congregated between Le Havre and Dieppe. After moving sixty miles in a single day against minimal opposition, Rommel found himself faced on the 11th, in the vicinity of St. Valery-en-Caux, with an opponent who was not prepared to give way. Here, the French fought well and the British 51st Highland Division surrendered only after a stiff resistance, efforts to evacuate it by sea having largely failed. While his artillery engaged ships of the Royal Navy, resistance on shore was gradually overcome, and a rich haul of prisoners taken, including one corps and four divisional commanders.

For the Germans, it was now simply a matter of mopping-up France, while the French called for an armistice and the British pulled back across the English Channel. The final operations by the 7th Panzer Division, launched forth from a bridgehead that had been seized over the Seine near Rouen, saw the Division making full speed for Cherbourg, mopping-up stragglers and demoralized French formations on the way, but failing to reach the port in time to prevent the evacuation of the British 1st Armoured Division.

By this time, Rommel's sense of achievement was unsurpassed in an army that could congratulate itself on one of the greatest campaigns of annihilation of all time. To Lu, he described in exultant terms the capture of Cherbourg, as he carried out "the Führer's special order to take the port as quickly as possible". Heavy bombing of the forts and rapid exploitation of success, against an enemy he reckoned at thirty to forty times his superior in numbers, achieved the desired result with the minimum delay, and brought an end to the fighting for his Division. Since 10 May, for the loss of 682 killed, 1,464 wounded, 296 men missing and 42 tanks totally destroyed (losses higher than those in other Panzer divisions that had seen quite as much action), it had taken 97,648 prisoners, 277 field guns, 64 anti-tank guns, 458 tanks and armoured cars and over 4,000 lorries, besides a mass of other material. Josef Goebbels could congratulate himself upon the success of the man his judgement had backed. The feats of the air and tank arms were trumpeted on high, the names of air aces and Luftwaffe commanders were linked with the Panzer leaders, especially the charismatic Guderian and Rommel. The 7th Panzer Division came to be known as "The Ghost Division", and its photogenic commander was firmly emplaced on the peaks of public esteem. The book he wrote extolling his troops' feats played down or ignored the part played by the rest of the German Army and the Luftwaffe. It was illustrated by the pictures he had taken with the camera given him by Goebbels.

Naturally, the 7th Panzer Division was among the formations selected for a part in the invasion of England that was planned for September. To this task, Rommel bent himself with a lot more enthusiasm than many of the Wehrmacht's upper hierarchy. Had the operation not been called off, it is not impossible that he would have been at the head of a spearhead driving on London. Even so, his future glory was assured. For the next three years or more, he would be Hitler's first choice for some of the most dramatic tasks on offer, as the German frontiers were pushed farther afield.

4

'A big and important job'

Right:
Italians surrender in hordes. The last scenes of the Italian collapse in 1941, which triggered off the German intervention and brought Rommel to North Africa. (Imperial War Museum)

Initially, there was no German intention to become involved in the North African conflict, for it stood within the Italian sphere of political influence. When Italy entered the war in June 1940, at the moment of France's collapse and when it appeared certain that the British would soon have to seek terms, there seemed little in the Italians' condition for Germany to be concerned about. Although the Italian economy was shaky, her Navy short of fuel and no match for that of the British, and her Army ill-equipped, it was scarcely expected that the nation would be put seriously to the test.

In the autumn, however, the British remained very much in business. The Italian Navy was inactive, and her Army had failed in a tentative advance into Egypt. The strain upon Benito Mussolini's Fascist government was heavy. Even so, the Germans were loath to go to his assistance when Mussolini asked for material aid, for Hitler had already settled upon his next major aggression, the invasion of Russia. This would place demands upon everything at his disposal, and diversions to any other theatre of war in the crucial year of 1941 were to be avoided if possible.

Nevertheless, in October 1940, after the proposed invasion of England had been called off, the Germans suggested that a mechanized force might be sent to Libya to aid the Italians, and a tank expert, Generalmajor Wilhelm Ritter von Thoma, was sent to investigate possibilities. In reporting adversely upon the Italian Army, he also said that supplies would be very difficult to provide in such vast and arid desert conditions far from German bases. Hitler, who was angered by the Italians' abortive invasion of Greece at the end of October, then let the matter drop until December, when the Italians suffered a series of disastrous defeats at British hands in Egypt, and were bundled in rout back into Cyrenaica. Pursuing, with a verve equalling

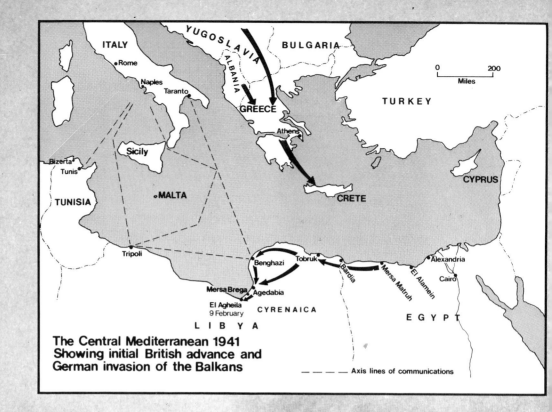

The Central Mediterranean 1941
Showing initial British advance and
German invasion of the Balkans

– – – – Axis lines of communications

that of the Germans in France, the British rapidly captured the important port of Tobruk on 21 January 1941, and seemed poised to continue their advance to the west.

Both Hitler and Mussolini were seriously alarmed by this. If Africa were lost, there was a possibility that the Fascist régime would collapse, removing Italy from the Axis partnership. Reluctantly, the Germans were compelled to intervene: it was decided on 11 January to send X Fliegerkorps (Air Corps) to Sicily to operate against the Royal Navy, and plans were also made to send the 5th Light Division to North Africa in mid-February. On 5 February the last remnants of the fast-retreating Italian Army were cut off by the British at Beda Fomm, to the south of the port of Benghazi, and two days later were annihilated. Only weak and demoralized Italian troops now stood to prevent a British invasion of Tripolitania.

The North African campaign

To Hitler, the deteriorating situation could no longer be ignored and, with Mussolini's agreement, he decided to send a Panzer Corps to Tripolitania at once. This would consist initially of the 5th Light Division, and be made up to strength in March, as shipping became available, by the 15th Panzer Division. It would be called the Deutsches Afrika Korps and its commander, by Hitler's choice (and certainly not that of the Army), was to be Erwin Rommel. This Corps was to be under the Italian commander-in-chief in North Africa, General Italo Gariboldi, but it was to be employed operationally as a single formation under Rommel, who had right of appeal to the German Army Command (OKH) in Berlin should the name and reputation of German troops be placed in jeopardy by any 'dubious' Italian orders. Rommel would also be allowed to give orders to certain nominated Italian formations. The Luftwaffe's contingents would remain directly responsible to its Commander-in-Chief, Hermann Goering, but a Fliegerführer Afrika, Generalmajor Stefan Fröhlich, would filter Rommel's demands for air support and pass them on to whatever units of X Fliegerkorps could be made available to the Army.

Rommel was now committed to fight in terrain with which he was entirely unfamiliar, employing a scratch force controlled by a staff who were quite unaccustomed to his methods. For the first time, he was placed in a position from which he could exercise the nearest thing possible to independent command, divorced from close surveillance by an immediate superior officer. Indeed, at the outset, it was clear that he had little intention of complying with Italian wishes, even though it was incumbent upon him to work closely (and, of necessity, tactfully) with a foreign ally for whom he could evince little sympathy or respect. Rommel was not an officer who readily forgot past failures. The combat performance of the Italians at Caporetto he faithfully remembered. Accounts of their recent débâcle, reinforced by what he saw when he flew to Tripoli on 12 February, merely stimulated his contempt.

Already, German administrative units were setting up a base, and supplies were being flown in. Soon, the leading elements of the 5th Light Division and fresh Italian formations to join their Ariete Armoured Division would arrive. Determined to defend Tripolitania by a forward deployment at El Agheila in the Gulf of Sirte, Rommel at once found himself in disagreement with Gariboldi, who preferred a position farther to the west. But a rapid air reconnaissance of the terrain satisfied his original opinion and so, without delay, he overrode Gariboldi and sent each unit, as it arrived, hurriedly eastward to confront the British.

From the outset, the restrictions of logistics hampered everything that Rommel wished to accomplish: unproven German equipment soon proved inadequate to the conditions; engine performance was degraded by the clouds of erosive dust; clothing was found to be ill-designed to meet extremes of temperature; stoves designed to burn wood were useless in a land without trees; and the men's rations were unsuitable for the climate, with the result that their health, as well as Rommel's own, deteriorated. A conflict arose between the base staff, who wished only to establish a base, and the demands of the 5th Light Division, who wanted everything sent forward. The British official history significantly and succinctly comments: "General Rommel appears not to have concerned himself with such matters, but expected necessary supplies to be produced wherever they were wanted, a difficult task for his staff who often did not know what he intended to do next." Here, indeed, was the nub of the question. For Rommel, battle was everything – even as Corps commander, he saw it as a tactical subject to which strategy was subordinate.

Rommel's first desert offensive

Strategic directives came from Rome, but the real control was applied from Berlin, and it

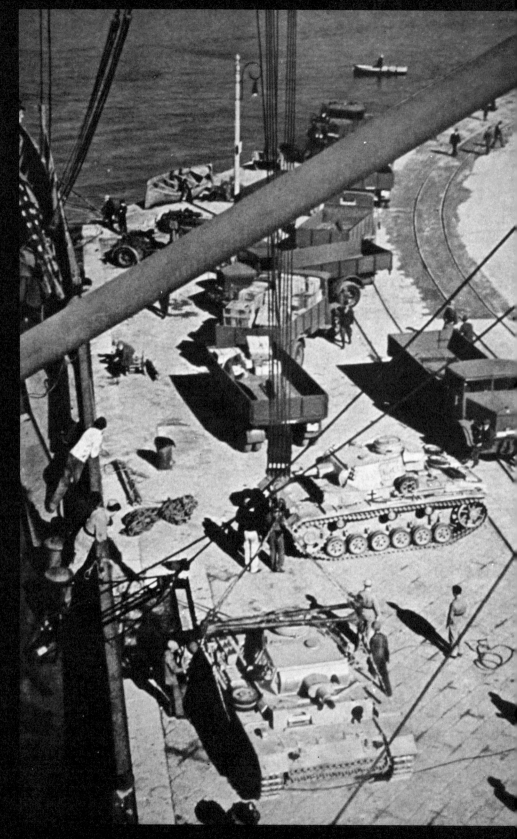

Right:
The dominant
weapons arrive.
Pz Kpfw III tanks
are unloaded in
Tripoli.
(MacClancy
Press)
Far right:
The first
contingent of
Afrika Korps
troopers deplane.
(MacClancy
Press)

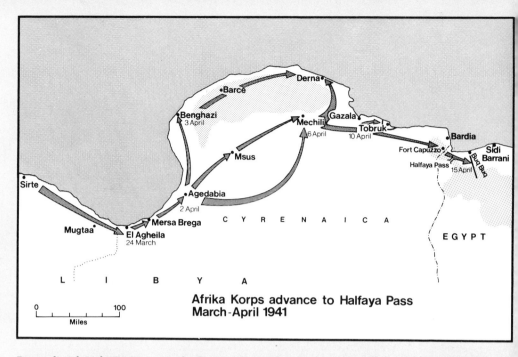

**Afrika Korps advance to Halfaya Pass
March-April 1941**

Rommel's 5th Light Division attacks the mixed covering force of the inexperienced British 2nd Armoured Division at Mersa Brega on 31 March, and seizes his initial objectives after a stiff fight that might not have gone his way had the British at once committed their armour. With the enemy in retreat, Rommel presses his pursuit and, despite initial Italian objections, extends his penetration rapidly eastward with the assistance of Italian troops. Under pressure, the British armoured division is defeated in detail and driven back on Tobruk. By 4 April, Rommel has taken Benghazi, and the 9th Australian Division, with remnants of the 2nd Armoured Division, is about to begin its withdrawal from Mechili into the Tobruk perimeter. Lunging eastwards in pursuit, Rommel captures nearly all the British commanders and arrives outside Tobruk on 10 April. By now, his original force is depleted and short of supplies, but elements of the 15th Panzer Division are beginning to reinforce him. Pushing light forces forward to the Egyptian frontier, where they are held by British mobile forces, he launches a heavy assault against besieged Tobruk on 12 April. The garrison holds firm and repels this attack, as it is to repulse each Axis assault during the weeks to come. By 1 May, Rommel has reverted to the defensive.

was there, during a visit on 19 March, that Rommel received fresh instructions. The 5th Light Division was now firmly established alongside the Italians at Mugtaa, and British patrols had been pushed back, their Army having made no further effort to advance in strength. Hitler decorated Rommel with the Oakleaves of the Iron Cross, and the Commander-in-Chief, Walter von Brauchitsch, laid down that he must concentrate on the defence of Tripolitania and only plan for the recapture of Cyrenaica. Upon his return to the front on the 23rd, however, Rommel received reports that the British had thinned out at El Agheila. This was irresistible. At once, he told the 5th Light Division to seize the place next day, successfully carrying out a plan he had formulated prior to the Berlin visit. With El Agheila in his hands and the 5th Light Division again released for mobile action, success prompted him a step further. Since it was among his principles that a supine enemy must need be harried, he ordered his forces to probe forward against the defile at Mersa Brega, which was known to be strongly held by the British. Its possession would considerably improve his water supplies. At the same time, he made plans for a reconnaissance 160 miles to the south-east, to the oasis of Jalo, which posed a threat to his flank so long as it was occupied by the enemy.

Both the German and Italian High Commands were lukewarm about the Mersa Brega scheme, which was launched on 31 March and the British noticed too that the initial assault itself was pressed with caution.

Rommel, of course, had good reason for a careful approach to the British—the Arras experience was still fresh in his memory. By nightfall, indeed, the attack had stalled, and it needed but one firmly executed counter-attack by the British armour to throw him back to El Agheila in a state of mind more willing to obey the High Command's cautious instructions. But the commander of the British 2nd Armoured Division doubted the feasibility of an attack in the hours of daylight remaining and, instead, authorized a withdrawal. In this moment of weakness, he did far more than open the way into Cyrenaica: he let loose the genie of Rommel's ambition and brought upon himself the full destructive onslaught of which his formidable German opponent was capable. As Rommel wrote, "It was a chance I could not resist ... Accordingly, on 2 April, the 5th Light Division moved forward ... to Agedabia ... The Italians followed along the coast road ... Meanwhile the 5th Panzer Regiment [which contained the sixty light and sixty medium tanks that represented the total armoured strength of Afrika Korps at that time] ... ran up against British tanks and a skirmish developed. Soon seven enemy tanks were burning on the battlefield. We lost only three."

Already Rommel had exceeded his orders. Von Brauchitsch had not envisaged an attack on Agedabia until May, but here it was already taken and the enemy in flight, leaving behind a large 'bag' of prisoners and equipment. To the Germans, monitoring the British radio network, it was obvious that the enemy was in confusion. General Wavell, the British commander-in-chief, was as astonished as

von Brauchitsch, since he too had made an orthodox appreciation of the situation, which made no allowance for so headstrong and precipitate a battle leader as Rommel. Moreover, it is likely that he was fooled by actually knowing too much of German intentions: the British had long since found a way of deciphering the German 'Enigma' code machine, and were therefore well supplied with many vital orders sent from Berlin to the Afrika Korps. How could Wavell guess that Rommel would disobey?

Arrogantly, but with ample justification, and ignoring all demands and pleas from above to restrict a further advance, Rommel now broke the rules and divided his forces. With armoured cars he pursued the enemy northward to Benghazi, which fell on 4 April, while a column of tanks and guns moved north-eastward to the key route-centre of Mechili, where the 5th Light Division commanded by Johannes Streich arrived on the 6th. With the enemy in disarray, the main risk was an administrative one, to which Rommel gave little attention until the 6 April when a column making from Mechili via Msus ran out of petrol. Unable to move his artillery into position at Mechili in time for a combined assault with another column, the local commander cried for help. Rommel's reaction was typical, immediate and personal. Finding it hard to trust those other than tried comrades, he felt bound to do the job himself. "All petrol reserves held by Divisional headquarters were immediately collected together – thirty-five cans in all – and at 0300 hours I set off with my Gefechtastaffel [tactical headquarters] to get the artillery into position before daybreak," he wrote. But, losing his way, he ran foul of an enemy column and was fortunate to evade capture. By now, his forces were dispersed all over the desert, some lost, some out of fuel. In a furious temper, he flew here and there in his Storch in desperate attempts to bring them together and, on at least one occasion, narrowly avoided landing among the British. All in all, his papers transmit a sense of panic – certainly, he was more worried than he admits. To Lu, he wrote only of his successes; his mistakes he covered up. His subordinates came to know the lash of his tongue when things went wrong (as they were bound to do when he followed order with counter-order). Streich he called a coward, and Streich answered back. If the British had not suffered a breakdown in command, and had launched a co-ordinated attack on Rommel's scattered and stranded forces, there might

have been little between him and total annihilation. He was lucky to survive. As it was, however, on 11 April he could look upon the defences of Tobruk. The enemy had been driven off and then enclosed; as captives, he had taken nearly every senior British desert leader, including General Sir Richard O'Connor who had earlier beaten the Italians. It was an astonishing and well-nigh miraculous performance.

The first siege of Tobruk

The thirty-mile perimeter defences of Tobruk, built originally by the Italians, were most tenuously held by a garrison of Australian and British troops, protected only by meagre air cover and a few anti-aircraft guns, and supplied by sea along a coastal route that was ever vulnerable to interdiction. Minefields, an anti-tank ditch and well co-ordinated artillery fire were the rocks upon which the garrison's resistance was founded when Rommel launched his initial assaults. These attempts were ill-prepared, however, and asked too much of troops who had outrun their strength. Rommel chose to call the first attacks "raids", which was close enough to the truth. But the main assault of 14 April also broke down under heavy artillery fire. The 5th Light Division was hard hit, its infantry element accusing the tanks of 'leaving them in the lurch', and Rommel blaming everybody except himself for the failure. The Italian Ariete Division also failed to advance into the artillery storm, and aggravated Rommel's contempt for their fighting qualities. Mutual recriminations pervaded the Axis camp as the losses piled up for nothing. Nevertheless, the British at the frontier were unable to counter Rommel's light reconnaissance troops, who seized the important defile of Halfaya Pass. Moreover, the 15th Panzer Division was daily gathering its strength as its units were brought forward from Tripoli. With Benghazi of increasing assistance as a port, it now seemed only a matter of time before Tobruk – an essential logistic feature, as even Rommel admitted – would fall.

In Rome and Berlin, meanwhile, there was mounting concern about the situation. Already, the campaign in Russia, scheduled for June, was in jeopardy. To Rommel's excessive expenditure of material had to be added the cost incurred by the, admittedly, outstanding German achievement of conquering the whole of Yugoslavia and Greece in April. These expended resources were lost for ever. Franz Halder, the German Chief of the General Staff, fumed at Rommel's methods and complained that he had "not sent in a single clear report". To clear up the mess, he sent his Deputy Chief of the General Staff, Friedrich Paulus, to North Africa, where he arrived on 27 April. After a cool study of the position, however, Paulus accepted the fait accompli, and sanctioned another assault on Tobruk on the 30th. But this, like its predecessors, ran into a fore-warned defence, and suffered grievous losses. Rommel blamed it on the inadequate training of the soldiers, who were pitched into a positional warfare that is always more costly than mobile operations (a situation he had precipitated himself, by acting against orders and taking the offensive so soon). He sacked Streich, in whom he had "lost confidence"; he blamed the Italians (of course); and he accused the Luftwaffe of incompetence, claiming that it would have been much more effective if it had been placed under his direct command instead of operating via Stefan Fröhlich. Indeed, Fröhlich's life he turned into sheer misery, roughly bullying an accomplished airman who was merely carrying out the orders of his superiors and making

the best use possible of the small number of fighters and bombers at his disposal. By the end of April, Rommel was at loggerheads with OKH and OKW in Berlin, distrusted by the Italians and disliked by Fröhlich, who, as time went by, went out of his way to avoid the commander of the Afrika Korps – to the detriment of future co-operation between the land and air forces. (It is even possible that, had he not been Hitler's favourite and Goebbels' protégé, Rommel might himself have been removed. It is worth recalling that when, in 1917 in Rumania, one of Rommel's platoon commanders had gone too far against Rommel's orders, Rommel had refused to go to that young man's aid, and had abandoned him to his fate despite a fine display of initiative. Perhaps Rommel forgot that in 1941.)

On the other hand, Rommel had recaptured Cyrenaica and dealt the enemy a deadly blow, at a cost of about 1,300 men. Feared and disliked though he might be by some of his own officers, and dangerously erratic though his methods were, he had given his followers a taste of victory, and his success had been a terrific boost to their morale. The officers, notably the staff and higher commanders, were wary of him, but the men followed him without question. His position was guaranteed, too, by a fanfare of praise on the German radio and in the press. Once more, Rommel was closely attended by one of Goebbels' most trusted young men: Hanke had been replaced by Deputy Reichspresschef Leutnant Dr. Ingemar Berndt, whom, writes Rommel's son, his father distrusted to begin with, but later came to like. Like his predecessor, Berndt was thrust into the thick of the fighting, and was to prove a fanatical soldier. But the full extent of his influence in Germany and with Rommel was yet to be exposed.

Right:
The Fliegerführer Afrika, General-major Stefan Fröhlich, who suffered, like so many others, from a bad relationship with Rommel.
(Bundesarchiv)
Below:
Stuka dive-bombers prepare for action.
(Image Press)

Left:
A 25pr field gun
in action – the
most potent
British defensive
weapon in
Tobruk and the
desert in 1941.
(Robert Hunt
Library)
Right:
German infantry
ride to the attack
on Pz Kpfw IVs.
(Image Press)
Below:
105mm field
artillery supports
the attack on
Tobruk.
(Bundesarchiv)

Right:
Mechanical wear and tear was very high in the dust-laden desert atmosphere. Engine changes such as this placed a heavy tax on the supply and maintenance services. (Image Press)

The British counterattack: Operation 'Brevity'

For the rest of the year, Rommel was forced on to the defensive. Pursuit into Egypt (which he plainly had in mind) was unthinkable until his strength was rebuilt and Tobruk had been taken. But supplies were denied him both by his masters in Europe and by the British, who sank so many of the Italian supply ships at sea. For this, too, he blamed the Italians, whose fleet had been driven into port by the British and whose convoy movements were almost invariably known in advance to the enemy – indeed, the breaking of their coded instructions revealed so much to the British that Rommel began to suspect his allies of treachery. Be these things as they may, it was now Rommel's turn to withstand assault: for, after withdrawing from Greece and being driven out of Crete by an airborne invasion, the British now managed to assemble a strong force of armour in the desert with the purpose of relieving Tobruk.

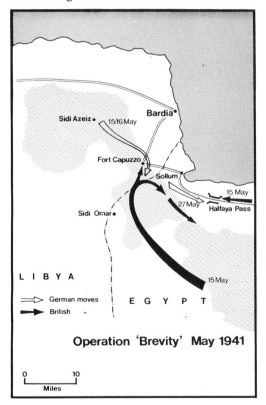

Operation 'Brevity' May 1941

Three British columns manoeuvre around the Halfaya Pass on 15 May and drive the Axis forces out, while receiving a rebuff in the tank battle that develops to the south-east of Fort Capuzzo. On 27 May, a German counterattack develops from the north-west and retakes the Pass, which Rommel then proceeds to fortify with 88mm guns.

The difficulty of every tactician in his endeavours to outmanoeuvre his enemy close to the North African coast lay in the limited permutations of deployment offered. With sea on the northern flank, a desert void to the south, and few topographical features to impede movement by mechanized forces, armies were compelled to operate within relatively close proximity to the coast road, restricting their inland forays to light forces except where established tracks made it possible to give them adequate logistic support (for example, along the route from Agedabia to Mechili, which Rommel had just exploited with such difficulty). To survive in a stand against tanks and their associated artillery units, infantry needed to find shelter in the few rocky locations, such as the rugged Halfaya Pass. There, for survival, they must fortify themselves behind minefields, covered by anti-tank guns and supported by mobile tank forces. Tank forces found – as had Rommel at Tobruk – that attacking such localities could be expensive and unrewarding. The mobile formations were therefore compelled to adopt a stereotyped approach via the desert flank, committing themselves to a thoroughly predictable course of trying to isolate and cut off the less mobile units clinging to the coast. The British and Italians had used this unavoidable gambit from the outset in 1940. Rommel had no option but to copy them; there was little scope for originality. Victories would be won by the side that made the best use of the resources at its disposal in campaigns that, in the final analysis, were governed by logistics. It followed that Rommel, an outstanding leader and tactician provided with well-trained and well-armed mobile forces, had an immediate superiority over British opponents whose battle leadership was wanting after the most experienced men had been eliminated in April. Logistically, however, the issue was open to question. It was due to Rommel's inferior logistic condition that, throughout May and June, he stood on the defensive, capable of only limited operations, while his enemy was enabled to employ more expansive, offensive tactics, using the predictable moves.

The first challenge by the British came on 15 May and was no surprise to Rommel, whose radio intercept service had provided adequate warning of their intentions. The British had scraped up twenty-nine of the faster, but lightly-armed and unreliable cruiser tanks, plus twenty-four of the heavy Matilda II tanks of the kind that had so shaken Rommel at Arras. The latter were to tackle the

Halfaya Pass by a direct assault, while the cruisers sealed off the area from the desert flank. British logistic support for Operation 'Brevity', as this was called, was tenuous, and they lost a number of tanks against the well dug-in German guns. They also suffered from a sharp armoured counterattack by the 5th Light Division, which might have achieved even more had not its refuelling arrangements broken down, leaving the tanks temporarily stranded. Throughout the engagement, Rommel remained uneasily on the defensive, worried that the Tobruk garrison might attempt a simultaneous breakout. From his point of view, the skirmish was disappointing. Three tanks were lost, 258 casualties sustained, Halfaya Pass forfeited, and clear evidence provided that coordination between his battle groups had not been all it might. His reaction to this setback was characteristic: failing to understand the reasons for the British operation being so restricted, he interpreted this as a sign of weakness, and tried a bluff on the 26th and 27th to eject them from Halfaya. Using every available drop of petrol – and well knowing that there simply was not enough fuel to supply them if an intensive battle developed – he assembled 160 tanks on the frontier. But the limited assault he delivered proved sufficient. The British, faced by superior numbers and harried by Oberst Herff (a very determined German battle-group leader to whom much credit must go), withdrew hurriedly with heavy losses. Letting them depart, Rommel dredged up every gun he could find, including many abandoned Italian pieces and a few 88mm dual-purpose guns, and heavily fortified the Halfaya Pass.

Operation 'Battleaxe'

The next encounter was to be a much more serious affair, designed by the British as a genuine relief of Tobruk. Having brought 238 new tanks through the Mediterranean by sea, brushing aside opposition by the Axis air forces and the Italian Navy, they were anxious to launch them quickly into action (despite technical teething troubles and lack of time for training) at a time when the Axis – as 'Enigma' told them – were severely restricted in mobility by fuel shortage. The British attack, Operation 'Battleaxe', would be a conventional 'left hook' through the desert, aimed on Sidi Azeiz, while heavy tanks and infantry assailed the Halfaya Pass. They would confront the lately-arrived 15th Panzer Division, the 5th Light Division having been withdrawn by Rommel into

reserve near Tobruk to recuperate after two months of hectic activity. Adequately forewarned, as usual, by the insecure British radio traffic, Rommel alerted his troops the previous evening. In consequence, the assault on the Halfaya Pass next day was met by a storm of accurate gunfire, made all the more effective by the British failure to coordinate their artillery support with the attacking units, allowing the 88mm gunners to aim undisturbed (just as at Arras). But the Germans made similar mistakes themselves. Although their guns and infantry in the desert fought resolutely against the initial British flank attacks, the local tank commanders copied the British by lunging headlong against the guns of emplaced British tanks.

On the evening of the 15th, the issue was in balance: although the Halfaya garrison remained intact, it was cut off and short of supplies, while, in the desert, the 15th Panzer Division had sustained high tank losses. The arrival of the 5th Light Division and Rommel himself at Sidi Azeiz, coupled with the assembly of such fulsome information that Rommel actually over-estimated British tank strength by a factor of two, was the moment for the commander of the Afrika Korps to display that tactical flair for which he is justifiably celebrated. He would attack southward next morning, using the 15th Panzer Division to strike at the mass of British armour near Fort Capuzzo; the 5th Light Division was to circle to the west before making for Sidi Suleiman.

Two short extracts from *The Rommel Papers* provide valuable insight into the man at work under pressure, and give an understanding of his battlefield techniques. At 0230 hours on the 16th, having completed the issue of orders for what he believed would bring a decision, he wrote a short note to Lu in which he said, "It's going to be a hard fight, so you'll understand I can't sleep." Rarely could he relax, and all too frequently, as his staff complained, he over-involved himself in details that were more their concern. After the 15th Panzer Division had suffered a sharp rebuff the next morning, and he had called off their attack in order to switch their axis to move in conformity with the 5th Light Division on the right flank, he was to comment that "it is often possible to decide the issue of a battle merely by making an unexpected shift of one's main weight". While this combination of unrelenting, hard work allied to close supervision of the staff placed a severe strain upon them all, it also produced results. And, guiding him for much of the

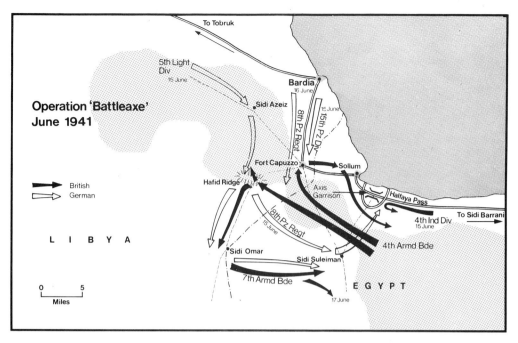

Operation 'Battleaxe'
June 1941

British
German

5th Light Div
15 June

To Tobruk

Bardia
16 June

Sidi Azeiz

8th Pz Regt

15th Pz Div
15 June

Fort Capuzzo

Sollum

Hafid Ridge

Axis Garrison

Halfaya Pass

To Sidi Barrani

L I B Y A

8th Pz Regt
15 June

4th Ind Div
15 June

4th Armd Bde

Sidi Omar

Sidi Suleiman

0   5
Miles

7th Armd Bde

E G Y P T

17 June

As the preliminary to an attempt to relieve Tobruk, the British launch two divisions supported by more than 200 tanks to the assault of the Halfaya Pass, linked with an enveloping move through the desert directed upon Sidi Azeiz. On 15 June, the attack on Halfaya is repelled with heavy losses by the well-emplaced Axis artillery, although a British column manages temporarily to enter Sollum in its rear early on the 16th. In the meantime, the 15th Panzer Division moves southward to tackle the British outflanking force near Fort Capuzzo, while the 5th Light Division is brought down from Tobruk. German anti-tank gunners on Hafid Ridge hold out all day and inflict heavy losses, but the same treatment is handed out to the 8th Panzer Regiment that evening when it, too, charges unavailingly against well-positioned British tanks at Fort Capuzzo. Taking personal control on the evening of the 15th, Rommel directs the 5th Light Division to drive south and then swing eastwards to Sidi Suleiman via Sidi Omar, while the tanks of the 15th Panzer Division again attack Fort Capuzzo. Although the 15th Panzer Division receives another drubbing, the British, wary of their flank, swiftly withdrew.

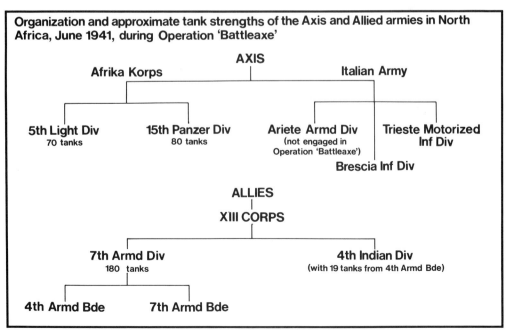

Organization and approximate tank strengths of the Axis and Allied armies in North Africa, June 1941, during Operation 'Battleaxe'

AXIS

Afrika Korps   Italian Army

5th Light Div   15th Panzer Div   Ariete Armd Div   Trieste Motorized
70 tanks   80 tanks   (not engaged in   Inf Div
                                            Operation 'Battleaxe')

                                                     Brescia Inf Div

ALLIES

XIII CORPS

7th Armd Div   4th Indian Div
180 tanks   (with 19 tanks from 4th Armd Bde)

4th Armd Bde   7th Armd Bde

Right:
The spoils of victory. A captured British 26-ton Matilda tank with an obsolete German Pz Kpfw I alongside. (Bundesarchiv)

Below:
Armoured cars, trucks and motor cycles of the Afrika Korps roll towards the Egyptian frontier. (Bundesarchiv)

time, of course, was that animal-like instinct of which he was fully aware. "I sniff through the country like a fox," he would often say – and thereby acquired for himself a nick-name, the 'Desert Fox'.

On 16 June, the 'Desert Fox' started in pursuit of the British who had intended to hound him. By the morning of the 17th, it dawned upon the quarry that they were in danger of being cut off should the combined German armoured columns link up with the Halfaya garrison and establish a barrier at their rear. They did not wait, but pulled back fast, their mobile artillery harrying the flank of the 5th Light Division as it raced eastward. Yet the British retreat was not a complete débâcle, as the German tank crews discovered: their opponents fought to the bitter end, and often gave as good as they got. The fight, as Rommel had foretold of an enemy he sometimes underestimated but never despised, was hard; although the British were driven back, they were not destroyed. And, in fact, more British losses came from mechanical breakdowns than from actual battle damage: ninety-one tanks were left behind on the battlefield, while the Germans lost but twenty-five. As Rommel bitterly complained, the victory might have been one of annihilation had not his flanking columns kept moving side by side, instead of establishing 'stop' lines to block and seal off the enemy pocket.

Above:
The swastika flies above a captured Matilda, near the Halfaya Pass. (Bundesarchiv)
Right:
Afrika Korps infantry trudge to their new defensive positions. (Bundesarchiv)

The repulse of Operation 'Battleaxe' taught Rommel two lessons, which are of immense importance in understanding his conduct of subsequent battles in this part of the desert. He felt he had learnt, by a study of panicky British radio traffic, that a raid aimed at their rear was an assured method of inducing fear and persuading them to bend to his will. Here was the psychologist at work. On the other hand, he took note that he had lost direct control of his two Divisions by remaining too remote from the action itself. To blame his subordinates, the Divisional commanders, for failure to co-ordinate their tactics was typical of Rommel when things went wrong; he should have foreseen the error. When next he essayed forth in the same locality, bent upon a similar aim, he would ride with the armour in person—with results of highly questionable value, as will be seen.

For the time being, however, he was on the crest of a wave. Five days later, the mass of the German Army would roll into Russia and capture the imagination of the world with victories of a magnitude that made the desert war look like a skirmish. Even then, however, Rommel would by no means be ignored by the propagandists, who made the most of his latest success. (It did, after all, clinch Churchill's decision to remove Wavell from command in the Middle East.) On 1 July, a grateful Hitler promoted Rommel to General der Panzertruppe, while the recipient, well knowing (as he told Lu) that "our stubborn friends on the other side will be back sooner or later", began to look around for ways of forestalling them.

5

The Vortex

Despite the way Rommel regarded his achievements, how generously the British paid tribute to his prowess, or how extravagantly Hitler and the German propagandists praised him, the German High Command saw the Afrika Korps as a mere detachment, which warranted only the barest essentials for its support in a secondary theatre of war. To the Italians and the British, on the other hand, this region was of supreme importance. The former were anxious to preserve the last remnants of their Empire; the latter eager to win victories for political prestige in the one and only theatre where their relatively small army was engaged, to free the Mediterranean shipping lanes from Axis domination, and to protect the vital Middle East oil sources.

To Hitler and von Brauchitsch, with the immense Russian campaign absorbing their attention to the full and demanding every available man, tank, gun and aeroplane, there could be no question of sending more than a dribble of reinforcements to Rommel, even if they could get past the Royal Navy. Only on the assumption of a successful conclusion to the campaign in Russia was draft Plan 'Orient' ordered by Hitler on 11 June, the intention being the eventual link-up of an advance through the Caucasus with an attack into Egypt. So not until the middle of August

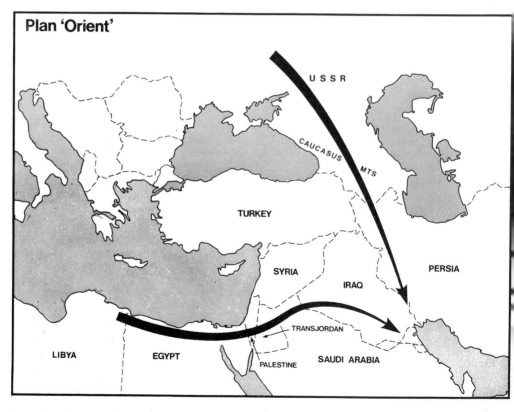

Plan 'Orient'

Right:
General Sir Alan Cunningham, who was removed from command of Eighth Army during Operation 'Crusader'. (Image Press)
Below:
Catching Rommel by surprise, British 19-ton Crusader tanks with 40mm guns race across the desert in the attempt to relieve Tobruk. (Imperial War Museum)

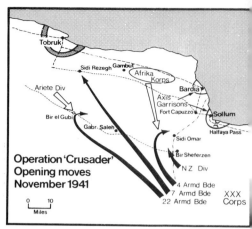

Operation 'Crusader'
Opening moves
November 1941

0   10
Miles

The British columns wheel round from the frontier to confront German armour concentrated to the east of Tobruk, where it is in readiness for the forthcoming German attack upon the port. The dispersal of the Afrika Korps eastwards on 19 and 20 November permits the British to seize Sidi Rezegh as a preliminary to a sortie from Tobruk on the 21st.

Relative strengths for Operation 'Crusader', November 1941

	Aircraft	Tanks	Armoured divisions	Infantry divisions
Axis	510	400	3	6
British	700 plus reserves	756 plus 50% reserves	3 equivalent	6 equivalent

1941, when victory in Russia seemed within reach, as the superbly trained and led German armies swept forward, was serious consideration given in Berlin to doing something positive to stimulate the North African venture. It was agreed, at last, that the lines of communication must be made more secure, and that the island of Malta would need to be neutralized as a matter of priority. There was agreement too that, prior to any advance on Egypt, the port of Tobruk had to be taken. In September 1941, even the Italians, whose forces in the desert had been much increased in numbers (if not in quality), came to concur with that. Meanwhile, Rommel, who was planning a November assault on the Tobruk perimeter, became anxious in August that the British had schemes to pre-empt him.

Signs that a desert supply dump was being created near Bir el Khireigat led him to project for mid-September, a carefully-planned 'reconnaissance in force' to destroy it, using the 5th Light Division, now upgraded and renamed '21st Panzer Division'. Movement by moonlight and well-timed refuelling were essential to the security of this long-range stroke by such a large force. Subsequently, it was discovered that the dump did not exist, but Rommel, ignoring all the danger signs, nevertheless proceeded with the raid with the revised intention of eliminating the British light forces that infested the frontier zone. He accompanied it in person, with the Divisional headquarters under Johann von Ravenstein. Everything went wrong (and it is interesting to note that the incident is omitted from the published version of his Papers). The British kept out of harm's way, contenting themselves with long-range shelling, while the German refuelling arrangements once more broke down,˙ with the result that the 21st Panzer Division was caught immobile in daylight by enemy bombers. The Division's effective tank strength dropped from 110 to 43 (although only 5 were actually abandoned) and had still not recovered by the middle of November. Rommel's chief of operations, Oberstleutnant Siegfried Westphal, remarks that this setback caused the postponement of the attack on Tobruk, because the losses could not be replaced. He found Rommel very depressed at an event that was "caused by our own fault". *The Rommel Papers*, however, only record how uplifted Rommel was when, at the end of September, a large shipment of supplies and equipment got through to Benghazi. He meanwhile continued to disbelieve the growing signs of an impending British offensive.

Operation 'Crusader'

By the autumn of 1941, the Axis forces were much enlarged to meet what was recognized as a considerable concentration of British troops in Egypt, whose long-term intentions were assumed to be the clearing of the entire North Africa coastline. In July, Rommel relinquished command of the Afrika Korps and took charge of a newly-created Panzergruppe Afrika with Alfred Gause as his chief of staff, Westphal as chief of operations and Friedrich von Mellenthin as intelligence officer. (Rommel, in fact, had bridled at the arrival of these formidable General Staff officers under Gause, and they had to take care not to ruffle his feathers too much while proving their indispensibility.) He had now to contemplate and control operations on a far larger scale than before, a task for which his previous training was scant preparation. By November, he had under his command the Afrika Korps (under Ludwig Crüwell), which now consisted of the two German Panzer Divisions, a Motorized Division (later to be known as the 90th Light Division) and the Italian Savona Infantry Division, as well as the Italian XXI Corps of four infantry divisions ringing Tobruk. Near by and likely soon to come under his control, though remaining under direct command of the Italian North Africa Command under General Ettore Bastico, was the Italian XX Motorized Corps, consisting of the Ariete Armoured Division and the Trieste Motorized Division. Under strength though he still was on 15 November, Rommel prepared to attack Tobruk on the 20th.

Axis strength and intentions were known to the British commander of the Eighth Army, General Sir Alan Cunningham, and it was therefore to his advantage to get in the first blow. He opened Operation 'Crusader' on the 18th, with the intention of destroying the Axis armour in battle as well as raising the siege of Tobruk and eliminating the Axis garrisons that had been established at the Halfaya Pass and Bardia.

The British advance in the direction of Gabr Saleh and Tobruk, as viewed from Panzergruppe headquarters, was cloaked in mystery, since the British wireless silence was complete, Axis air reconnaissance impossible because of heavy rain and flooded airfields, and ground reconnaissance of only limited capacity and accuracy. Since there was nothing von Mellenthin could tell Rommel that might convince him that anything more dangerous than a spoiling raid was in progress, Rommel, who professed not to

Right:
Rommel debating tactics with the Afrika Korps Chief of Staff, Fritz Bayerlein. It proved difficult to divert Rommel from his obsession in desiring to conquer Tobruk when the Afrika Korps stood in peril from the British offensive. Rommel was all too often at loggerheads with his subordinates and staff, besides those set above him. (Image Press)

believe in a British major effort, refused to abandon his cherished attack on the fortress. He rejected the anxiety expressed by von Ravenstein, whose 21st Panzer Division was already in contact with the leading British patrols, and by Crüwell, whose principal concern it was to fight the Afrika Korps as a unified force. It was not until the following morning that the presence of strong British armoured forces near Sidi Rezegh (within striking distance of Rommel's own location at Gambut) and Crüwell's warnings persuaded Rommel to admit to the existence of a full-scale enemy offensive. Even so, his reaction was tardy: he merely permitted the 21st Panzer Division to move against Gabr Saleh, while retaining the 15th Panzer Division on the coast until the evening. Almost casually, it seems, he delayed until after lunch before driving forward to watch the 21st Panzer Division enter battle.

Because Rommel failed to write a personal account of this battle, we are denied many of his innermost thoughts at this juncture, and must depend on the records and accounts of others for an explanation of what took place. The best of these come from Westphal, von Mellenthin and Fritz Bayerlein (who was Crüwell's chief of staff). Their stories of the opening gambits of 'Crusader' are broadly consistent, even though Bayerlein in The Rommel Papers draws attention to a controversy as to whether or not Rommel should have gambled in prosecuting the attack on Tobruk in the hope of completing it before Cunningham's offensive took effect. Bayerlein, who is not always a reliable witness, uses this as an example of Rommel's disinclination to gamble. The fact remained that Cunningham's armour was so close to Tobruk by the morning of the 19th that any suspicion of ignoring it until the 20th or 21st was ludicrous. Rommel had no option but to react to the British move. His error, as von Mellenthin points out, was in doing so just that much too precipitately to allow Crüwell to concentrate his Corps, a mistake that was mitigated by the British when they split their armoured forces into smaller groups and also sacrificed concentration. The fact is that Rommel had still not totally abandoned hope of attacking Tobruk next day: hence his delay in moving the 15th Panzer Division.

Yet it was this reluctance on Rommel's part to face the enemy offensive that persuaded the British to divide their forces in order to seek out the German armour. As a result, the initial clash between British tanks and a German battle group of tanks, field guns and 88mm dual-purpose guns on the afternoon of the 19th found the Germans in a local superiority of strength, resulting in a balance of losses in their favour. They had, moreover, another new weapon, which, aggressively handled, was to give them a distinct advantage in the armoured battle: this was the long and relatively lightweight 50mm anti-tank gun. On its low-slung field mounting, it could be brought speedily into action in the forefront of the battle, to engage from one, inconspicuous position before being shifted rapidly to another, safer fire position. This gun outranged the existing British tank guns, and could, at optimum distances, penetrate all but the thickest armour on the British heavy Matilda tank.

Rommel was right when he wrote to Lu on the 20th that "the battle has now reached a crisis". That day, the Afrika Korps managed to concentrate for the first time against an enemy who was spread all over the desert. By then, it was mainly a question of sifting the available information and allowing Crüwell, "with a free hand", to encompass the enemy's destruction. The main trouble, however, was the paucity of information available. Air reconnaissance was still difficult because of the inclement weather, and ground reconnaissance was poor. So the actual pattern of British dispersion was still unknown. Moreover, the initial concentration of the Afrika Korps was immediately undone when the 21st Panzer Division (as was its wont at critical moments) ran out of petrol. So the 15th Panzer Division was sent ahead on its own, and the vital gathering of German armour was again postponed. The 21st Panzer Division wasted its time on 21 November, while the 15th, more from luck than judgement, hit one of the dispersed British armoured brigades (the 4th) and gave it a drubbing east of Gabr Saleh.

Only now, as it at last became clear that the British had a firm grip on Sidi Rezegh and that a breakout from Tobruk was to be expected next day, did Rommel allow himself unreservedly to accept the blatantly obvious signs that this was a full-scale British offensive. At fault though his information services may have been, it is scarcely to be believed that, as was claimed, it was a British radio announcement from Cairo that convinced him! His instincts were more sensitive than that, and he had repeatedly rejected the evidence before him. Now, however, he shook off the torpor that seems to have marked his behaviour throughout the first three days of 'Crusader'. Just before dawn on

The long, towed 50mm Pak 38 anti-tank gun, which proved such a menace to the British armour. (Bundesarchiv)

the 21st, he signalled Crüwell that, "the situation in this theatre is very critical", in his efforts to launch the Afrika Korps swiftly westward for a concerted attack against the British at Sidi Rezegh. But, before it could do this, the Afrika Korps had to disentangle itself from the British armour with which it had become engaged at Sidi Azeiz the previous evening and, while so doing, news came in that the British had begun their major sortie from Tobruk, also in the direction of Sidi Rezegh. Simultaneously, reports arrived of a fresh enveloping thrust at the frontier, curling round from Sidi Omar in the direction of Sidi Azeiz with the obvious intention of isolating the frontier garrisons. The Afrika Korps could not be in two places at once, and nor could Rommel: Crüwell had to be left to his own devices in executing his attack on Sidi Rezegh, and the frontier positions had temporarily to be abandoned to their own defence. As for Rommel, he reckoned his presence in demand at the most critical point – as he saw it – where the British were debouching from Tobruk. This fascinated him. Here he spent the rest of the day leading, in person, the battle groups of the 90th Light Division and Italians against the hostile incursions, an exercise in leadership that availed him little, for the British only stopped when they had advanced 4,000 yards and taken over 1,000 prisoners. Indeed, the sole reason for the British halt was news that their armour at Sidi Rezegh (part of the 7th Armoured Division) could not come immediately to their aid, since the Afrika Korps had put in its appearance from the east at about the time the sortie had begun. This had thoroughly absorbed the 7th Armoured Division's attention, besides inflicting heavy losses upon it, and was therefore the crucial factor. Add to that the danger to Panzergruppe headquarters, which found itself in all-too-close proximity to the New Zealand Division as it swept by on either side of Sidi Azeiz, and 21 November was not a day for rejoicing in the German camp.

Some idea of the tension under which they were all working can be obtained from Westphal, when he describes Rommel's retort to an officer who reported that he had to leave Africa immediately on doctor's advice because of heart trouble: "That is out of the question. You are looking all right and standing upright. This theatre of war will only be left in a horizontal position, on a stretcher." The day would come when Rommel, in connection with his own health, would adopt a different attitude. But, on this "macabre

evening", as Westphal put it, when Panzergruppe headquarters had of necessity to be transferred to El Adem, south of Tobruk, General Hans-Ferdinand Geisler, commander of X Fliegerkorps, took his leave of them, and a signal, full of praise, arrived from von Brauchitsch at OKH. "One had the feeling that we were already partially written off," remarks Westphal.

The risks that Rommel took on the following day, the 22nd, further reduced confidence in the outcome of the battle. Because of his close proximity to the Tobruk perimeter, where the British breakout looked to be the main threat, Rommel became obsessed with the detailed fight in this sector rather than standing back as overall commander and analysing the broad situation. His orders were narrow, those of a divisional leader rather than a Panzergruppe commander of mature and wide outlook. By causing Crüwell to shift the 21st Panzer Division to Belhamed in order to counter the Tobruk breakout, Rommel again brought about the splitting of the Afrika Korps. It was Crüwell's wish to gain "complete freedom of manoeuvre" by regrouping at Gambut, where he moved the 15th Panzer Division on its own. But these two movements enabled the British 7th Armoured Division, for the first time, to concentrate near Sidi Rezegh, separating the Afrika Korps into two elements eighteen miles apart. This division of strength was a procedure that ran quite contrary to German practice, and it was Rommel, by interfering with Crüwell's more sensible and orthodox approach, who was wholly responsible for it.

It was fortunate for Rommel that Crüwell pulled his chestnuts out of the fire for him. Realizing that Rommel, who had virtually taken direct command of the 21st Panzer Division at Belhamed, was intending to launch it against Sidi Rezegh early in the afternoon, and that the 15th Panzer Division seemed to have shaken off enemy surveillance, he brought that Division round from the east to catch the 7th Armoured Division between two fires. That evening, everything went the German way. The 21st Panzer Division's attack, delivered with the élan and confidence that only Rommel was able to impart in such circumstances, overran Sidi Rezegh after one of the British armoured brigades (the 4th) had been detached to pursue the 15th Panzer Division to the east. But the 15th, moving in from the east at dusk, crashed into the headquarters and part of the 4th Armoured Brigade and captured fifty

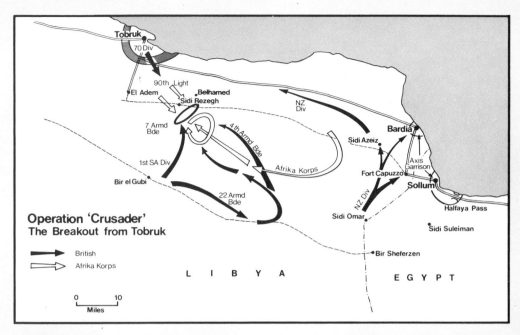

Operation 'Crusader'
The Breakout from Tobruk

➤ British

⇨ Afrika Korps

Tobruk
70 Div
90th Light
El Adem • Belhamed
Sidi Rezegh
NZ Div
7 Armd Bde
4th Armd Bde
1st SA Div
Afrika Korps
Bir el Gubi
22 Armd Bde
Bardia
Sidi Azeiz
Axis Garrison
Fort Capuzzo
Sollum
NZ Div
Halfaya Pass
Sidi Omar
Sidi Suleiman
Bir Sheferzen

L I B Y A   E G Y P T

0   10
Miles

Below:
A Pz Kpfw III rolls past a burning lorry at the height of the battle. (Bundesarchiv)

The breakout from Tobruk takes place on 21 November, and compels Rommel to recall the Afrika Korps to relieve the pressure by attacking the British armour at Sidi Rezegh. Simultaneously, the previously scattered British armoured units also begin to converge on this vital spot. At the same time, the New Zealand Division and the 4th Indian Division begin to encircle the Axis frontier garrisons, occupying ground vacated by the Afrika Korps when it is drawn off in the direction of Tobruk. The struggle between armoured formations to the south-east of Tobruk is decided for the moment in the German favour at Sidi Rezegh, where the Afrika Korps, joined by the Ariete Division on the 22nd and 23rd manages, with its armour concentrated, to trap the 5th South African Brigade and cause the British heavy tank casualties. Here too, on the 23rd, the New Zealanders are repelled as they advance on Sidi Rezegh.

tanks, besides eliminating this important element of control. Gradually, the Afrika Korps was coalescing at the vital spot. And now – at last – Rommel called for a positive Italian involvement in the mobile battle by asking Rome to place XX Motorized Corps (which included the Ariete Armoured Division) under his direct command. The request, which should surely have been made much earlier, was immediately granted, and the Ariete was instantly given orders to join forces with the armour of the Afrika Korps.

Next day, 23 November, was to mark the zenith of German achievement in this battle, and it is instructive to note that this came about only partly as the result of Rommel's directions, and mainly because of the exper-tise of Crüwell. While it is true that Rommel now fully recognized the importance of the ground between Bir el Gubi and Sidi Rezegh, and appreciated that the enemy in that area was vulnerable to a counter-stroke, he sent such a long and detailed radio signal to Crüwell on the night of the 22nd/23rd that there was simply insufficient time to decode and transcribe it. So next day, Crüwell, know-ing only Rommel's outline intention, made and executed his own plan by concentrating *all* his tanks (including the Ariete Division) at Bir el Gubi, and launching them northward en masse, catching the British in a vice

between the 21st Panzer Division's infantry and guns at Sidi Rezegh. Crüwell's conduct of the fighting on 23rd was a masterpiece of improvisation, as he deftly steered his armour (150 tanks) past scattered enemy opposition to reach the desired assembly area. It was all the more praiseworthy since almost his entire headquarters had been cap-tured at dawn by the New Zealanders, and he had therefore to control the battle with a makeshift command organization through-out the day.

This day, 23 November, was the German Totensonntag, the day of remembrance for the dead of the First World War and, in 1941, it was to be commemorated by the loss of many officers and men. But, by nightfall, their sacrifice could be set against the total disruption of the British supply columns hit by the 15th Panzer Division on their way to Bir el Gubi, the destruction of the 5th South African Brigade and further heavy losses inflicted on the remains of the 7th Armoured Division. The German casualties were serious as a result of a tactical experiment on Crüwell's part, which (as von Mellenthin sardonically points out) was an innovation for the Germans. Instead of manoeuvring for good fire positions, as was customary, Crüwell drew his force up in a phalanx and charged. At least sixty tanks paid the penalty

Above:
Rommel in a huddle with his staff after the failure of his drive to the frontier. (Image Press)
Right:
Desert sand grimes members of the battle-weary Afrika Korps. (Image Press)

*General Sir
Claude
Auchinleck, the
British
commander-in-chief,
who soon felt the
need to supersede
Cunningham and
impose his own
authority on the
battle against
Rommel.
(MacClancy
Press/Imperial
War Museum)*

for this folly, and it can only be asked if Rommel would have permitted it had he been present (as was his intention). But Rommel was once more inextricably mixed up in a local battle of his own, helping to fend off the same New Zealanders who had overrun Afrika Korps headquarters that morning. It was only at nightfall that he got back to Panzergruppe headquarters to discover what had happened elsewhere.

Rommel's mood that night was of exultant excitement, though Westphal felt he greatly overestimated the extent of the German achievement. Probably harking back to the experience of his dramatic and successful psychological counter-strike during 'Battleaxe' in June, he determined to repeat the master blow. With 106 tanks remaining to the Afrika Korps, reinforced by the Ariete Division, he would sweep scythe-like next day to the frontier, erect a barrier in the enemy rear and, at the same time, relieve the frontier garrisons. Westphal, who was highly sceptical, writes: "Rommel was determined to lead the advance ... Gause would go with him. I would be responsible for the Tobruk front. I pointed out the danger of the British and New Zealanders, who would not easily

give in. Rommel said I exaggerated, that I did not understand the British."

Rommel's 'dash to the wire'

Next morning, 24 November, Rommel removed the Axis armour from the vital point (against Crüwell's advice) and took a weakened Afrika Korps (less than a hundred tanks) in some confusion (over conflicting orders from Rommel and Crüwell) upon a raid for which the logistic arrangements were inadequate. As von Mellenthin remarks, "no cool or accurate appraisal was possible". Rommel had correctly judged the character of one Briton—his immediate adversary, Cunningham, who certainly lost his nerve as his administrative troops recoiled to the frontier and panic set in—but he had underestimated the British as a whole. As soon as Cunningham proposed calling off the offensive, he was removed by his Commander-in-Chief, General Sir Claude Auchinleck, who took personal charge, and restored the situation by his calm presence. When that happened, whatever remote chance Rommel might have had of stampeding his opponent evaporated. His psychological blow forfeited conviction because he was unable to press it home,

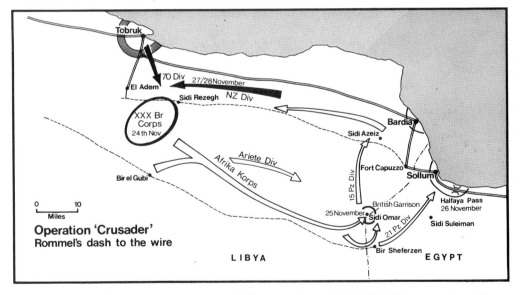

Operation 'Crusader'
Rommel's dash to the wire

Convinced that he has won a great victory at Sidi Rezegh, Rommel, on 24 November, takes the Afrika Korps in a raid to the east, hoping to seize the initiative, cut the British supply lines, and also relieve the coastal garrisons. He is harried all the way, and firmly rebuffed at Sidi Omar on the 25th. But he causes a notable British panic (which results in the commander of the British Eighth Army being relieved by the British commander-in-chief in person), and manages to reach the Halfaya Pass and Bardia. In the

meantime, the British, left in occupation of the vacated crucial battleground to the south-east of Tobruk, are able to repair many broken down and damaged tanks and to seize, once more, the Sidi Rezegh area. On the 26th, they link-up with the Tobruk garrison, and compel Rommel to abandon his raid, which has already largely failed in its object. At Sidi Rezegh once more, the Afrika Korps engages British armoured formations that have been reinforced and are a lot wiser from experience.

through lack of resources. It was revealed as a misjudgement and an underrating of his adversary.

On the 25th (the day on which Lieutenant-General N. M. Ritchie assumed command of Eighth Army), the 21st Panzer Division reached the Halfaya Pass, but the 15th Panzer Division was repulsed at Sidi Omar, and that ended the chance of sealing off the British. Worse still, from the German point of view, Rommel was frequently out of touch with Afrika Korps headquarters and entirely cut off for four days from Panzergruppe headquarters because of the breakdown of his radio vehicle. On the night of the 24th, Rommel and Gause were alone in the desert in their broken-down vehicle, and were fortunate to be seen and picked up by Crüwell as he motored by. While it is true that a battlefield is a very untidy place, a good higher commander will normally endeavour to make it tidier and avoid spreading unnecessary confusion among his own troops. On this occasion, Rommel's behaviour, out of radio touch and rushing from one crisis spot to another, was in distinct contrast to the calm and inspiring example set by Auchinleck. For example, it was Rommel who had reversed a properly thought-out order by Crüwell on the 25th, and sent the tanks of the 21st Panzer Division to their destruction against the British at Sidi Omar; and, while Afrika Korps headquarters plaintively echoed Rommel's complaints of "Where are the German fighters?", and enemy aircraft ravaged its scattered columns, it was his ill-considered strategy that had detached the Afrika Korps from the airfields at Gambut, which had now fallen.

Meanwhile, Westphal, suffering at that moment from jaundice, was becoming anxiously aware of a sinister accumulation of enemy strength to the south and east of Tobruk. Throughout the 25th, the Italian commander-in-chief, Bastico, had been at Panzergruppe headquarters, and he also was growing increasingly worried about the situation. On the 26th, Westphal, who had implored Rommel on the radio to send the Afrika Korps back to the west, had made no contact with his commander or had been ignored. At last, in desperation, he (a mere lieutenant-colonel) sent a direct order to the 21st Panzer Division calling it back. It was not a moment too soon. As von Ravenstein told Westphal, they had all come to the conclusion that they were being driven into a British prison camp, and von Ravenstein gave his officers time off to write farewell letters! But

Rommel was furious, and threatened to court martial Westphal. Only when he at last arrived back at his own headquarters on the 27th, looked at the map, and read the signals, did he comprehend the peril from which Westphal had saved him. It is, indeed, almost incredible to read about Rommel's personal exploits at the time of the frontier raid: the catalogue of his narrow shaves and flukey escapades, as he raced about the battlefield from one unit to another, frequently driving among the British, produced a legend of invincibility more in tune with a dashing young subaltern from a boy's journal than with a mature army commander. He got away with it, but that is no reason for adulation. In any case, he had thrown away what might have been a German victory.

The return of Rommel and the Afrika Korps to the vicinity of Tobruk in an attempt to retain the initiative came too late. They would win a series of local tactical successes in the ensuing days and the British would see their tenuous link-up with the Tobruk garrison broken. But already, on the 27th, the Italians were asking for a withdrawal. And, although von Mellenthin claims that by the evening of the 30th "on paper we seemed to have won the 'Crusader' battle", he had to admit that the price had been too heavy and that the Panzergruppe had been worn down. It had not, in fact, received a single new tank since the start of the battle and, by now, the sixty or so remaining machines were in a mechanically parlous state. The enemy, meanwhile, was steadily being reinforced with new and repaired tanks, some manned by relatively fresh troops. The 30th certainly marks a turning point in the North African campaign. Though, Rommel had written to Lu on the 29th saying that he was "full of confidence", he was, as von Mellenthin remarks, "reluctant to face the hard facts of the situation", and he admitted to Bastico (who, when times were good, he normally ignored) that the outlook was grave. Jointly and urgently, they asked Rome for men, machines and supplies, but these would not arrive overnight. On 2 December, he was reduced to exhortation: "Soldiers! This magnificent success is due to your courage, endurance and perseverance ... Forward then to the final knock-out of the enemy."

Retreat from Cyrenaica

The unsatisfactory state of affairs in North Africa had long been realized in Rome and Berlin. Gradually, the proposals for a deeper German involvement, which had been mooted in August, had been converted into a positive plan and, in mid-November, Mussolini had been compelled to admit a further German intervention in the 'Italian' theatre. To secure the lines of communication from Europe to Africa, the Germans would raise their air contribution from a Fliegerkorps to a Luftflotte brought in from Russia. At its head would be Generalfeldmarschall Albert Kesselring, who would also assume the title of Commander-in-Chief, South, without, however, being accorded direct command over Rommel. Kesselring had arrived in Rome on 28 November, and would soon visit Cyrenaica to see for himself the state of the game. But, by the time he and Rommel met on 15 December, the entire position was in a state of flux.

On 4 December, Rommel, who the previous day had actually (and incredibly) been tempted once more to attempt the relief of the long-isolated frontier garrisons by another drive to the frontier, belatedly sanctioned a withdrawal from Tobruk. If maintenance of aim is a virtue of generalship, then Rommel was well endowed, for he persisted to the end in his determination to seize Tobruk. Perhaps it was plain obstinacy. Informed on the 5th that reinforcements were unlikely until the end of the year, when Luftflotte 2 would make its presence felt, he lapsed into deep pessimism and hastened his retreat, making for a previously prepared Italian line of defence south of Gazala. The troops that could be extricated took post on the 8th (a day on which, according to Bastico, Rommel yelled

Right:
British 25pr guns pummel the retreating Germans. (Imperial War Museum)
Below:
The German infantry enter new defensive positions as a sand storm brews on the horizon. (Bundesarchiv)

THE VORTEX   83

at him that he had "now decided to take his divisions to Tripoli and have himself interned in Tunisia").

Certainly, Rommel had now concluded that it would be wiser to abandon Cyrenaica altogether—he rarely did anything by half-measures—but he could no longer ignore the Italians. The matter had become political. He needed their support and could only obtain it by diplomacy. So he had started on the 8th by roundly condemning the Italian Army to Bastico's face and, in almost every succeeding confrontation, made their collaboration less willing by the tactlessness of his behaviour. A few useful concessions were made in the command structure, however, with all the Italian formations now placed under Rommel's direct command. But the exchanges reverted to a rude confrontation when, on the 16th, as the British began to outflank the Gazala Line, he announced uncompromisingly that the position must be abandoned and Cyrenaica given up. From the military angle he was undeniably right, since the Axis

position had become untenable in every respect. Had he been on better terms with the Italians he might have won their agreement at once, but it was among Rommel's failings in high command that his relationship with allies was so frequently acrimonious—as, indeed it was with most subordinates who did not toe his line.

There is complete unanimity in the testimony of those present at the meeting on 16 December concerning the atmosphere. As Ugo Cavallero, the Italian chief of staff, put it, "feathers flew". Rommel gratuitously insulted the Italians by frankly stating that the defence of Agedabia had to be entrusted to German troops, the only ones he could rely upon. At this, Bastico lost all restraint. Kesselring, who entered the discussion that afternoon, tried hard to smooth things over and tended, in so doing, to take the Italians' part. With ample military justification, Rommel rejected Kesselring's suggestion that the withdrawal might be delayed. Kesselring, he said, was not in full possession of all the

facts, and his promise of strong Luftwaffe assistance was the last thing likely to sway Rommel at a time when he was thoroughly disenchanted with the Luftwaffe contribution to date. In conclusion, Rommel pointed out that the decision was his in any case, and the withdrawal would begin at once. It was not a moment too soon. At that very moment, British armoured cars and tanks were advancing rapidly and unopposed to cut the coast road to Tmimi and place a barrier across the Axis rear. Had this enemy formation not run short of petrol and been forced to withdraw to meet its supply lorries, the better part of the Axis Army would have been reduced to fighting its way out, and must surely have lost heavily in the engagement. (It is noteworthy, however, that Crüwell judged it possible to hold the British at Gazala, and that he sided with Kesselring and the Italians.)

It was typical of Rommel that, once he had decided upon retreat, he executed the movement with a verve equivalent to his fastest advance. Small rearguards held off the British, but the main body was withdrawn at full speed in a single bound, to evade the enemy pursuit. He had sent what remained of the 90th Light Division to Agedabia to pro-

vide a safe base, but little thought seems to have been given at first as to where the rest of the Army might make a stand. To Lu on the 20th, he merely said it would be "somewhere", but that he had "little ammunition and petrol and no air support". The final assertion is untrue, of course; but the air support already being provided by Kesselring had made a poor showing on the 18th. Delighted to be making a contribution, Kesselring had boasted to Rommel of an attack that was in process of being made by his dive-bombers upon the British. Unfortunately, at that precise moment, a signal arrived from Crüwell complaining bitterly that the attack had fallen upon the Afrika Korps, with most unhappy results. The relationship between Rommel and Kesselring had thus got off to a very bad start. It would be futile (and incorrect) for Kesselring later to claim that, had it not been for the Luftwaffe, the Panzergruppe would not have escaped. He would have been on firmer ground if he had taken credit for the arrival at Benghazi on 19 December of a ship bringing twenty-two tanks—the first to arrive since September—and another ship with a further twenty-three tanks at Tripoli. Though rep-

Above:
Newly-shipped Pz Kpfw IIIs arrive to sustain the Afrika Korps near Benghazi. (MacClancy Press)

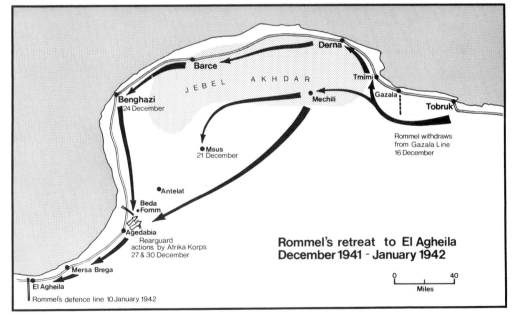

**Rommel's retreat to El Agheila
December 1941 - January 1942**

Derna
Barce
J E B E L   A K H D A R
Tmimi
Benghazi
24 December
Mechili
Gazala
Tobruk
Rommel withdraws from Gazala Line 16 December
Msus
21 December
Antelat
Beda Fomm
Agedabia
Rearguard actions by Afrika Korps 27 & 30 December
Mersa Brega
El Agheila
Rommel's defence line 10 January 1942

0   40
Miles

Deprived of reinforcements, and faced by an opponent whose strength has been maintained, Rommel withdraws from Tobruk on 5 December and heads for the Gazala Line, where the Italians are strengthening the existing defences. On 15 December, the British direct their 7th Armoured Division through the desert to curl northwards against Rommel's rear at Tmimi. Rommel,

against Italian wishes, begins a precipitate retreat to Agedabia. At Beda Fomm and to the east of Agedabia, the Afrika Korps turns and prevents the Axis armies from being cut off and pressed too hotly. By 10 January, the German troops have gone into reserve behind the Italians at El Agheila, and the British, short of supplies, have halted.

resenting but half the total despatched (the remainder having been sunk at sea), this infusion of tanks provided a psychological as well as material boost to the Germans. Of this, Gustav von Vaerst, the latest commander of the 15th Panzer Division, took full advantage when a column of British tanks became over-extended near Beda Fomm on the 23rd. His swift raid provided a local success for the Germans, which ensured that there would be no repetition of the disaster that had befallen the Italians on the same ground the previous February.

Rommel was able to extricate the bulk of his men and a certain quantity of material from Benghazi before the coast road was cut. Moreover, when the British followed-up on the 27th, during the final stages of the German withdrawal to Agedabia, they found themselves in trouble once more. Crüwell, that fine tactician, noticed that a gap had opened between two British groups. With the sixty tanks at his disposal, he seized the chance of striking a numerically superior but qualitatively inferior enemy force of ninety tanks and, with Rommel's approval, hit back hard on the 28th, destroying thirty-seven British machines for the loss of only seven German tanks. And yet again, on the 30th, Crüwell struck, this time destroying twenty-three out of the sixty-two British tanks, and putting paid to any enemy hopes that remained of preventing the Axis Army from gaining the shelter of El Agheila. Here, on 10 January 1942, the long retreat ended, practically unhindered by the British, who had run short of fuel. That day, for the first time since 18 November, the Afrika Korps went into reserve.

Rommel had been through some bad moments, and there is little doubt that the strain had told upon him. His stomach, always unreliable, had behaved well but he had been worried about it quite often. In almost every letter to Lu, he dilated upon his misfortunes and the shortcomings of the Italians, of whom he noted on 25 December, "there are shocking signs of deterioration". But by then he detected a ray of hope. At lunchtime, he shared a bottle of champagne with Gause, Westphal and von Mellenthin in the Intelligence truck; in one of those brief moments when he felt able to take his mind off their predicament, he remarked, "I wonder if your families are thinking of you?" In fact, their families might have been shocked if they could have seen them then: Crüwell and Westphal had jaundice, and Gause was badly 'run down' by 10 January.

Now was the time for both sides to tidy up and reinforce. The British maintained light covering forces east of El Agheila, while they began to drag supplies forward and endeavoured to reopen the badly-damaged port of Benghazi. Meanwhile, in four days of siege warfare, they eliminated the Axis garrisons of 14,000 men that had been abandoned at the Halfaya Pass and Bardia. Rommel's spirits, however, were beginning to rise again. He had managed to execute his escape to his own satisfaction, his tank force was expanding and, by 20 January would stand at about 140. The Luftwaffe, under Kesselring's experienced command, was beginning to

take such a toll of the British at Malta that the Axis flow of supplies across the Mediterranean to Tripoli was already improving. From Rome, where he was recuperating, Gause wrote to say that the Führer had "approved" of all he had done and was "full of praise and admiration". This was important – especially because it came in the aftermath of Hitler's comprehensive sacking of generals (including von Brauchitsch and Guderian) for alleged failures in Russia. Genuinely disenchanted with the Army's leadership, Hitler had personally assumed the appointment of Commander-in-Chief, in addition to that of Supreme Commander. From now on, Hitler alone (through Field Marshal Keitel and General Jodl at OKW) would be Rommel's immediate superior.

And so, on 17 January, a revitalized Rommel could look to his own future with confidence, and confide to Lu: "The situation is developing to our advantage and I'm full of plans that I daren't say anything about around here. They'd think me crazy. But I'm not; I simply see a bit further than they do . . . I work out my plans early each morning, and how often, during the past year and in France, have they been put into effect within a matter of hours? That's how it should be and is going to be in future."

6

Backlash to Gazala

The situation that had been "developing to our advantage" had been drawn to Rommel's attention by the General Staff officers he tended to denigrate. By piecing together the information gleaned from air and ground reconnaissance reports, snippets from agents planted behind the enemy lines and, above all, from the interception of radio traffic, von Mellenthin had been able to arrive at certain positive conclusions, which immediately convinced Westphal as to the possibilities of profitable offensive action. They owed much to the brilliant work of Lieutenant Alfred Seeböhm, who, by dint of hard practice listening to enemy radio operators' exchanges, had managed to 'think' his way into the minds of the British until he could tell which units were active near the front, and what their strength and intentions were. Additionally, certain high-quality information was being received from another radio intercept unit, which, with knowledge of an American diplomatic code, was reading some revealing signals from an American liaison officer operating with the British in Cairo; these both confirmed and amplified Seeböhm's discoveries. From this multiplicity of sources, it became apparent to Seeböhm, von Mellenthin and Westphal on 12 January 1942 that, throughout the next fortnight, the enemy to their immediate front would be their inferior both in numbers and experience. They now knew that the British 1st Armoured Division, fresh to the desert and with only 150 tanks, had replaced the hardened 7th Armoured Division, and that its vehicles were in bad order. Against them, Rommel could pit 117 German tanks (mostly the reliable Panzerkampfwagen IIIs and IVs manned by seasoned crews) and 79 of the inferior Italian tanks. Indeed, by 21 January, the Axis would have in the region of Mersa Brega three German mobile divisions (about 12,500 men all told), plus the Italians' two mobile divisions

and three infantry divisions (about 25,000 men). Whereas the British would comprise but two mobile divisions – one of the rare occasions on which Rommel significantly outnumbered his opponents.

The records show that it was Westphal who initially and strenuously proposed attack and Rommel who at first demurred, on the grounds that the administrative backing was insufficient. This was a revelation in itself, but not necessarily an indication that he fully understood the essential logistic situation. There existed just sufficient supplies for a limited offensive. So he misled Lu when he suggested that the idea of a local offensive was his own. Once convinced that the logistics were feasible, however, he became his old driving self again. The horizon brightened ahead, and he planned with his inherent zest – at the same time taking the precaution of keeping OKH and the Italians in the dark as to his intentions. Kesselring, however, was in the know: because the initial planning had to include the Luftwaffe, the plan was discussed with him. With a spirit as bold and as daring as Rommel's, he saw no tactical objection to the raid, but he had to be wary of Italian reactions, since he was engaged at that moment in delicate negotiations to gain their collaboration for his plan to invade Malta. Only that way could a permanent solution to the logistic problem be enforced: by taking Malta, the Axis supply lines to the North African theatre of war would be made safe.

Kesselring, however, harboured deep reservations about Rommel's qualities as a higher commander charged with the task of co-operating with allies. It was bad enough that Rommel was at loggerheads with the Luftwaffe (to which Kesselring, as one of its founders, bore a strong allegiance) and that Generalmajor Stefan Fröhlich, the Fliegerführer Afrika whose task it was to translate

Rommel's requests into air action, now did his best to avoid the Army commander; but it was far more serious to Kesselring that Rommel seemed to go out of his way to aggravate the Italians. And all this was in addition to the clash of personalities that already existed between Kesselring, a General Staff officer of immense charm and culture, and Rommel, who was not only anti-General-Staff, but often offensive in behaviour. Kesselring was to write of Rommel after the war: "To his subordinates he was insultingly rude. Were it not for the fact that he was a Württemberger, it might have been worth speaking to him about it." In more significant and practical terms he writes in his memoirs: "Rommel's great reputation, then at its zenith, was an obstacle to the introduction of any change." From the start, Kesselring aimed to minimize Rommel's influence and eventually remove him from the Mediterranean stage, a policy that he would pursue with subtle thoroughness for the next eighteen months until he had achieved his aim. To begin with, he replaced Fröhlich with a much tougher officer, Hoffmann von Waldau, who had but recently been displaced as Deputy Chief of the Luftwaffe General Staff because he had presented Hermann Goering, his commander-in-chief, with too many unpalatable truths concerning the Luftwaffe's overall decline. Von Waldau was the last man on earth to be bullied by Rommel. From now on, German air support would be controlled with firmness as well as outstanding practical aptitude.

When Kesselring learnt of Rommel's plan, he kept it to himself. Indeed, the conspiratorial silence among the Germans was one reason why the British remained in ignorance of what was in store, since nothing was given

Far right: *Planning the surprise, opportunist offensive — Bayerlein, von Mellenthin, Rommel and Nehring. (Image Press)*
Right: *Von Mellenthin and Westphal. (Author's Collection)*

away via radio intercept. Their only warning came from a single air-reconnaissance report on 21 January, which told of many enemy vehicles concentrating at Mersa Brega. Nevertheless, air power was to play but a minor rôle in the opening stages of the forthcoming battle, since heavy rains had converted the British airfields into a morass and sandstorms obscured the German concentration areas.

Rommel's plan, as the British Official History remarks, was "simple and modest". Its tactics were conventional. While the Italian infantry was left behind to hold the pivot at Mersa Brega, the Afrika Korps would execute a flank attack through the desert, twelve miles from the coast, and the Italian XX Motorized Corps would advance along the coast road, braced by a German Battle Group under Colonel Werner Marcks. The start of the advance, which began on 21 January, was marked by honours and upgrading for Rommel. He received news that Hitler had awarded him the Knight's Cross to the Iron Cross. At the same time his formation was redesignated 'Panzerarmee Afrika' and (most important of all) took under its direct command all three of the Italian Corps.

Heavy dive-bombing by the Luftwaffe unsettled the outposts of the British 1st Armoured Division. As it had been the previous April, so it was again in January 1942: the British initiated a premature withdrawal, the troops abandoning their equipment and broken-down tanks as they departed. Rommel followed hard, hitting the nail on the head when he told Lu next day, "our opponents are getting out as though they'd been stung". There was more to it than that. For, on the 22nd, Crüwell had enveloped part of the 1st Armoured Division and had taken 117 tanks, 33 guns and thousands of prisoners. Many more were to 'drop into the German bag' as they hounded the British towards Msus. Buoyed up by victory, Rommel cast aside all restraint. His estimation of British morale at that moment was as low as it had been of the Italians' at Caporetto. He would plunge farther and deeper among them for just so long as his supplies held out, prudently keeping enough in hand to retreat to safety if necessary.

Angered as well as scared by what they calculated to be the extravagant risks Rommel was taking, the Italian commanders nevertheless delayed their intervention and remonstration until the 23rd in order to see what might happen. Cavallero, backed up by Bastico, was all for gathering such fruits of victory as were to be had. He was simply repeating an order from Mussolini when he told Rommel: "Make it no more than a sortie and then come back." Foremost in Cavallero's mind was the continuing difficulty of supporting operations to the east of Mersa Brega until Malta had, at least, been neutralized. Kesselring was present, too, and gave tacit support to the Italians – not because he was against Rommel seizing the Benghazi area with its strategically-useful airfields and port, but because he understood how important it was for him to acquire, personally, the Italians' confidence in himself, and so gain approval for his essential attack against Malta. But, as Kesselring had already appreciated, once Rommel's ambition had been stimulated and he saw glory within his grasp, there could be no stopping him. In a rancorous meeting, Rommel told the Italians that he would move east and then north-east to strike the enemy. He could always withdraw to Mersa Brega, he argued, but he left no doubt that Benghazi was his true objective – as indeed it was. "Nobody but the Führer could change my decision, as it would be mainly German troops who would be engaged," he told Cavallero. And so the visitors left empty-handed (and hungry too, since they had declined the frugal lunch that was offered them).

On 24 January, Rommel was with Westphal in a Storch, scouting ahead for fresh routes by which to capture Benghazi, and again he nearly had his career terminated. "We saw a camp," writes Westphal. "Rommel shouted, 'There's the Afrika Korps'. In fact it was a British camp ... and we narrowly missed being shot down." But, by then, the outcome of the opening engagement was beyond doubt. General Ritchie had reported to Auchinleck that, with the 1st Armoured Division unable to hold the desert flank, there was no possibility of defending Benghazi. A withdrawal to the area of Gazala and Tobruk was almost unavoidable if total envelopment was to be avoided, and the British situation became even less tenable when another lunge forward by Rommel reached the area of Msus late on the night of the 25th, and placed him across one more escape route from the port. Yet, at that moment, Rommel was in difficulty too. His forces were split up, while his spearhead units had outrun their supplies and were in danger if the British counterattacked. Moreover, it was deemed necessary to secure the vast booty left behind by the enemy in the desert: the lesson of Sidi Rezegh, when the enemy had been given time

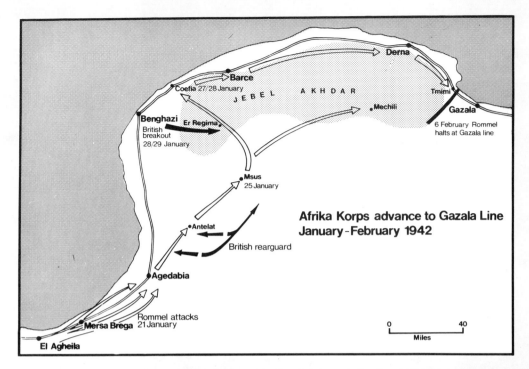

**Afrika Korps advance to Gazala Line
January–February 1942**

Derna

Barce

Coefia 27/28 January

J E B E L   A K H D A R

Tmimi

Mechili

Gazala

Benghazi
British breakout
28/29 January

Er Regima

6 February Rommel
halts at Gazala line

Msus
25 January

Antelat

British rearguard

Agedabia

Rommel attacks
21 January

Mersa Brega

El Agheila

0   40
Miles

Restored in strength, and aware that the enemy forces opposing him are inexperienced and temporarily weakened, Rommel concentrates at Mersa Brega with the Panzerarmee Afrika and, on 21 January 1942, makes a three-pronged advance towards Agedabia. The British covering forces retire, are brought to battle and, in a series of disastrous encounters, are virtually deprived of their tanks. The British try to hang on to Benghazi even after the Afrika Korps has taken Msus on the 25th, but are compelled to halt in order to bring up supplies. As a result, when Rommel leads his Germans through terrible terrain towards the coast at Coefia on the 27th and 28th, it is to cut off many troops to the southward. Only a daring breakout by night on the 28/29th prevents a disaster for the British, who withdraw to their new line at Gazala.

eft:
talian M13/40
elf-propelled
5mm L/18 guns
ive armoured
upport to one of
heir many vul-
erable infantry
livisions. (Image
ress)

8elow left:
Heavily
andbagged and
bsolescent
talian M13 tanks
et ready for the
ssault, but are
hen held back
vhen Rommel
upsets the Italian
enerals.
MacClancy
ress)

to recover broken equipment, was faithfully remembered.

Rommel's pause inspired Ritchie with thoughts of a counter-stroke against the divided German forces. But Ritchie was over-optimistic and certainly too late. By the 27th, Rommel had closed up his front, and the advance upon Benghazi had been resumed. At once, Ritchie took the advice of his local commanders, ordered the demolition of the port facilities, and began a general withdrawal to the north-east. But Rommel was too quick for him. Leading the pack himself, and making his way at the head of Group Marcks across appallingly difficult country from Msus to Er Regima, he executed a brilliant example of 'the indirect approach' by moving through terrain the enemy had not thought it necessary to guard. His column arrived at the coast to the north of Benghazi on the evening of the 28th, ambushing an enemy column as it passed, and cutting off those remaining at Benghazi. But the German net was wide open in many places, and a bold move that night by the British out of Benghazi enabled the bulk of their troops to escape.

Benghazi was again Axis property, Rommel's arrival coinciding with a signal from Mussolini in which the Duce gave his permission for an advance to the port if the circumstances were "exceptionally advantageous". Laconically, Rommel replied that he had just arrived. Next day, Hitler rewarded him with promotion to Generaloberst, and Goebbels seized the opportunity to present his timely victory to the German people in full (for events on the Russian Front were going anything but well), extolling Rommel as "an exemplary character and outstanding soldier and revelling in the manner in which the British and American press was playing up ... one of the few figures in the German Army with a world reputation". Rommel had timed his gem of a stroke to perfection, and carried it out with exemplary élan and economy of effort. This was, perhaps the finest of all his manoeuvres, perfectly judged and executed as it was. For, by 29 January, his logistics could carry him no farther. Only light covering forces could be supported to keep in touch with the British as they withdrew to their new line at Gazala – the same line the Axis had evacuated under such pressure only six weeks before.

Future strategy
Both sides had now to rebuild and reshape their plans. For the British, to whom this theatre of war was of prime strategic and political importance in the war against Germany, it was essential to restore prestige and, as soon as possible, clear the North African shore, so that the sea route through the Mediterranean could be re-opened. This would mean an immense saving in shipping, which was in short supply under the pressure of U-boat attacks. It would also help confront their new enemy, the Japanese, who were rapidly overrunning the Far East, an event that was draining resources from General Auchinleck. In nine months' time, all would be in the Allies' favour, but, until then, American help would not be effective. For their part, the Axis powers had to defeat the British and, if possible, seize the Middle East before the effects of American intervention became overwhelming. The war in Russia had swung against them in December, but they had stabilized the situation, would muster strength for one more enormous effort in 1942, and would drive into the Caucasus aiming to seize the oilfields there. The gigantic pincer movement by Rommel to link up with it through the Middle East, mooted in June 1941 in Plan 'Orient', was not seriously contemplated, however, though it was fully expected by the Allies.

Kesselring, a strategist of clear vision, by no means dismissed the desirability of reaching the River Nile and cutting the Suez Canal; but, before that could be done, he reiterated, Malta had to be taken and then Tobruk. In February, Rommel agreed with him. The closer he stood to Tobruk, the more he desired to complete the conquest of the port that had been denied him in November. Rommel at first operated only upon the periphery of the Malta debate, which was conducted by Kesselring and Admiral Raeder (the Chief of German Naval Staff) with Hitler, Mussolini and the Italian High Command. At heart, the Italians were terrified at the prospect of invading Malta: they recalled (as did Hitler and Goering) the appalling losses suffered by the German parachutists and sea-borne troops at Crete in May 1941. They preferred to let the Luftwaffe neutralize the island. And in any case, they announced, they could not be ready for the invasion until August. Hitler, for his part, reckoned the Italians would decline to commit their fleet. In attempting to bring the Italians to his side, Kesselring agreed to demonstrate that Malta could be dominated from the air and, throughout March and April 1942, in one of the most concentrated and successful air offensives ever executed by the Luftwaffe, Luftflotte 2 did exactly that.

In his own narrative of the events leading up to the next offensive phase in the desert war, Rommel makes the point that, in the absence of a positive German strategy in North Africa, he had to make do with only three German divisions as a "lost cause". He appreciated that the British preferred to fight a positional campaign instead of the mobile kind he preferred, and resolved to impose his methods upon them "... for I had decided to strike first". This oversimplifies the intricate negotiations that allowed him to proceed, bearing in mind, also, his initial agreement that Malta must first be taken. The outstanding success of the Luftwaffe, in thoroughly neutralizing the island at relatively small cost by the middle of April, made possible a considerable increase in supplies for Panzerarmee Afrika, since the British submarines and surface forces had been withdrawn from there. Von Mellenthin's intelligence appreciation disclosed that parity had been reached with the enemy on land and that a British offensive could soon be expected at Gazala. But, when von Mellenthin later remarked that Rommel's only hope was to out-manoeuvre the enemy he went to the heart of the matter. His calculations were far adrift: the British actually had two armoured brigades and three infantry brigades more than he had thought.

Gause and the Italian generals were against further advance: they counselled waiting until the autumn. Westphal says that he was the only one in favour, and reckons that it was the new Chief of the General Staff to Bastico, Count Barbasetti, who settled the issue by a psychological error in telling Rommel that it would be "irresponsible" to attack in May. "That", says Westphal, "was too much for Rommel", for whom calculating General Staff officers in any army were suspect. But the Italians, of course, were lukewarm to aggression in any form, including the invasion of Malta—in respect of which, they let it be known, they thought the Luftwaffe had achieved the aim, and therefore there would be less urgency about the airborne and sea assault. On or about 10 April, Rommel judged that, by the end of May, he would be in a position to attack the British at Gazala—just before their impending attack upon him. At this moment, he merely proposed another spoiling offensive, with the object of capturing Tobruk. Kesselring agreed with this: taking Tobruk before Malta would push the British airfields back from the island, isolating it further from RAF intervention. On 1 May, in a meeting at Berchtesgaden with Hitler and Mussolini, Kesselring won approval for Rommel to attack Tobruk in May (Operation 'Theseus'), as a preliminary to the assault upon Malta in July (Operation 'Hercules').

These bare outlines of the story leading up to Rommel's most celebrated offensive are complicated enough, but it must not be assumed merely that he made a suggestion to Kesselring and that Kesselring carried it forward from there without further involvement by Rommel. Rommel was fostering his own interests with every means at his disposal, and using his personal link with Hitler to implant the need for a desert offensive. He failed to obtain more German troops, however: everything was required for Russia. And, even with the improved supply situation, calculations indicated that extra forces in the desert would place too heavy a demand on transport facilities.

The Goebbels connection was now of greater importance than ever to Rommel. From the Propaganda Minister's acolytes came eulogies that spread throughout the world press—with especially generous helpings on the pages of the British and American newspapers. One such offering, which portrayed Rommel as a true Nazi who had risen to the top from lowly beginnings, gave Rommel great offence. (It was a treatment to which Guderian also objected in 1941, when he told his wife that he did not want to be treated "à la Rommel".) Kesselring was to remark, however, that Rommel, "despite his simple nature, put up with publicity men around him". Rommel was becoming a legend and, for as long as that was so, there was little chance of Kesselring or anybody else usurping his position. Kesselring, on the other hand, was a favourite with Goering, and also a man with an excellent popular image, though not in quite the same category as Rommel or Guderian. He had led his Luftflotte to victory in Poland, Holland and France; had played an important part in the Battle of Britain, and had commanded with outstanding success the largest portion of the Luftwaffe in the initial attack against Russia. He was, moreover, a master of political and bureaucratic manoeuvre, with the touch of a diplomat in his amiable handling of allies and colleagues alike. As an opponent, he had proved himself formidable and, beyond doubt, he could now be rated as one of Rommel's opponents—one who was only awaiting the right moment to have the 'Desert Fox', whose manner and methods were repugnant to him, replaced.

7
Objective Tobruk

On the night of 26 May 1942, the Italian Corps in the north, commanded overall by Crüwell, moved forward to distract British attention, and the mass of the Axis mobile troops mounted their vehicles, in their assembly areas along the Trigh Capuzzo, in readiness for the night drive that would take them south of Bir Hakeim, en route to strike the British in rear. Rommel wrote with strength and tenderness to Lu: "There is no need to tell you how I will go into it. I intend to demand of myself the same as I expect from each of my officers and men. My thoughts, especially in these hours of decision, are often with you." He wrote these words at one of the turning points of the war, just a few days before the mass of the German Army would storm forward again in Russia, on the roads that would take them deep into the Caucasus and to the city of Stalingrad on the River Volga. But it was also a moment of change in the nations' balance of forces, not only in the matter of numbers but in terms of quality too. The disparity between Panzerarmee Afrika and the Eighth Army at the Gazala Line was:

	Axis:	British:
Tanks	560 (including 223 Pz Kpfw IIIs and 19 Pz Kpfw III Specials)	849 (including 167 Grants)
Aircraft	704 (497 serviceable)	320 (190 serviceable)
Men	90,000	100,000

Significant to that balance sheet, however, was the advent of the latest tanks—the German Panzerkampfwagen III Special with its more powerful 50mm gun and the American-built Grant with its all-purpose 75mm gun. The Panzerkampfwagen III Special could stand greater punishment than its predecessor, and had much improved hitting power. The Grant's 75mm gun not only had a far superior armour-penetration capability than the 40mm guns on the other

Below:
*A British Grant
tank of American
manufacture,
which gave
German tanks
and 88mm guns a
shock; weight 28½
tons; armour
(max) 57mm,
guns 75mm,
37mm, speed
26mph, crew 6.
(Imperial War
Museum)*

Below:
The latest Pz
Kpfw IV, with its
thicker armour
(60mm) and the
long 75mm gun
which made it a
match for the
enemy's Grants.
But there were
always too few of
them.
(Bundesarchiv)

British tanks, but also fired a useful high-explosive round that enabled it to shell the high-standing German 88mm dual-purpose guns from beyond their effective anti-tank range. In artillery, there was something approaching parity, although the German 50mm and 88mm anti-tank guns were superior to the British guns, even allowing for the arrival in British hands of their latest 57mm (6pr) piece. On balance, however, the British had acquired the capability to defeat the enemy by technical means, providing they made the best tactical use of their new weapons, and the Allied preponderance in sheer quantity of material was becoming irresistible.

As Rommel well knew, the British had ensconced themselves within fortified localities behind deep minefields, around, and among which, their tank formations would operate. It was now his intention to circle round Bir Hakeim and get astride the British supply lines in the Acroma area. By this means, he hoped to disrupt the British front and bring their armour to battle on his own terms – a plan, it may be noted, that bore some resemblance to the original British plan for Operation 'Crusader'. And, like the earlier British plan, Rommel's suffered from the defect that it forced his massed Afrika Korps (now under Walther Nehring) and the Italian XX Motorized Corps to fan out to achieve

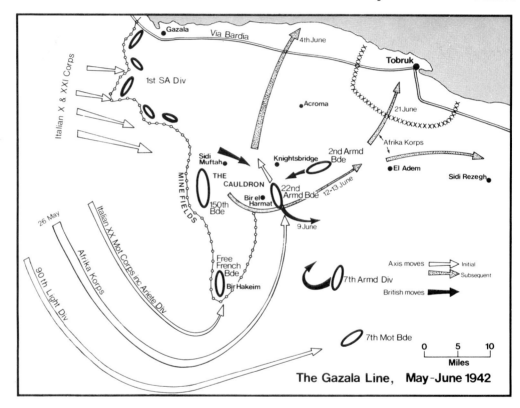

The Gazala Line, May–June 1942

On 26 May, as German/Italian holding attacks try to give the impression of a main attack towards Gazala along the coast road axis, Rommel, with his entire mobile force, sweeps round Bir Hakeim by night and heads for the coast in the British rear. Heavy tank fighting breaks out, and the German advance is contained in the area of Sidi Muftah. Because the French in Bir Hakeim interdict his supply lines, he is forced to cut a new route through 150th Brigade's area and its minefields, or face surrender. He manages to do so on 4 June, with a few hours to spare. Too late, the British launch counterattacks to relieve the Brigade and, during the ensuing days, lose heavily in tanks. On 9 June, after many days of heavy air bombardment, the garrison is withdrawn from Bir Hakeim. Having smashed a badly executed British counterattack on 12–13 June, Rommel again heads for Tobruk, and drives the British pell-mell to the frontier or within the weakened perimeter of the port. By 21st, Tobruk is at last in German hands.

Relative strengths, 26 May 1942

	Aircraft	Tanks	Armoured divisions	Infantry divisions
Axis	704	560	3	6
British	320	849	3 equivalent	6 equivalent

their objectives, and this eventually obliged these formations to come into action piecemeal.

Rommel went with the leading troops, motoring through the night in what he described as a "state of high tension". On his left, the Trieste Motorized Division was the first to diverge, in error, from the prescribed course, while the Ariete Armoured Division soon found itself embroiled with a British motorized brigade and then held up by the 1st Free French Brigade defending Bir Hakeim. In the wishful hope that his approach had been undetected (while, in fact, the British had known since 10 May through radio intercept that Rommel would get in his blow

before theirs, and it had been shadowed and reported all night long by South African armoured cars), Rommel thundered northward at dawn, and burst upon the British armoured formations. At first all went his way. The sheer weight and momentum of the initial impact carried the Afrika Korps through the British weakly-defended southern flank, and plunged them largely intact among the British armoured brigades to the south of a point they had named Knightsbridge. It was Rommel's good fortune that, forewarned though they had been, the British had been laggardly and were caught short of their pre-planned battle positions. The British armour suffered heavily from the

gunners of the 15th Panzer Division, which in turn grew overconfident and charged the British without waiting to co-ordinate its artillery fire, as Rommel had insisted it always should. A furious tank-versus-tank battle broke out, with both sides suffering heavily, and the Germans ruefully coming to appreciate the immensely powerful effect of the new Grant tank.

Rommel, as usual, interpreted the slightest indication of an enemy setback as an augury of victory: positive by midday that the battle was won, he urged his divisions on. But, though he had disrupted the armoured brigades of the 7th Armoured Division, he had far from defeated them. They hit back or stood fast – to such effect that, by the end of the day, one-third of the Afrika Korps was out of action, and the rest were leaguered in the desert, short of fuel and ammunition. Moreover, the 90th Light Division, which had been sent north-eastward towards El Adem, had been intercepted and pinned down by British tanks. To make matters worse, the Free French based upon Bir Hakeim were sending out patrols and intercepting the German supply columns as they tried to reach their beleaguered tanks. By nightfall on the 27th, Rommel appreciated that he was in real trouble. It was von Mellenthin's opinion, in retrospect, that the British had only to concentrate their armour on the 28th for a concentric attack and the Afrika Korps would have been crushed. But the British did no such thing. They remained excessively cautious, and reacted ponderously, partly because of the collapse of the 7th Armoured Division's command system after its headquarters had been overrun and its commander taken prisoner. (That windfall was Rommel's second stroke of good luck in this battle.)

Another commander might well have abandoned his original aim at this moment, but Rommel never gave in easily when he scented success. He stuck to his plan, and told Nehring to continue the advance next day – even though only the 15th Panzer Division was capable of movement, the 21st having run out of fuel. Again, the fighting was fierce and, once more, Axis losses mounted fast. The Germans were repulsed far short of their objectives, and it was now the turn of Rommel's command and control system to disintegrate, partly as a result of Panzerarmee headquarters being overrun by British tanks, and partly through his own impatience. For, having despatched Westphal on a personal errand to Nehring,

and having promised faithfully to await the return of his chief of operations, he at once drove off in another direction. When Westphal came back it was to find empty desert, and to realize that his commander was now totally divorced from direct contact with his communications and staff.

Once more, at the end of the day's hard fighting, things looked grim, even though Rommel later managed (in person) to lead the supply columns through to his tanks. But this dramatic rescue act, frequently praised as an example of leadership, was in itself an abdication of his true function as a commander. It was again Westphal who, when his commander could not be found, felt bound to take upon himself Rommel's part by ordering Crüwell to attempt a breakthrough of the minefields in the region of Bir el Harmat. Axis tank casualties now stood at about 200, although not all of these were total losses. Nehring was disappointed with the results of the day, and transmitted his misgivings to Gause, who concurred and suggested to Rommel that they must abandon the operation and simply announce that it had been no more than a reconnaissance. At this, Rommel let fly, according to Westphal, in a rough and coarse fashion to which no chief of staff should have been subjected. He would not give up, though he realized now that the plan must be changed and that, first and foremost, a lane must be cut through the minefield to allow a 'short cut' for supplies from the west. But attacks by Crüwell that night foundered among the minefields, and became the target for a torrent of British fire. And, next day Crüwell himself was captured when he was brought down in his Storch behind the enemy lines.

Kesselring arrived at Crüwell's headquarters when the loss of its commander was reported. Von Mellenthin, who was acting on the spot as the senior German staff officer, asked Kesselring to take command, to which the Field Marshal replied, with characteristic irony, that he could "hardly take orders from Colonel General Rommel". But, when von Mellenthin pointed out that it would hardly suit the Germans to have an Italian take over at that moment, the Field Marshal agreed. Kesselring's comments on the situation (biased though they may be) are pertinent in any assessment of Rommel, and he was later to write: "I then learnt the difficulties of a commander whose hands are tied by subordination to a headquarters that issues no orders and cannot be reached. Moreover, the stimulating effect of Rommel's presence on the decisive flank was offset by his immediate exposure to the fluctuations of battle." Indeed, by the end of the 29th, Rommel's spirit had succumbed to the fluctuations of battle, made worse by further gloomy reports from Nehring and the staff. Kesselring recommended that the drive for the coast should proceed, and that a planned landing from the sea behind the enemy lines be allowed to continue (on the assumption that such an event would have the desired, unsettling effect upon the British). But Rommel had lost confidence. The exact nature of the situation on the ground was in fact obscure to the Germans, while von Waldau was complaining that his direction of air attacks could only be by guesswork. That night, Rommel decided to simplify matters and place his forces on a firmer footing: he pulled back to the area of Sidi Muftah and gave instructions for the forces on either side of the minefield to clear gaps in it to enable the supply column to travel by a shorter route and no longer have to pass in the vicinity of Bir Hakeim.

The 'Cauldron'

Once again, German intelligence was at fault. The existence of a British infantry defensive 'box', held by 150th Brigade and blocking Rommel's prospective route through the minefields, was unknown to them. The gapping operation was now seen to be dependent upon eliminating the box; that could not start until the 31st, and might take a further three days. Rommel saw clearly that the situation was critical. At any moment, the British might launch a massed armoured assault, which his severely reduced troops could not for long withstand. They were short of ammunition; water was running out; and the men were receiving minimum rations. To a captured British officer who complained about this in person to Rommel on the 31st, there came the reply: "You are getting exactly the same ration as the Afrika Korps and myself – half a cup. But I agree we cannot go on like this. If I don't get a convoy through tonight I will have to ask General Ritchie for terms." The deadline he set was noon on 1 June.

The British in the Sidi Muftah box, meanwhile, held out with singular determination and skill. Slow progress was made by the Germans, despite intensive dive-bombing support, and it really only needed one well co-ordinated attack by the British on the 31st, or even the morning of the 1 June (when the 150th Brigade's ammunition began to run out) for the Germans to have been overwhelmed. The British higher command seemed to operate by committee, however,

with long discussion of the pros and cons, and no clear command decisions emerging. So what few probes were made against the German defensive hedgehog were tentative, while their tactics of advancing with armour straight into the fire of German anti-tank guns that had not been shelled by the artillery were the ineffectual products of an ill-founded tactical doctrine – an invitation to suicide. Rommel was well served by his opponents' ineptitude.

As for Rommel himself, the sheer desperation of the situation propelled him into an act of 'do or die' bravery. As a supreme act of leadership, he placed himself at the head of the leading platoon in the decisive assault on the 150th Brigade box, and led it towards its objective. Perhaps he already perceived the enemy's weakness: prior to this attack, he had felt free to withdraw troops from the threatened northern and eastern edge of the defensive hedgehog (known as the 'Cauldron') in order to concentrate maximum forces against the 150th Brigade. On the other hand, it can be accepted that if he had not used so many troops in the final assault, and taken this risk, then within the next few hours it would not have mattered very much where the German troops stood – they would have been compelled to lay down their arms. But, by midday on the 1st, the exact deadline Rommel had set himself, it was the British who had to surrender. The way to the west for the Axis had been unbarred. Soon the supplies would flow in, and the Panzerarmee would quickly rebuild its striking power against an enemy who persistently wasted tanks in abortive charges against unshaken guns. The initiative was returning to Rommel. With that, he was at his most dangerous.

German losses were by no means light, and among the wounded were von Vaerst, Gause, and Westphal. The latter had been standing on top of an armoured car with Rommel, watching the commencement of a dive-bombing attack upon the 150th Brigade and arguing over certain points of reference, when they were shelled. A row broke out between them as to whether, as Rommel claimed, it was German fire. Rommel insisted that Westphal should come down inside the armoured car with him, but Westphal wanted to complete his observations, with the result that he was hit and flung to the ground. Rommel made no attempt to determine the fate of his best staff officer, but drove off to cover. A little later, Westphal was rescued by nearby troops and made his way back to the headquarters, where everybody was surprised to see him – for Rommel had returned and announced that his chief of operations had been killed!

Fritz Bayerlein now replaced Gause as chief of staff, and Rommel turned once more to the attack. It was at last felt that Bir Hakeim must be eliminated prior to any further advance on the enemy rear, though why this was now desirable, in view of the fact that a direct link through the minefields at Sid Muftah had been made, is questionable. In retrospect, Kesselring came to doubt the need for the attack, but at the time he strongly encouraged Rommel to carry it out. His complaint, however, concerned the intensive and wasteful employment of aerial bombing uncoordinated with the ground attacks that were designed to take advantage of them. For a week, the Free French held out, and the Luftwaffe suffered losses and used up bombs and fuel it could ill afford. Finally, on 8 June, Kesselring sent an ultimatum to Rommel, saying that further air attacks would be made only if the army really attacked! In an extremely bad humour, Rommel began a properly-studied attack, providing the tank support he had denied in the earlier stages – a denial linked with his reasonable desire to preserve the armour for mobile operations and to avoid using it up on costly direct assaults against prepared positions in the British manner. By the 9th, Bir Hakeim was in bad shape. On the 10th, it was in Axis hands.

In the meantime, the British had assisted Rommel by further dissipating their armoured strength in attacks on the 'Cauldron'. When at last they made a full-blooded attack with tanks and infantry on the 5th, no single British officer was actually made responsible for co-ordination. Tanks and infantry worked as separate entities; artillery fire was badly orchestrated with the advancing units; worst of all, the attack was not directed at the centre of Axis strength, and fell foul of massed German anti-tank gunfire. The result was disaster. By nightfall, the British had lost not only some fifty of the seventy heavy tanks committed to the attack, but had laid themselves open to a riposte in the classic Rommel style. Seeing that the attack had exhausted itself, Rommel sent the 21st Panzer Division, part of the 15th Panzer Division and the Ariete Armoured Division through a gap in the minefields to drive the British eastwards, away from the areas to which they had returned for replenishment and reorganization. Gun positions were overrun by this single, mighty and quickly-arranged heave. With their guns knocked out, the British infantry were easy prey. It was this sort of superb command and control in a fluid situation that Kesselring praised when he wrote: "It was a joy to watch Rommel's amazingly expert technique in directing a desert command." But it must be recalled that, on this occasion, the enemy's intention had been clearly foreseen, and that the plan to counter-attack had been carefully prepared beforehand. This was no improvisation, but the prelude to a much farther-reaching scheme designed to break out of the 'Cauldron' once Bir Hakeim had fallen and all the armour could be concentrated for a single blow.

The breakout

Rommel's personal narrative of what ensued reflects the confidence he undeniably felt at the time: despite his pronounced numerical inferiority in tanks (there being but 184 Axis machines to pit against the 247 British), he felt sure of success. His plan was not new. It was still the intention, as it had been on 27 May, to swing north-east and then northwards towards Acroma/El Adem and the coast, in the hope of persuading the British to give way before an incursion into their rear. As von Mellenthin states, "it would not have succeeded if the British had not made serious mistakes". The British, in fact, were involved in their characteristic command pastime of arguing against orders. On 12 June, for example, the German radio intercept picked up a message from the 4th Armoured Brigade flatly declining to obey an order. The customary debate between commanders was taking place, as subordinates followed their own dictates instead of implicitly obeying the orders they had received from Ritchie – who was himself subject to a great deal of advice (and encouragement) from Auchinleck.

No such divisions weakened the Axis command this time. Rommel was in charge, the Germans did as he said and, by imaginative local tactics, improved upon his ideas. The Italians followed too, and played their part to the best of their ability, 'corsetted' at key points whenever possible by the interweaving of German formations and units. At midday on the 12th, the Axis motorized formations stood before Knightsbridge and hoped the British would attack them. But nothing so helpful took place; the British command debate had yet to be resolved! So Rommel eased forward with both Panzer Divisions, feeling for soft-spots until he began to outflank his opponent – who sent out radio calls for help and attracted from the north an additional armoured brigade to the slaughter. Boldly pushing his anti-tank guns forward among his tanks, and using the tanks as bait to lure the British closer (while also taking full advantage of the dust and haze), Rommel at last came to grips with the British in a position of distinct advantage. The crack of anti-tank fire rose to a crescendo, advancing British tanks burst into flames or pulled back, harried by German tanks and guns that continued to edge ahead from position to position in well-controlled unison. This was where superior German training, based upon a well-understood tactical doctrine, paid enormous dividends. The diffident British performance was the product of their amateurish preparation for battle: gallant though they were, they were slow on the move, rash in the attack and indifferent in gunnery. But even gallantry falters on a day when tank losses amount to 138 and the local commander has no notion of the extent of the disaster – as was the case with Ritchie by the evening of the 12th.

Rommel knew all about it, because this time he was in the right place to see and yet keep closely in touch with his communication 'tentacles'. Ritchie, on the other hand, now began to fear the very thing Rommel intended he should: that the infantry south of Gazala would soon be effectively cut off by superior German armour. Throughout the 13th, Rommel hammered home his advantage, which by now was immense in both morale and physical terms. His tanks had suffered but lightly and, in any case, the damaged machines lay within his territory and were recoverable. The British had only seventy tanks remaining, had been driven away from many machines which might have been repaired, and had also lost heavily in guns. By midday on the 14th, Ritchie grasped the extent of the disaster he had suffered, and realized that a retirement to the frontier was unavoidable, since he could not hope to hold the enemy south of Tobruk. He debated with Auchinleck as to whether Tobruk should once again be placed to withstand a siege and, despite a decision (taken in February) that in circumstances such as these it should be abandoned, decided to hold it once more. The orders to withdraw from Gazala went out that afternoon, but the Germans had already detected a rearward movement that told its own story.

To Rommel at that moment, it mattered little what Ritchie did. His own aim was clear – to throw a barrier across the retreat of the enemy from Gazala. Yet it was almost an irrelevance that, in the early hours of 15 June, the 15th Panzer Division shot forward on the last leg of its dash for the coast, cutting the Via Balbia and, theoretically, closing the escape route. For, as Rommel had discovered the previous June during Operation 'Battleaxe' (and as the Germans had since frequently experienced in Russia), it was one thing to complete an encirclement and quite another to enforce it. Light forces that have over-extended themselves in stretching for an objective leave weak links behind them. Again, his men were too few and too tired to fight. They slept, and the seven tanks left to block the Via Balbia were swept aside as the tide of British retreat flooded past them. Although Rommel could justifiably boast to Lu that night that "the battle has been won and the enemy is breaking up", he was premature in claiming that "we're now mopping up the encircled remnants of their army". A great many had escaped and were on their way to Tobruk, his next objective. Victory, however, stimulated him, and it is interesting to read in the same letter, "my health has stuck it all right".

The fall of Tobruk

While the 15th Panzer Division cut the Via Balbia, the remainder of the Afrika Korps was on its way eastwards, crashing through isolated British 'boxes' to the south of Tobruk, managing to avoid the worst effects of British heavy bombing, chasing the surviving British mobile units towards the frontier, and occupying their forward airfields and desert supply bases. The booty that had fallen into German hands was considerable, and the vast majority of it could be put to instant use; but, once again, the question of supply was beginning to raise serious difficulties. No sooner had Kesselring switched the Luftwaffe from the neutralization of Malta in order to throw it into the desert battle, than the beleaguered island revived and its garrison began again to impede the supply lines. Because Hitler had placed a temporary ban upon sending across men in ships, Rommel was denied a much needed reinforcement of 8,000 soldiers who were ready to sail. Moreover, his losses from air attack in the desert now started to rise as elements of the Luftwaffe were drawn off to deal with Malta and to reinforce the Russian front where the new offensive was impending.

The British, however, eased his difficulties. Dispersing some of their mobile land forces into raiding columns, they deprived their main armoured and infantry formations of essential artillery support. In consequence, the well-balanced and excellently led Afrika Korps units nearly always came into action

Above:
From positions they had occupied in November 1941, German 150mm guns open the culminating bombardment of Tobruk in June 1942. (Image Press)

Right:
German engineers maintain an improvised bridge across Tobruk's anti-tank ditch after the assault has passed over. (Bundesarchiv)

with a better chance of success than their opponents. Throughout 16 and 17 June, they inflicted heavy losses upon British armour and, on the 18th, the 21st Panzer Division reached Gambut, capturing huge quantities of supplies, and completing the encirclement of Tobruk – an encirclement that this time would be unbroken. Indeed, as Auchinleck well knew, the chances of holding the port were remote in the extreme. The defences had been partly stripped of mines to fill the Gazala barrier, and the garrison was short of armour. Moreover, Rommel had a plan ready – the original 1941 version – and was determined to implement it forthwith. To help him further, it was discovered that artillery ammunition dumped at the sites designated for the attack that should have taken place the previous November was still untouched. The British had not even bothered to remove it.

For two days, the Panzerarmee enjoyed its first hours of relative tranquillity since 26 May, although Rommel meanwhile drove the officers to frenetic efforts in making adjustments and last-minute preparations for the assault he intended to launch against Tobruk on the 20th. Kesselring was sending across every aeroplane he could lay his hands on in Southern Europe; even so, he would eventually assemble only 150 assorted bombers for the operation. Nearly everything would depend upon the ground forces, for Rommel had over 200 tanks and ample artillery,

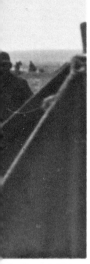

against 52 British tanks, about 70 anti-tank guns and approximately 100 field guns. Throughout the 19th, the German reconnaissance of assault positions and the enemy defences went ahead, against a background of faint protests from Nehring who thought that to delay the occupation of the assembly areas until the night before the attack might invite disaster, owing to the difficulties of moving troops across unfamiliar ground in darkness. But Rommel overruled him, insisting that absolute reliance must be placed upon achieving surprise. As so often in the past, when it came to judging the capabilities of his troops, he was proved right. Indeed, Westphal, speaking in general terms about Rommel's conduct of the moves leading up to the assault upon Tobruk, says: "Rommel's

unshakeable steadfastness ... was admirable and rewarded. His assessment of situations was proved correct in every detail. His seemingly over-stubborn perseverance in a decision, even when not understood, was vindicated. He showed himself as at the height of his ability."

At 0520 hours on 20 June, the Luftwaffe began to bomb the designated sector in the south-east corner of the Tobruk perimeter. A little less than two hours later, behind an intensive artillery bombardment, the German infantry and engineers advanced to seize crossings and, in less than three-quarters of an hour, were across the main anti-tank ditch. This was one of the few successful set-piece attacks launched by Rommel in North Africa, and it went 'like clockwork'. By 0830 hours,

the leading tanks of the 15th Panzer Division were crossing the ditch and fanning out beyond, soon to be followed by the 21st Panzer Division after it had breached a minefield. Enemy fire was at first desultory, so the initial incursions were cheaply and easily bought. Close behind the leading Divisions came Rommel, who had slept but two hours the night previously. He perfectly sums up the vital moment of the assault in his own words: "Towards 1100 hours I ordered the Ariete and Trieste who, after overcoming the anti-tank ditch, had come to a halt in the British defended zone, to follow up through the Afrika Korps penetration. The German attack moved steadily on and the Afrika Korps, after a brief action in which fifty British tanks were shot up, reached the crossroads at Sidi Mahmud at about midday. We held the key to Tobruk."

Twenty-four hours later, British resistance ceased. A vast haul of some 33,000 prisoners was gathered together, with a fabulous collection of equipment and supplies, for the British had failed to remove or destroy much that lay within this important supply base. Over 2,000 vehicles (much in demand by the Panzerarmee), thousands of tons of ammunition (which could be of only limited use) and 5,000 tons of food were collected. Most important of all were the 2,000 tons of fuel, which put an entirely different complexion on future plans. The capture of Tobruk had cost the Germans 2,490 casualties since 26 May, and was the greatest victory Rommel would ever win. It shook the British to their roots, caused Auchinleck to sack Ritchie and take command of Eighth Army in person, and forced the British Prime Minister, Winston Churchill, to defend himself against a vote of no confidence in the House of Commons. But the very magnitude of the success was in itself the stimulus to fatal troubles to come for Rommel, as his ambition overcame reason.

The Trap at El Alamein

On the day Tobruk fell, the minds of the Axis commanders in the Mediterranean turned to divergent plans. Kesselring, of course, was delighted that Rommel had completed Operation 'Theseus' to time and in such an exemplary manner. The crises of a battle so nearly lost were forgotten when he came to Rommel on 22 June to offer his congratulations and, a few days later, sealed Hitler's promotion of Rommel to Field Marshal by presenting him with his new badges of rank. 'Hercules', he believed, must come next: but Kesselring, just for once, was badly out of touch.

Already, at the beginning of June, at about the time Rommel was fighting his way out of trouble in the 'Cauldron', Hitler had come to the final conclusion that the invasion of Malta was not a practical operation of war. While he accepted the possibility that parachute troops could seize a bridgehead, he did not trust the Italians to mount a sea-borne expedition. So the Führer was entirely receptive to Rommel's personal message to himself and Mussolini on 22 June in which something more ambitious was proposed than a push in the direction of Sidi Barrani by light forces. Announcing the large quantities of stores and equipment he had captured, and describing the state of confusion in which the depleted enemy lay, Rommel requested permission to advance in strength with the aim of capturing Cairo, and he asked for all the Italian troops in North Africa to be placed under his command without restriction. It was very much a case of 'now or never', before the British recovered. Once 'Hercules' was cancelled, Malta would revive and again make the movement of supplies to North Africa too costly. But, if the British could be driven out of the Suez Canal zone quickly enough, Malta would lose its significance, and supplies would arrive safely via Tobruk from Greece. Above all, however, the Rommel plan offered the two dictators the sort of bait – political prestige – they could rarely resist. To Mussolini, Rommel's suggestion that he should ride through Cairo on a white horse was charming; to Hitler the conquest of the Middle East would match splendidly the imminent drive into the Caucasus. Hitler said yes, and Mussolini, though worried by the doubts of his advisers, agreed. It was Hitler whose backing really mattered, of course, and to ensure this Rommel had sent Berndt to Berlin, briefed to employ his profound influence through Goebbels, as well as making use of his own persuasive tongue direct to the Führer.

Since Berndt plays a highly significant part in the Rommel story from this moment, his character must be understood. As an extremely resourceful officer, he had quickly won Rommel's confidence in 1941. In 1942, he was back in Berlin for a few months helping Goebbels "in drawing up a plan demonstrating how we could enlist the aid of the occult in our propaganda", to quote the Doctor, whose respect for Berndt was unstinting. To Westphal, however, Berndt was "a man to avoid". He recalls an occasion when Mussolini, Rommel and he were engaged in a confidential conversation from which the rest of the staff had been deliberately excluded. Almost at once, both Mussolini and Westphal noticed a pair of boots protruding below the curtain that hung over the door. And it could be seen, from the curtain's movements, that whoever occupied the boots was busy taking notes. Mussolini was clearly embarrassed, and quickly excused himself. Westphal then found that the culprit was Berndt, whom he severely reprimanded. But Rommel seemed to approve and, indeed, was evidently cognizant of the eavesdropping. The fact remained that Berndt, in the summer of 1942, was a vital link between Rommel and Hitler, besides being a faithful reporter of Rommel's deeds to his master in Berlin.

When Kesselring came to hear of the change of plan, he opposed it with all the power at his command. In a signal to Hitler and OKW, he forecast a logistic breakdown; Malta was daily growing more aggressive, and the supplies captured at Tobruk would not last for long; the Panzerarmee's tanks numbered little more than 100; and the Luftwaffe, temporarily exhausted, would be unable to provide air cover over the length of advance Rommel proposed making in the teeth of the enemy defences. But Hitler had made up his mind, and Kesselring was brusquely instructed to give maximum support.

As the Panzerarmee began to advance against the next British defensive system at Mersa Matruh on 26 June, Kesselring, accompanied by Cavallero and Bastico, arrived at Rommel's headquarters to examine a situation about which none of them felt really assured – for even Rommel was to admit that his gamble would be abandoned if things went wrong. The so-called 'meeting of the marshals' has been the subject of several different versions, some of which lack corroboration, but it is important, because the day on which it was held marked the opening of the German offensive towards the Caucasus, so any move in the direction of Egypt was bound to be interpreted as part of a master plan (which in practical terms, in fact, did not exist). Cavallero, despite his doubts, was not in a position to argue with Rommel, since Mussolini had approved the advance; but he made plain his reservations, particularly with regard to the tenuous logistic situation. Kesselring argued strenuously against the attempt. (Any suggestion that he did otherwise is firmly refuted by Nehring and others who were present.) Von Mellenthin's account of the various meetings seems to be somewhat confused, but he eventually makes it clear that Kesselring maintained that the correct plan was the original – to take Malta

first. Rommel stood unyielding against them, his mind made up. His contempt was explicit in a letter to Lu when he referred to a probable effort "to put the brakes on, as far as they can. These beggars don't change!!" Nor, for that matter, had he; like Napoleon after Austerlitz, he felt bound to go on seeking glory.

Rommel's opponents had not changed their ways either. The British held the fortified position at Mersa Matruh, locating their mobile troops on the desert flank. It was not Auchinleck's intention – he had sacked Ritchie on the 25th – to stay there for long, however, since he preferred to meet Rommel in the far stronger position he was preparing at El Alamein, where Rommel would be at the end of very long lines of communication. To confuse the British commanders at the front further, they had not only to contend with a change of leader but also a radical alteration of doctrine. They were told to operate as 'battle groups' (on the German model), and to fight a fluid action, despite the fact that their training had accustomed them to working from position to position. Worst of all, their mobile troops, under Lieutenant-General Gott, had become, like him, weary, inured to defeat and lacking in new ideas.

The advance to El Alamein
When the Panzerarmee tackled the Mersa Matruh defences on the evening of 26 June, and thrust its mobile troops deep into the British centre, severing those in the fortress from the rest in the desert, cries of British alarm spread confusion throughout the night. Yet, next morning, when the Germans resumed their advance, matters still hung in the balance. The 90th Light Division, attempting to complete the encirclement of Mersa Matruh, ran into heavy fire and was stopped. The 15th and 21st Panzer Divisions, along with the Italian XX Corps, edged their way between the British formations and

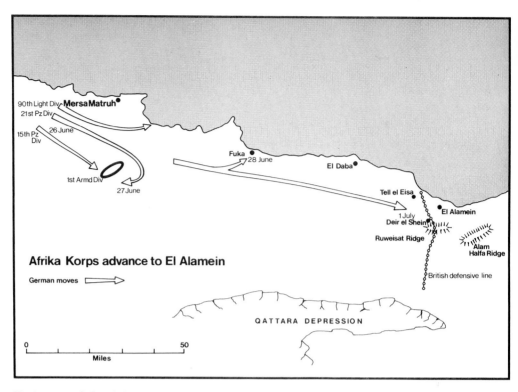

Afrika Korps advance to El Alamein

German moves ⟹

90th Light Div	Mersa Matruh
21st Pz Div	
15th Pz Div	26 June
1st Armd Div	
27 June	

Fuka — 28 June

El Daba

Tell el Eisa

1 July
Deir el Shein — El Alamein

Ruweisat Ridge

Alam Halfa Ridge

British defensive line

QATTARA DEPRESSION

0 ——— 50
Miles

Having overwhelmed the Tobruk garrison on 21 June, Rommel receives permission to advance to Cairo and the River Nile. On 26 June, he assaults the first major British defensive position at Mersa Matruh and, after executing a conventional and none-too-successful right hook, is happy to see them withdraw, materially undefeated though they be. On 1 July, with seriously attenuated forces, he arrives to the west of El Alamein and is met by heavily reinforced British troops, who fight with such determination that he can no longer advance. Throughout July, repeated Axis attacks and British counterattacks are respectively repelled in the relatively narrow strip of firm terrain between the sea and the impassable Qattara Depression. A battle of attrition brings the Panzerarmee to the point of desperation, but the British are unable to break through. Both sides adopt defensive postures and race to build up strength for the next contest

Right:
A British petrol lorry, caught by an Axis bomb. (Imperial War Museum)
Far right:
An ammunition dump explodes at Mersa Matruh, as the British retreat gathers momentum. (Image Press)

118   THE TRAP AT EL ALAMEIN

became involved in tank-versus-tank combat. Confident in the knowledge (obtained by radio intercept) that the British would withdraw once an encirclement was achieved or even threatened, Rommel went in person to the 90th Light Division to urge it on, in the meantime telling Nehring to attack again and scatter the British units along the escarpment to the south. Nehring's attack had the desired effect, for it developed as Auchinleck was already talking of withdrawal, and when Gott had already made the incorrect assumption that the New Zealand Division, upon which the attack had fallen, was in process of disruption. In fact, the New Zealanders were able to hold the 21st Panzer Division throughout the afternoon, the Italians were almost stopped dead to the south, and the 15th Panzer Division was making little impression either. Indeed, as the light began to fade, the Panzerarmee, with the exception of the 90th Light Division, which had worked

Above left:
Rommel poses
with British
prisoners. (Image
Press)
Below left:
A pre-war British
Medium tank,
used as a pill-box
at Mersa Matruh,
is investigated by
a German soldier
who might well
have wondered at
the presence of
such a relic.
(Bundesarchiv)
Below right:
British Bren-gun
carriers await the
advancing
enemy. (Imperial
War Museum)

its way a little closer to its objective on the coast road, was stalled, and its staff was engaged in its customary concern about logistics and the exorbitant quantity of petrol being consumed by vehicles driving almost exclusively through sand. It was true that the British had lost a number of tanks, but the same could be said of the Axis forces, which had by no means come off lightly.

Once again, Rommel was lucky. Already, Gott had issued confused orders to his XIII Corps to withdraw, and the movement had begun. Next day, X Corps at Mersa Matruh would be compelled to conform. Throughout the night, there was wild upheaval as the British began to pull out, crashing among the exhausted Germans. In the midst of this turmoil lay Rommel's own battle headquarters, which came under heavy fire and was ringed with burning vehicles. For the rest of the night, it had to disperse to seek safety. Von Mellenthin was in no doubt about Rommel's

danger, pointing out the widespread dispersion of the Panzerarmee by daybreak, and how easy it would have been to annihilate it had the British possessed the will and the organization. Perhaps Rommel did not see this. More likely, he believed the radio intercepts. On their own admission, the Germans had only a rudimentary knowledge of the enemy deployment and had advanced in a tentative manner, to say the least. But, whereas Gott concluded he had lost the battle when that was far from the case, Rommel, deprived of adequate tactical information, worked on the correct assumption that he had won it, and gave orders to the 21st Panzer Division, which was in peril of extinction, to pursue the enemy. What looked like a gamble the British ineptitude turned into a certainty.

Mersa Matruh fell into German hands on the morning of the 29th, by which time the 21st Panzer Division was close to Fuka and in hot pursuit of the fast-retreating British.

Again, a quantity of material and a number of prisoners fell into Axis hands, but of the vital petrol there was insufficient to make up for the consumption to date. Furthermore, the Axis timetable had been delayed. Now more than ever, Rommel (who told Lu on the 29th, "I'm fine") felt the need to lead and cajole his weary and under-strength troops from the front. Bayerlein quotes a pre-war lecture by Rommel to his students at Wiener Neustadt when he told them: "Never spare yourself . . . Always be tactful and well mannered and teach your subordinates to be the same. Avoid excessive sharpness or harshness of voice, which usually indicates the man who has shortcomings of his own to hide." The lecturer himself, as has already been shown by several examples, was by no means innocent of the traits he denounced. His own shortcomings at this moment were aggravated by fatigue, as he drove himself too hard. But he might have avoided many of his worst problems: by the time the leading elements of his army reached the main British line of resistance at El Alamein on the 30th, it possessed but fifty-five tanks and had virtually outrun support from the Luftwaffe – just as Kesselring had predicted. The Axis troops struggled forward under persistent harassment from the enemy air force. Ahead stood a forty-mile front between the sea to its north and the impassable Qattara Depression to its south. Pressing Rommel from behind was Mussolini, who had arrived on the 29th in readiness for his entry into Cairo. It was all the more necessary, therefore, to justify the Duce's visit. But with understrength and exhausted troops, who fell asleep whenever they stopped, the only chance of breaking through lay in hustling the British. And this time the British were not to be hustled. Resolute they stood, under control and – perhaps of the greatest significance – with their artillery grouped and organized to enable heavy concentrations of fire to be brought down quickly upon the Axis columns. No longer would the guns fight in 'penny packets'. In each battle to come, the British were to use their artillery and their tanks concentrated, and to terrible effect. Mersa Matruh had been the last battle in which Rommel could throw the British totally off balance.

Left:
Afrika Korps tank crews take a breather as a Storch approaches with fresh orders.
(MacClancy Press)

Left:
*A water point.
(Bundesarchiv)*
Right:
*Petrol supply
lorries struggle
forward.
(Bundesarchiv)*
Below left:
*Rommel eating
'Empire Selected
Fruit' on the
march. (Image
Press)*
Below right:
*20mm
Flakvierling 18
AA guns
guarding the
vulnerable
supply lines.
(Imperial War
Museum)*

Right:
*An Afrika Korps
battle group is
held up at El
Alemein.
(Bundesarchiv)*
Below:
*The 88mm guns
race forward to
help check the
British counter-
attacks.
(Bundesarchiv)*

Stalemate

There was little scope for originality of plan when Rommel found himself up against the stiff British defences stretching southward from Tell el Eisa. Like Gott, he was tired and had run dry of new ideas. So his orders for a quick attack on 1 July made no concessions to the fatigue of his troops, or to the fact that they had been delayed by enemy resistance, a sandstorm and rough terrain. The 90th Light Division, alone in starting on schedule, lost direction and fell foul of the defenders of El Alamein, who could not be stampeded. Battered throughout the day by ruthless artillery concentrations (which Rommel shared as he tried to lead the Division in the same rôle that it had performed at Mersa Matruh), it was stopped dead at nightfall. The Afrika Korps, cannoning into a steadfast British position at Deir el Shein, spent a costly day reducing the defences and could get no farther by nightfall. Though Rommel seemed to believe he had broken through, this was far from being the case. And only thirty-seven tanks remained to him. Next day, the 90th Light Division did no better, and its morale began to sag as it endured a regular succession of air attacks at thirty-minute intervals. The Afrika Korps, instructed to assist the 90th, ran into the British 4th Armoured Brigade and could not break free. Its tank strength was further reduced to twenty-six – and still Rommel was determined to attempt to push on next day, having made no real progress on the 2nd. Of course, there was no hope. This time, the British tanks waited behind crest lines, and picked off the Axis forces as they advanced, while the artillery fire crashed down, reducing the infantry to impotence and preventing the Germans from combining their anti-tank guns with the tank thrusts, as so often they had done in the past. Rommel had shot his bolt, as he told OKH by radio that night. Now was the time to pull right back.

As if to show him the way, Auchinleck initiated offensive operations on 4 July, aimed at the Panzerarmee's flank and rear at Deir el Shein. The Germans had now to concentrate more than ever upon bolstering the Italians' morale, for they were rapidly losing heart. An improvised anti-tank gun screen, held in place by some 1,500 infantry and less than a score of tanks, was all that could be raised, and still the Panzerarmee was wide open to outflanking. But the British had grown over-cautious of Rommel, and Auchinleck decided against risks, rationing himself to frontal pushes under close control. Thus, the Panzerarmee was in truth saved by Rommel's reputation, quite apart from its own remarkable prowess. Nothing else could have saved them at that moment if a resolute attack had been pressed home hard.

But the British attacks were not pressed hard, and the initial Axis despondency began gradually to be replaced by a semblance of its old confidence when the Stuka dive-bombers appeared again. Rommel, indeed, began once more to think of mounting an outflanking movement to the south, but was instantly checked when, on the 10th, the British attacked towards Tell el Eisa and Deir el Shein, behind what was described by one German as "a bombardment with the sound of the drumfire of the First World War". It fell upon the Italian Sabratha Division, which broke in rout – a collapse that might have undermined the entire Axis position had not von Mellenthin intervened by inserting a nearby German unit into the gap. Continuing their progress next day, the British hit the Trieste Division, and this too gave way in panic. It was fortunate for Rommel that, at this moment, units from the German 164th Light Division (the first new formation he had received for nearly a year) began to arrive by air. It was they who stemmed the tide. But, as Rommel wrote later, "there could be no question of launching any large-scale attack in the future. I was compelled to order every last German soldier out of his tent or rest camp to the front, for, in the face of the virtual default of a large proportion of our Italian fighting power, the situation was beginning to take on crisis proportions." That day, too, something else of quite fundamental importance happened, as told by David Kahn in The

Codebreakers. The British attack overran the radio intercept unit that, under the inspired control of Alfred Seeböhm, had provided so much invaluable information to Rommel and his staff. Not only was Seeböhm killed and his personal expertise lost, but many of his vital records were captured and the secrets of his access to so much British activity revealed. At once, the British were able to deny these sources to the Axis and, almost simultaneously, the leak in the American diplomatic codes was detected and stopped. From this moment, Rommel was groping in the dark.

To reduce the El Alamein position, Rommel launched attacks to the north of the key Miteiriya Ridge on 12, 13 and 14 July, but once more the 'drumfire' fell upon his infantry (for it was now becoming an infantry battle) with devastating results. The British preponderance in strength was now so apparent that to continue offensive operations against them could only be suicidal. True, Rommel's tank strength had risen to 100, but each day's battle saw it whittled away, as machines broke down through lack of maintenance, quite apart from battle damage. At last, on the 14th, he was forced to the conclusion that he must revert to the defensive. That day, the British made a two-division assault upon the central Ruweisat Ridge to the east of Deir el Shein, and Rommel was forced to throw in the last of his reserves to hold them. By miracles of improvisation and courage, the Germans again managed to stabilize the position with well-conducted counterattacks, but Rommel's letter to Lu on the 17th sums up his despair "Things are going downright badly for me at the moment ... the enemy is using his superiority, especially in infantry, to destroy the Italian formations one by one, and the German formations are much too weak to stand alone. It's enough to make one weep.'

He conferred with Cavallero and Kesselring on the subject of supply, and the feasibility of staying where they were. Kesselring, of course, came in for criticism, even though this was the very situation he had foretold and had tried so hard to avert when the advance on Cairo was proposed. Wise after the event, Rommel now criticized the supply authorities and, above all the Italians, for having failed in their duties. In The Rommel Papers he wrote a diatribe on the subject in such a way that one has the clear impression of an attempt to shift the blame from himself and to find a scapegoat. Kesselring comes off quite lightly in this section of The Rommel

Papers, but Cavallero (who was dead before they were written) is not spared for "belittling our supply difficulties again" – a most unjust remark. And von Rintelen, the German Military Attaché in Rome, is persistently criticized for failure: "He constantly lets himself be done in the eye." Yet, the very next day, Rommel was writing to Lu and described himself, in this moment of gloom, as "an incurable optimist".

By the 21st, after four days of relative inaction, the British attacked again along the Ruweisat Ridge, with a mass of armour heavily supported by infantry, artillery and aircraft. This was a set-piece battle of the kind relished and much practised by the British. It broke right through, rolling forward until it hit the main line of German anti-tank defences, where heavy casualties were sustained by the advancing tanks. Again, the Italian troops, many of them fresh, panicked and did badly, but the conduct of a mobile defence by the Germans with minimum forces and few reserves was admirable. The brunt of the British attack was borne by the Afrika Korps, which could fight on this occasion without having to look over its

shoulder at faltering allies. Nehring kept his head, and the divisional commanders operated as of routine, absorbing the leading enemy waves in depth and countering once momentum had slackened. Nearly 140 British tanks were put out of action or destroyed, and the main attack foundered – as did subsidiary efforts in the north, where the Australians also were stalled in some desperate fighting which stretched the Germans to the limit. The Axis had won a decisive defensive success, for, although Auchinleck was to try (and fail) once more to push ahead from the Miteiriya Ridge on the 26th, this final attack lacked the strength and purpose of the one that had been defeated on the 21st. At this, he decided to accept the stalemate, and to take his time over the preparation of a major offensive. Rommel was absolutely correct when, on the 26th, he wrote telling Lu of time off he had taken to visit the Qattara Depression (probably to see for himself that it was impassable), remarking, "The worst of our troubles are disappearing."

The ailments of the Panzerarmee, its men and its commander now began to assume an ever-increasing significance, however, as the crisis intensified, even though, from the point of view of its equipment and supply there was a steady improvement as July gave way to August. Malta had been brought under renewed heavy attack by Kesselring, and Axis ships were getting through, though heavy losses continued. New tanks were now arriving, many of them the up-armoured Panzerkampfwagen III and several of the fine new Panzerkampfwagen IV with thicker armour and a long 75mm gun that gave it a superiority over the Grant. The 164th Light Division also helped fill the gaps that were so frequently created when the Italian infantry defaulted. The German commanders, meanwhile, were in poor shape. Gause, wounded in June, brought back a few days later and concussed again by a shell in the July battles, was a sick man. Westphal returned in August, to be greeted by Rommel with delight and the remark that he was "worth a whole division". Von Mellenthin would soon have to leave, suffering from the dysentery that crippled so many members of the Axis forces. The

strain of action, compounded by the badly-balanced German diet, weakened them all. As for Rommel himself, it is worth recording in the light of the events of the next few weeks, that on 2 August he wrote to Lu of the prevailing sickness among the older officers, and reported that he was feeling "very tired and limp, though I have a chance to look after myself a bit just at the moment ... We've all got heat diarrhoea now, but it's bearable. A year ago I had jaundice and that was much worse."

The Axis had now either to advance and take the objectives Rommel had set on 25 June, or retire. An advance demanded a wholesale strengthening of the system of supply, and it was on this subject that Rommel addressed a long letter to Keitel at OKW on 8 August. He needed more troops, he wrote, and an increased volume of supplies to satisfy his daily needs and restore his strength for attack. This would require a complete reorganization of the administrative situation, placing it completely under

Below:
Ruweisat Ridge, strewn with wrecked Valentine tanks. (Bundesarchiv)

German jurisdiction. To do this, there was only one man who came to his mind – Albert Kesselring, whom he later described as having "considerable strength of will, a first class talent for diplomacy and organization and a considerable knowledge of technical matters". So, at last, Rommel was recognizing Kesselring's special importance, for he had "the Luftwaffe and Goering behind him ... to tackle questions of high policy in relation to Italy". Although not immediately acted upon, his suggestions were at once given serious consideration, and moves were set afoot to place Kesselring in a stronger position with a more closely-unified command organization.

On 10 August, Rommel was writing that "the situation is changing daily to my advantage". This cannot have been on account of any improvement in the supply situation, since the difficulty of getting men and supplies across the Mediterranean was as intractable as ever, and irreparable damage to Tobruk harbour had been inflicted by British

bombing on the 8th. At a later date it might have been so, because, on the 16th, Bastico was cut out of the chain of command, and the Panzerarmee made directly responsible to Cavallero at Comando Supremo. Maybe Rommel believed this new arrangement would simplify supply – for that was the intention – but it would take a long time to put into working order and, in the meantime, there were battles to be fought that could not be long delayed. Nor is there evidence to suggest that, when the British replaced Auchinleck with General Sir Harold Alexander and sent Lieutenant-General Bernard Montgomery to command Eighth Army, the Germans took much notice.

At this point, however, Rommel's health went into sharp decline. The old stomach troubles made a reappearance and a specialist was called in. According to Bayerlein, Rommel was having frequent attacks of faintness. A medical report said that he was suffering from a multiplicity of intestinal complaints, together with circulation problems. With the next Axis offensive but eight days away, Rommel signalled OKH on the 22nd to say that he was ill, and suggested that Heinz Guderian should be sent out as a substitute. But Guderian (who had been sacked at the end of 1941) was still out of favour with Hitler, and all the Führer would agree to was that Kesselring should take over as Supreme Commander in North Africa with Nehring to command the Army. That was too much for Rommel. Telling Lu on the 24th that he was well enough to get up occasionally but that he would soon need six weeks of treatment in Germany, he added, "I'm not going to leave my post until I can hand over to my deputy without worrying. At the rate we've been using up generals in Africa – five per division in eighteen months – it's no wonder that I also need an overhaul some time or other."

So, unfortunately for the chances of Axis success, it was a debilitated Field Marshal who was to lead their troops in a final attempt to reach the Suez Canal. Indeed, it was hard to replace him. Goebbels was worried that the reputation of his propaganda idol might suffer, and kept a wary eye on the situation; but the German people had come to believe in the miracles Rommel worked – and Germany would certainly need miracles before long. It had been alarming enough for Goebbels, in May, when he heard of Rommel's narrow escape from capture in the Gazala battle. It would be extremely difficult in August to explain why the all-conquering hero had been replaced in his command.

Downfall at Alam Halfa

Opposite page:
*The Axis Armies
go to ground. A
command post
near El Alamein.*
(Image Press)

Although it is true, as Westphal reports, that Rommel was constantly absorbed throughout August with planning the assault upon the El Alamein position and the advance to Alexandria, it was Kesselring who played the leading rôle in getting that offensive started. For Rommel was consumed by doubts as to the wisdom of attacking, his mind filled with trepidation over the supply situation. The morale and fighting capacity of his troops seemed at as high a level as ever, further enhanced as it was by the arrival of several more of the up-gunned Panzerkampfwagen IVs. But von Mellenthin says that consideration was given to withdrawing the marching troops – the bulk of the army – to Cyrenaica, leaving only the mobile forces at El Alamein to engage the enemy to their best advantage, freed from having to consider the safety of the Italian infantry. At the end of July, however, Hitler had insisted upon there being no cession of territory. Once more, the matter of Italian fidelity was paramount, and Mussolini's ambitions must not be thwarted without a struggle. (Nevertheless, he would soon return to Rome, deprived of his early triumph in Cairo.)

Kesselring brought heavy pressure to bear on Rommel in an effort to stiffen his resolve in the crucial days prior to the planned attack on 30 August. For, strongly against the advance into Egypt though he had been in June, Kesselring now appreciated that, in the light of the Führer's orders, there could be no question of retreating, so the Panzerarmee's only hope of survival was by way of another step forward. Moreover, there was little time to spare before British strength became overwhelming. Soon, a protracted German defence of the El Alamein position would be impossible at the end of such over-stretched lines of communication. Rommel was unlikely to receive the reinforcements he craved and, even in the event of their arriv-

ing, the effort involved would further distor Axis strategy. Troops sent to Egypt would b a diversion from the main aim of defeatin Russia before the impending avalanche o American men and resources finally tippe the scales in the Allies' favour. So Kesselrin used every form of persuasion to make Rom mel take the plunge, knowing that this wa the last moment when the war might be won

As late as the 27th, Rommel was stil unsure of the feasibility of the attack, becaus he believed there was insufficient fuel to sus tain the Luftwaffe's air effort, and onl enough to carry his 446 battleworthy tank (only 203 of them German, the others obsolet Italian types) a distance of 150 miles – a ver tight margin bearing in mind the extent o manoeuvre anticipated and dependence o deliveries yet to be made. On the 27th, Caval lero and Kesselring visited him, and th former promised delivery of 5,000 tons o petrol then in transit by sea to Tobruk, 25 miles away. Another 1,000 tons would b brought in by air, Kesselring announced – bu at once he was challenged by Westphal, wh pointed out that it would require 250 lifts b Ju 52 transport aircraft and this, even unde ideal conditions and without enemy interfer ence, would be impossible. He was told b Kesselring to leave the meeting and, from distance, watched the two Field Marshal shake hands and heard Rommel say "Splen did!" Kesselring had evidently made promise, which Rommel accepted, an Westphal concedes that much fuel did arriv by air (while most of the fuel despatchec by sea was sent to the bottom). Unfortu nately – and very much to Kesselring's sur prise when he heard of it later – the fuel deli vered by air never reached the front. A investigation showed that it was consume along the lines of communication, where, a Paul Deichmann, Kesselring's chief of staff discovered, "fuel was freely issued in an

amount to the columns on the road". Deichmann continues, in a post-war letter to Kesselring: "Rommel's attention was drawn to this by teletype message, but he replied that

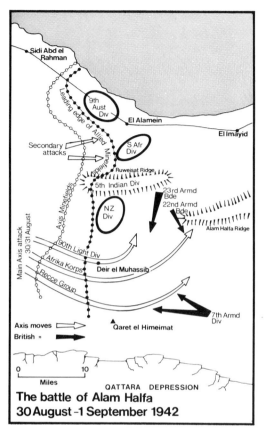

Attempting, by demonstrations in the north, to pin the British to their static defensive position between Ruweisat Ridge and El Alamein, Rommel concentrates his mobile forces on the southern flank and drives forward during the night of 30 August, with a view to positioning the Afrika Korps due south of the Alam Halfa Ridge at first light on the 31st. Delayed by an unexpected minefield, soon after crossing the start line, and further held up by soft sand that causes the vehicles to use more fuel than expected, the Panzerarmee's penetration has to be curtailed and sent north, not as far to the east as intended. As a result, it runs into the teeth of the British defences drawn up along the ridges. And, lacking surprise, there is never the slightest hope of the breakthrough to the coast that is essential to success. Caught in the open, the assault wilts under incessant bombing. Deprived of adequate fuel supplies when supply columns find the greatest difficulty in getting through, Rommel is forced to concede defeat on 3 September, and conducts an orderly withdrawal to the minefields. He is cautiously pursued by the British, whose commander, Montgomery, is careful to deny Rommel the chance of excecuting one of his celebrated ripostes.

he was only interested in the fuel we flew to his tanks. It was his quartermaster's job to bring the fuel from the rear to the front. Probably a scapegoat for the failure was sought at the time." Kesselring says that, if he had realized this at the time, he would have arranged for delivery to have been made nearer to the front, regardless of the risk to aircraft.

Rommel's state of mind on 30 August is difficult to assess. To Lu, on the eve of battle, he wrote: "Many of my worries have been by no means satisfactorily settled and we have some very grave shortages. But I've taken the risk . . . As for my health, I'm feeling on top of my form. There are such big things at stake. If our blow succeeds, it might go some way towards deciding the whole course of the war." His physician, Professor Horster, says that on the morning of the attack Rommel wore a very troubled expression. "Professor," he said, "the decision to attack today is the hardest I have taken. Either the Army in Russia succeeds in getting through to Grozny [in the Caucasus] and we in Africa manage to reach the Suez Canal or . . ." and he made a gesture of defeat.

"A reconnaissance in force"

From their usual reliable sources, the British were made perfectly well aware of the approaching storm, and had tracked the assembly of Axis forces on the southern flank, prior to their drive against the British rear. By the light of flares, the groups of hostile vehicles were bombed before they moved off. Except when sandstorms intervened, they were never to be spared a moment's respite from the swarms of RAF aircraft, and this the Luftwaffe could not prevent. Moving eastward by full moonlight, they ran into a deep minefield, the presence of which had not been suspected. This obstacle, defended by enemy artillery fire, not only cost Rommel time, but it lost him von Bismarck, commander of the 21st Panzer Division (killed by mortar fire), and Nehring, commander of the Afrika Korps, who was wounded. Bayerlein took over at once and, by forceful leadership, kept the Afrika Korps in motion until it at last broke through into open desert. But for his initiative, the whole operation might have been cancelled there and then. As the stream of adverse news reached Rommel, his thoughts switched to cancelling the attempt and retiring at once, before serious damage was incurred by his striking force. These were realistic considerations, since it was quite apparent that the attack had already forfeited the two elements upon which its success depended – speed and surprise – but it was not characteristic of the Rommel of old.

Hopes rose again, however, when rapid progress was made to the east, though already the timetable was far adrift. Then came another hold-up as the vehicles ran into soft sand, which hindered progress and used up much precious fuel. At dawn on 31 August, the Afrika Korps was not nearly as far east as Rommel had intended it should be, and he was compelled to make his first adjustment to the plan, in order to allow the northerly drive time to reach its objective on the coast by nightfall. Prematurely, he ordered the phalanx of armoured vehicles to turn north, while an inaccurate air report of additional enemy armour located to the east helped strengthen his disinclination to go that far. The centre of his thrust would now carry his tanks against the mass of the enemy, instead of round its flank – limiting the Germans' room to manoeuvre. Strategically, therefore, Rommel had already been thwarted. It remained to be seen if the élan and skill of the German troops would compensate for this by tactical verve, the Italian formations having already fallen behind and shown themselves, as the aerial bombardment intensified, less than enthusiastic. Speed of execution might have rescued Rommel, but this too was denied him when a fresh sandstorm blew up and retarded the Afrika Korps' deployment into attack formation. Not until 1300 hours did the 15th Panzer Division start feeling its way round the right flank of the British position on the Alam Halfa ridge in its endeavour to occupy the western spur. Meanwhile, the 21st Panzer Division, moving a little later, made the tactical error of chasing some decoy British tanks, which led it straight into the fire of the British heavy tanks standing back in hull-down positions. Now developed an almost static shooting match, since the British tanks were under precise instructions from Montgomery to resist the temptation to charge the enemy, a manoeuvre which, in the past, had caused them such terrible and unnecessary losses. The charging was left to the Germans, who tried to work their way forward in the manner accustomed and fell victims to an opponent who coolly reinforced his position and shot back with deadly efficiency. At nightfall, von Vaerst (who had assumed command of the Afrika Korps), in consultation with Rommel, called off the attempt and pulled back to refuel with what little petrol could be dragged forward.

Fuel shortage dominates Rommel's account of the battle, and is given as the main reason for making only a few desultory and

ineffective advances throughout 1 September. It was probably the decisive factor, although Kesselring had his doubts when he wrote afterwards that he thought the attack promised success and the troops could not understand the order to halt. Perhaps he is on shaky ground here, but he does have a point when he argues that, since there was still enough fuel to sustain the subsequent withdrawal (which was to start on the 2nd and go on until the 6th), there was surely enough to carry them forward the remaining twenty-five kilometres to Alexandria, where they would have found the main British fuel stocks. In point of fact, Rommel was dissuaded from any further attacks by the sheer strength of the enemy opposing him, and by the realization that the only offensive option open to him was the sort of 'butting against a brick wall' battle of attrition against which every fibre of his intelligence and experience rebelled. The events of 1 September served to convince him of the inevitability of retreat. He describes in *The Rommel Papers* the ceaseless and remorseless air attacks, the severe casualties suffered by bomb-bursts intensified by rock splinters, and the fact that no fewer than seven officers of the Afrika Korps staff were killed. "Between 10 and 12 o'clock we were bombed no less than six times by British aircraft. On one occasion I only just had time to throw myself into a slit-trench before the bombs fell. Swarms of low-flying fighter-bombers were coming back to the attack again and again, and my troops suffered tremendous casualties. Vast numbers of vehicles stood burning in the desert." Rommel had reached the breaking point. In the afternoon he was on the verge of calling off the battle, as the enemy artillery bombardment, well controlled, superbly concentrated and kept in action by mountains of ammunition, fired ten shells for each that the Panzerarmee could send back in retaliation. All movement had ceased. That night, Rommel signalled OKW his intention to pull back. The official version of events would be that the offensive had been only a "reconnaissance in force" – but those on the spot knew better.

Unlike the first abortive phase at Gazala, when the chance of renewing the offensive was always present, this retreat was to be conclusive, even though each German commander always kept his eyes open for a false move on the British side. But Montgomery kept up the pounding from long range, and followed-up the retiring enemy cautiously. The success of the British aerial bombing clearly made a deep impression on Rommel:

for ever after, he would be obsessed by fear of the enemy air threat whenever he contemplated a plan of battle. (In case the contribution credited to Allied air power might be overestimated, it is perhaps worth recording the extent of Afrika Korps losses to air attack up to 4 September, by which time the worst was over. These amounted to 406 men and 170 vehicles destroyed, a high proportion of the overall total; but, of the vehicles, only three were tanks, indicating that armoured vehicles still provided their occupants with a high level of protection, and that the main function of air power was the disruption of supply lines and, perhaps above all, the destruction of confidence and morale – Rommel's included.) After 1 September 1942, Erwin Rommel was never the same commander again. From that moment onward, the fire of battle was never to burn as brightly within him.

Yet his conduct of the withdrawal was masterly, the German battle groups stepping methodically backwards at their own pace, while infantry and guns were carefully dug-in to hold open the lanes in the captured British minefields and prevent any attempt at closing the escape route westward. For four days, the British were held at bay while the Luftwaffe put in a special (though largely unavailing) effort to curb the enemy air attacks. One purposeful British attack to close the gap at Deir el Munassib on the 3rd was held and pushed back by a classic example of armoured counter-stroke by the 15th Panzer Division. The British lost nearly a thousand

men in a matter of hours, this figure comprising the bulk of the 1,750 battle casualties suffered by Montgomery's Eighth Army throughout the entire six-day battle. For its part, between 30 August and 6 September, the Panzerarmee lost 2,910 men, 49 tanks (plus many damaged), 55 guns and 395 other vehicles. The losses themselves were not catastrophic; it was the complete lack of achievement that hurt, along with the realization that the exhilarating objective of June would not now be reached.

On the defensive

The immediate effects of the Battle of Alam Halfa upon Rommel were expressed in his irrevocable decision to go on the defensive (and to some extent his abandonment of the concept of mobile warfare), and his consideration of his own future. "Positions", he wrote, "had now to be constructed strongly enough to be held by their local garrisons over a long period." Kesselring was coming increasingly into the picture, not only in his efforts to improve the supply situation for the Panzerarmee, but in working closely with Rommel to consolidate a defensive barrier at El Alamein, which bore some resemblance to British practice at Gazala. Kesselring's mind turned also to the necessity of constructing a secondary position at Fuka, but this was never actually put in hand. At the same time, he was sedulously working upon his long-term aim of having Rommel replaced, his chief pretext to hand being Rommel's failing health, which seemed to fluctuate as an index

Left:
Rommel with Bayerlein, who so often stiffened Rommel's determination. (Bundesarchiv)
Right:
Italian infantry dug in behind the wire and minefields of El Alamein. (Bundesarchiv)

Above:
One of the 88mm guns upon which the defences so often depended, but which were now highly vulnerable to the 75mm guns of the American-built Grant and Sherman tanks. (Bundesarchiv)
Right:
Men of the Afrika Korps relax during a lull between enemy attacks. (Bundesarchiv)

Right:
Rommel's relief, Georg Stumme, in Russia just prior to his fatal posting. (Bundesarchiv)

of action and inaction. Already, it was agreed that he should be given a prolonged rest 'cure' in Germany and that a deputy, General Georg Stumme, should be sent to hold the fort in his absence (an appointment which, there is little doubt, Kesselring was fully determined to make permanent if he could). Pointedly, Kesselring was to write: "Both the troops and staff of the Panzerarmee had full confidence in him, and they worked well together." But neither Rommel nor Hitler saw it that way.

On 9 September, Rommel told Lu that his health was "fairly well restored and I hardly think anybody would notice anything. However the doctor is pressing me hard to have a break ..." Two days later: "I'm quite well so far. It goes up and down. It's high time I got out for a few weeks." But, although in these letters he registered anxiety at leaving his command in the hands of another, he exhibited unconcealed joy at the prospect of returning home to his family, allied to relief from responsibility. In those same letters, he grasped at straws of comfort—such as a report that Churchill had said the British could not hold Egypt much longer and that the British were worried about events in India and the Caucasus. He was greatly uplifted, too, at the failure of a British raid by land and sea against the oil stores in Tobruk on 13/14 September. His remarks upon this incident also demonstrate his understanding of the depredations of partisan warfare: he notes the hostile activities of a few dissident Arabs, but rejects the immediate instigation of reprisals against hostages which "only create feelings of revenge and serve to strengthen the franctireurs". It was not just a question of chivalry, but plain common sense.

Stumme arrived on the 19th, and was apparently disappointed to be informed that Rommel intended to return if the British launched a serious offensive. By then, Rommel, with Kesselring's complete agreement, had established the outline of a defensive system of fortified strongpoints among deep minefields consisting of 445,000 mines. This was to consume an immense amount of labour, but was to provide the framework of the Panzerarmee's effort to contain the expected British offensive—not that minefields could do more than impose delay, or that Rommel imagined static defences alone would suffice. The mobile troops would still play the major rôle; his reserves would be held back in the classical manner, to counterattack whenever a penetration was made, and restore the situation; but now they were to be closer to the front than in the past.

On 23 September, Rommel departed from Africa, and made his way to Hitler's headquarters via Rome. En route, he stopped to argue strongly his army's desperate need for supplies with everybody from Mussolini to Hitler himself. Everywhere he was made promises, few of which were kept, and he was probably right when he came to the conclusion that Cavallero hoped it would be a long time before they met again. He says he told Mussolini that, unless adequate supplies were sent, they would have to get out of Africa. Hitler showed him great kindness, informed him about the wonderful new weapons in production, hinted at the atomic bomb and gave the impression that all was well. But Rommel found it hard to convince Goering that the air war was proceeding so badly—which bears out Kesselring's testimony that "Goering did not want to

acknowledge the failure of his Luftwaffe policy". Nor, for that matter, did anybody in the upper hierarchy seem to have faced up seriously to the threat imposed by rising American weapon production and the inability of the German U-boats to prevent that production from being shipped to the various theatres of war. Rommel's contemporary reflections on these developments reveal as strong an obsession with the threat posed by American productivity and potential as with the use of aircraft against his troops on the battlefield.

Although, with hindsight, it appears that the accounts Rommel wrote in 1943–44 about events in 1942 give an impression that he had by then awoken to the likelihood of German defeat, there is no contemporary evidence in support of this contention. Too much should not be inferred from an optimistic interview he gave to the Press on 3 October. There is reason to believe that Rommel did not express himself as forcibly to Hitler as he claims to have done. For example, after a meeting with Hitler at a later date, he made a supplementary complaint to Goering, who at once asked, "Why did you not tell that to the Führer?" To this, Rommel replied that "he felt it wrong to speak too frankly to the Supreme Commander"–a reaction by no means unique among senior Army officers when face-to-face with Hitler. From now on, Hitler's voice in military decisions, which had been heard with ever-increasing volume and frequency since the beginning of the war, would hamper them all, with an erosive effect that dulled the initiative of even the most independently minded leaders at the front. Kesselring might declare, after the war: "I do not believe that OKW and Comando Supremo would have seriously resisted an urgent demand of Rommel to systematically evacuate the El Alamein position. Rommel proved often enough that he understood how to put his will into effect, or that he did not pay any attention to superior directives." But the atmosphere had changed dangerously for the worse since the days when Rommel could choose his way if the course seemed set for conquest. Retreat would now be the order of the day, despite the reluctance to relinquish ground that Hitler had demonstrated most forcibly during the previous winter retreat in Russia. And anyway, in the case of the El Alamein front, an orderly extrication of all the Axis forces was now deemed by the staff (and agreed by Rommel) as virtually impossible. With the transport available, they could not lift the mass of the Italian and the newly-arrived German infantry (the 164th Light Division) except in several stages. Under conditions such as these, it was reasoned, the enemy might launch a spoiling offensive that would overrun the forward positions and catch the remainder of the Army midway between locations. In other words, Rommel had led the Panzerarmee into a trap. It was now left to the enemy to spring it at his convenience.

Right:
*With Keitel in
Berlin, ack-
nowledging
the cheers.
(Image Press)*

10
El Alamein – a Study in Attrition

High up at Semmering, a mountain resort not far from Wiener Neustadt, Rommel was able to relax for the better part of October 1942. But, although he remarks in his *Papers* that he was "completely cut off from the outside world, except for the radio, newspapers and occasional letters from General Stumme and Colonel Westphal", neither his pen nor his mind could relax for long. He began setting down the story of his campaigning, so that, when the war was over, it would be possible to publish an account of his part, an auto-biography that would be illustrated by the many hundreds of photographs he had taken with this purpose in mind. He also took the opportunity to contemplate the state of his country as it approached the crisis of the war. It is hardly likely that he believed everything that the newspapers or radio told him, but there can be little doubt that, obscured though the truth was, he was at this time beginning to fully appreciate the dangerous situation into which Germany was being led. By applying his knowledge of the parlous circumstances in North Africa, it was poss-ible to arrive at conclusions that were far from reassuring. In Russia, little progress was being made in the Caucasus or at Stalingrad, where the battle swayed backwards and for-wards in a ruinous grapple. Over Germany, the British night-bombers were regular and numerous visitors, and the scars from their increasingly concentrated bombardments were beginning to become noticeable on the cities they had attacked. In the Atlantic, the U-boats were still having the best of it, but already there were signs of improved enemy defensive measures that might prevent them carrying out the crucial task of stopping American men and material getting across. (Rommel studied the Battle of the Atlantic, as he said, with particular anxiety, taking trouble to obtain for himself figures describ-ing American production.) Nevertheless, he did not at this moment believe that the war was lost, depressed though he had felt at cer-tain times in Africa when his own fortunes had fallen low.

In Africa, they saw things differently. Kes-selring, for one, was convinced that the British could not be pushed farther back, and was already unsure about whether the war could be concluded in Germany's favour. Both he and Stumme thought that they would do well to hold the El Alamein position, while the latter strained every nerve to stiffen the defences and put heart into his own troops (who needed little urging) and the Italians (whose outlook was pessimistic). A full-scale enemy assault was expected some-time in October as a matter of course, but its date was impossible to forecast with certainty now that the best sources of information had suddenly dried up. Nevertheless, Kesselring made a remarkably accurate estimate, based upon the scale and direction of the British air offensive as it built up to a crescendo prior to the predetermined date of 23 October. But the British were far ahead in the intelligence game: while reading the Germans' minds, they were devising measures to deceive the Axis as to their own forthcoming intentions.

Improved generalship and battlecraft on the British part also began to tell against the Axis to an even greater extent than it had done during the first encounters at El Ala-mein. Then, better grouping and artillery direction had played a significant part and the armoured formations had been kept under tighter control at Alam Halfa. Now, stricter discipline and caution were imposed by Montgomery upon his subordinates. Only very occasionally in the future would the German radio monitors hear bickering between corps and divisional commanders re-echoing down the channels of communi-cation in such a way as to undermine the morale of the fighting men. Rarely again

would the Panzerarmee find itself with a free rein to operate as it chose against British armoured forces that failed to co-ordinate their operations with supporting artillery and infantry. From now on, the artillery would fire against the Axis not only with the weight that had been so telling in July, but with a wonderfully improved flexibility, made feasible by sophisticated radio networks that enabled the concentrations of shells to be switched rapidly from one target to another with crushing effect. These advances in technique made it possible for Montgomery to dictate the terms of battle, and this he intended to do on 23 October by a carefully planned, set-piece offensive by artillery and infantry in the north, together with lighter, holding attacks in the south. These would be the preliminaries to breaking through the Axis minefields and 'boxes' prior to introducing the armoured forces to wage attritional warfare upon the Axis mobile formations.

Mobility for the Axis was, by comparison with the past, circumscribed. Rommel's basic admission that the only hope for the future lay in fortified positions had persuaded him to limit the amount of movement permitted to the tank forces, a limitation that was further compounded at El Alamein by his insistence upon mixing German forces with the Italians down to, and in places below, divisional level. The Germans invariably held the most sensitive sectors, such as the Ruweisat Ridge, domain of the Luftwaffe's Parachute Brigade 'Ramcke', which had but recently arrived. The most unusual feature of Axis deployment, however, was that of the mobile reserve. Afrika Korps headquarters, now under command of the tank veteran, Ritter von Thoma, was placed alongside the Italian XX Motorized Corps, under Giuseppe de Stefanis. To the north, the 15th Panzer Division was paired with the Littorio Armoured Division and, in the south, the 21st Panzer Division was alongside the Ariete. Each mobile group was located close behind the minefield zone, its artillery integrated with that of the forward infantry 'boxes', with several of the tanks dug-in, thus committing them to a semi-static rôle. Under these conditions, Axis command was intended to be joint, but, in practice, the Germans did the thinking and gave the orders with which the Italians complied—a system that worked quite well. Hence, the armoured formations were deprived of their customary rôle of outright mobility, and were not part of the Army reserve; that was a function handed over to the Motorized Infantry Divisions, the 90th

Light and the Trieste, which were held farther back along the coast road on either side of El Daba.

A hammering at El Alamein

When the British artillery opened a thunderous 908-gun artillery barrage at 2140 hours on 23 October, it came as a complete surprise to the Germans, whose communications system broke down under enemy fire and radio jamming. The process of the subsequent British infantry attack was only sketchily reported, and it was this meagre information that impelled Stumme to go forward early that morning to find out for himself the extent to which the enemy had penetrated the minefields on the northern front—incursions which, the initial reports suggested, had been by no means large. Coming under shellfire and turning about in his vehicle to escape, Stumme seems to have suffered a heart attack although for a day his fate was unknown, and his body lay in the open desert. For the moment, Ritter von Thoma took over, but, as everybody at Panzerarmee headquarters understood, that was only a temporary arrangement. There seems to have been little hesitation about the remedial action required. Kesselring, though reluctant to recall Rommel, took the view that there was very little choice in connection with such an important propaganda figure. Westphal had already signalled Germany with the news of the offensive and the suggestion that the designated commander should return at once, regardless of the fact that he had not yet completed his 'cure'. On the evening of the 25th and on Hitler's orders, Rommel was in Rome, battling once more with the failing supply system and railing at von Rintelen for not seeing to it that the Germans had a better share of shipments. That evening, he was back with the Army.

The situation he found was far from reassuring, particularly in the northern sector, where the remorseless enemy artillery fire and closely associated infantry attacks, with the tanks intervening, were grinding his infantry and guns to dust. The Trento Division was already reduced to half strength, the 164th Light Division had suffered losses, many anti-tank guns had been destroyed, and local counterattacks by the 15th Panzer and Littorio Divisions, though successful in limiting the penetrations to far less an area than Montgomery had hoped for, had also cut the strength of the 15th Panzer Division from 119 to 31 tanks. The Axis had entered the battle with 489

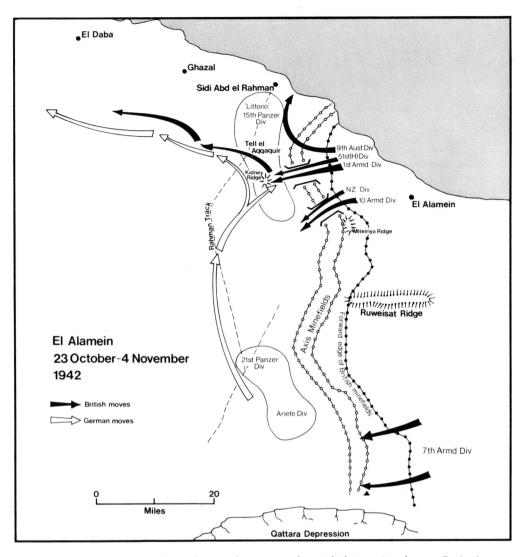

El Alamein
23 October-4 November
1942

British moves
German moves

0   20
Miles

To a considerable extent emulating the British policy at Gazala, the Panzerarmee adopts defensive positions at El Alamein on 23 October 1942, consisting of defensive boxes held secure by deep minefields. The forward zone is but lightly occupied, the majority of the infantry and artillery being located in a main line towards the rear; just behind lie the armoured divisions, ready to make instant counterattacks to eliminate penetrations of the main line. The principal British assault is aimed at the northern sector on the 23rd, while strong subsidiary attacks are initially launched in the south. As these die away, everything centres upon the northern thrust-line. To this sector, Rommel is compelled to send almost his entire mobile force, as the British chew their way into his defences and systematically eat up his infantry formations together with their anti-tank guns. Beginning on the 26th, he initiates a series of armoured counter-strokes which culminate, on the 27th, in an attack which makes no progress but incurs heavy tank losses. Still the British go on extending their gains towards Tell el Aqqaquir, until they stand, on the 30th, at the western edge of the Axis minefield. Realizing that a breakout is only a few hours away, Rommel begins, on 3 November, to thin out the forward positions and send what troops he can to establish a delaying position at Fuka. This withdrawal, postponed by 24 hours as a result of the ill-starred intervention of Hitler and Mussolini, gets into top gear on the 4th; but, by then, the British armour has burst into the open desert and is beginning to threaten the total envelopment of what few Axis troops remain on the run.

Relative strengths, 23 October 1942

	Aircraft	Tanks	Armoured divisions	Infantry divisions
Axis	675	489	4	8 equivalent
British	750	1,029	5 equivalent	8 equivalent

EL ALAMEIN–A STUDY IN ATTRITION   149

Below:
The British barrage on the night of 23 October signals the start of the Battle of El Alamein. (Imperial War Museum)
Bottom of page:
Scorpion mine-sweeping tanks advance to clear gaps in the mine-fields. (Mac-Clancy Press)

tanks, of which 278 were the almost-worthless Italian M13s and 14s, and only 30 were the good Panzerkampfwagen IV Specials. Casualties such as these were serious, even though many machines could be repaired locally. For their part, the British had 1,029 tanks, of which 170 were Grants and 252 Shermans (a new tank, which was the equal if not the superior of the Panzer-kampfwagen IV Special). So, although British tank losses amounted to about 300 (many of them repairable), they still had, by the morning of the 26th, over 900 available for action. They were winning the battle of

attrition. Rommel went on dancing to Montgomery's tune throughout the 26th, by ordering further, abortive counterattacks by the 15th Panzer and Littorio Divisions and by moving the 90th Light Division closer to the front. His uncommitted reserve was now down to the single Italian Trieste Division; steadily, he was being forced to commit his few tanks to destruction. Of fundamental importance was the decision he reached at noon to shift the 21st Panzer Division northward, despite the threat posed by the British 7th Armoured Division in the south. This was in no small part due to his fear that, if it were

not moved then, insufficient fuel would be left to shift it at all. Again, the fuel supply situation was abysmally poor – and not made any better by the news that two tankers, carrying 4,000 tons, had been sunk.

It was Montgomery who now dictated the course of events. His scheme of drawing the Axis armour into battle on unfavourable terms to counter local penetrations was working like a charm. Rommel, faced with the steady erosion of his infantry 'boxes', had to counterattack to support them. While he avoided the British mistake at Gazala of leaving 'boxes' unsupported, his attacks,

delivered with commendable speed as they were, turned out (relatively speaking) every bit as expensive in material terms. On the 27th, in an effort to eliminate a salient created by the British 1st Armoured Division on a slight rise in the ground called Kidney Ridge, Rommel took personal control, and threw in a co-ordinated counterattack employing the 21st Panzer and 90th Light Divisions in concentric thrusts aimed at the salient's tip. In conjunction with adjacent elements of the 15th Panzer and 164th Divisions, this amounted to the single biggest counter-stroke he was to attempt at any time in the

Above left:
On the brink of disaster; one of the outclassed Italian tank crews in their M13/41s. (Image Press)

Above right:
Lynch-pins of the Axis Army. Pz Kpfw IVs are thrown in to 'stop the rot'. (Image Press)

Left:
The loyal German soldiers. (Bundesarchiv)

battle. But the dive-bombing, intended to support it, suffered the fate of most Luftwaffe interventions in the battle: it was broken up by the overwhelming British fighter defence. So the struggle was waged exclusively as an Army affair, and the indomitable defence of 'Snipe' position by British anti-tank guns guarded by infantry brought the 21st Panzer Division to a halt with heavy tank losses; elsewhere, the furious British bombing and their interminable artillery fire held the 90th Light Division at arm's length. Rommel saw it all when, as so often before, he joined the 90th to watch it attack. By nightfall, he knew that his major effort had failed utterly, although he was unaware that this may well have been the turning-point in the battle. As he searched for a fresh expedient, he told von Thoma to abandon the attempt to break through and to hang on to whatever ground was then occupied by his troops. Von Thoma was nothing loath! The Afrika Korps' tank strength was down to 77 out of the 148 with which it had begun the day, and many

machines were a total loss. And still, implacably, the British steamrollered forward, consuming further irreplaceable elements of the 164th Division in addition to the less-determined Italian infantry.

For the next forty-eight hours, inexorable enemy pressure bore down upon Rommel and his Army, and revealed the pattern of Montgomery's strategy with frightening clarity. Having attracted the whole of the Afrika Korps to the north, it was here that the British attacks were concentrated, while the 7th Armoured Division remained to pose a threat in the south (though, in due course, it too would be brought north). Throughout the 28th, the Afrika Korps struggled to halt the steady British progress amidst the minefield belt and to prevent them from reaching their ultimate objective, the track passing southward from Sidi Abd el Rahman. It was no longer a question of smashing the British irrevocably. Now, the Panzer Divisions were being used in desperation to plug holes as they frequently appeared, and such losses as

Right:
*Axis infantry
surrenders as the
Allied assault
reaches their
positions. (Image
Press)*

they inflicted upon the enemy were little
more than those they suffered themselves.
Rommel's letter to Lu at the end of the 28th
indicated plainly that he had all but lost
hope, for he placed emphasis on the fact that
the enemy's resources were terrific and his
own very small. He spoke, too, of his survival
in defeat lying in God's hands, of the van-
quished's lot being heavy, and of being happy
in his conscience that he had not spared himself. This was a warning to Lu of worse to
come. On the morning of the 29th, Rommel
received news that yet another fuel tanker
had been sunk. Now it was all too plain: the
position would have to be abandoned.

But only now, as he accurately appreciated
that Montgomery was about to launch a fresh
and extremely heavy attack along the coast
with Sidi Abd el Rahman as its objective, did
he give orders for the preparation of a 'lay-
back' position at Fuka into which he could
retire. Far too late, he was forced to contemplate thinning out at the front and thus to
execute, under direct enemy pressure, the
manoeuvre he had deemed logistically impossible in September, long before the offensive began. It was to be an integral defect in
Rommel's conduct of his defensive campaigns of the future that he rarely gave much
long-sighted consideration to intermediate

'lay-back' positions. Inherently, his mind
dwelt on the place where he stood and, invariably, it was upon prospective advances
and counterattacks that he concentrated. But,
when he did decide to withdraw, it was never
by short distances – always he tended to
execute a great leap to the rear, regardless of
whatever potential delaying positions might
lie between.

". . . to victory or death"

In readiness for this withdrawal, Rommel
reverted to the procedures of old, cancelling
the close attendance of his armour in the
front-line and attempting to re-create a
mobile reserve. To begin with, the 21st
Panzer Division, with its sixty fit tanks, was
taken out of the line and replaced by the
Trieste Division, leaving the 90th Light
Division to hold the coastal sector against the
next British assault. But the 90th Light,
which was kept thoroughly busy from 28 to
31 October by a series of carefully-prepared
and well-executed Australian infantry
attacks, which gradually destroyed the
coastal defences (and demanded a rescue
counterattack under Rommel's supervision),
was to be spared the main onslaught. Montgomery changed his original scheme, and
aimed what was intended as the final break-

with ample targets. The leading British Armoured Brigade (the 9th) suffered the loss of seventy out of the ninety-four tanks they put into action. Yet still the pressure was maintained, even though the Axis gun-layers were finding it hard to tell the active from the wrecked among so many steel carcasses strewn and burning to their front. For Rommel, this was a Pyrrhic victory. His anti-tank guns were still being hunted down or hammered by shellfire from artillery and tanks. The 88s were particularly vulnerable (only twenty-four survived the day), but the long 50mm and ex-Russian 76.2mm guns were at a distinct disadvantage too, because they could only penetrate the frontal armour of the Shermans and Grants at short range, and therefore had to hold their fire too long for comfort. Although von Thoma told Rommel at 1815 hours that the line was holding, it was with the warning that it could not do so for much longer. The elements of the 15th and 21st Panzer Divisions that were not committed to the line could, and would, counterattack each side of the 4,000-metre British penetration, but it had to be at an inevitably high price. By the end of the day, von Thoma would be left with only thirty battleworthy machines, manned by exhausted crews.

All this Rommel appreciated, and realized that immediate withdrawal to the inadequate delaying position at Fuka was essential as a first step only. A few Italian infantry units were already installed there, stiffened by German detachments. The orders he now issued were complex in that they were hurried and applied to a fluid situation that was rapidly falling into decay. In principle, the mobile formations would provide a screen behind which the less-mobile infantry, German and Italian, might make their escape, using whatever transport could be found (of which there was precious little and for which fuel was fast running out). The whole scheme was tentative and, inescapably, political. Several formations were told they would have to get away "somehow". Much store was placed upon a hesitant British exploitation, in the hope that the magnitude of their superiority had been obscured by their high tank losses. Signalling his intentions to Hitler and OKW, Rommel admitted that shortage of transport must lead to the collapse of his plan, and that the "gradual destruction of the Army, in spite of the heroic resistance and exceptionally high morale of the troops" was to be expected. In fact, the Italian infantry were beginning to surrender out of hand already, and not all the

through attempt along a more southerly axis —mainly at the wilting Italian formations to the north of the Miteiriya Ridge. Operation 'Supercharge', as the British attack was named, would be executed on the night of 1/2 November by two British infantry divisions (assisted on the flanks by two more), backed-up by massed artillery, and eventually exploited by two armoured divisions that would pass through the gaps cleared in the Axis defences by the preceding infantry and mine-clearing parties. The British tank forces, depleted though they had been by the excellent shooting of the Axis gunners, were still immensely strong in number, with 152 Shermans and 133 Grants available in addition to the many obsolete British types. Against them, Rommel could only find 102 fit German tanks, with 52 under repair.

Subjected throughout the night to the sort of bombardment to which the Panzerarmee had become resigned, there was little the Italian and German infantry could do in the dark to check the remorseless infiltration of their defences. But, when dawn revealed British tanks in great numbers debouching into the open, with armoured cars attempting also to steal through the clouds of dust flung up by the churning of shells and tracks, the waiting anti-tank gunners were provided

Germans were as enthusiastic as once they had been.

Then, to make matters worse, Hitler intervened. As thinning-out of the forward positions went on during the night of the 2nd/3rd, two peremptory, yet controversial signals arrived. At 1330 hours on the 3rd came one from Hitler at Rastenberg, and another, couched in similar terms, from Mussolini in Rome. They commanded Rommel to stand fast, not to yield a yard of ground and to throw every gun and man into the battle. "It would not be the first time in history that a strong will has triumphed over the bigger battalions," exhorted Hitler. "As to your troops, you can show them no other road than that to victory or death." Although this seemed to come as a rejection of the message Rommel had sent to Hitler at 1950 hours on the 2nd, describing his plan of withdrawal, it is more likely that Hitler's message, delayed

by encoding and decoding procedures, was merely a personal one to stiffen Rommel's morale, possibly in response to worry expressed by Kesselring that Rommel's resolve was weakening. Be that as it may, the signal had a disastrous effect upon Rommel and his plans. Caught for the first time by an order from his Supreme Commander that was ridiculous and yet difficult to disobey, he hesitated and then mildly compromised. Hearing from von Thoma that the Afrika Korps, a 'thin grey line' facing massed enemy armour that was beginning to envelop its flanks, would be destroyed if it remained stationary, he authorized a limited withdrawal of six miles that night, at the same time telling the 90th Light Division and the Italians to stand fast. It was a lapse into obedience that he would regret, and one that prompts the question as to why, at this crucial moment, Rommel did not disobey Hitler's

Below:
An infantry assault covered by a half-track mounted gun. (Image Press)

demand—he had so often disobeyed the orders of many other superior officers in the past. There can be no satisfactory answer. Certainly, he was seriously disturbed in mind as the annihilation of his beloved Army looked certain. Unfortunately, it is impossible to omit the cynical suggestion that ambition's call warned him to play more carefully with the whims of his most powerful patron (whose wishes he had never yet felt the need to flout), than he would have done with a less-powerful superior officer. Undoubtedly, he was taken completely by surprise, and failed to evaluate the signal in its real meaning.

Rommel was angry as he contemplated the entirely illogical situation that had arisen. In a signal to Hitler, he pointed out the dangers that the standfast order created. He also sent Berndt on a personal mission to the Führer to describe the true state of affairs and to state that the North African theatre of war was probably lost. These pleas—which is all they were—would take too long in transmission to change the situation, but they may have helped relieve his feelings and his sense of helplessness. The wide swings of temperament to which Rommel was subject when under stress were exposed by a further manifestation next morning, when Kesselring arrived at Panzerarmee headquarters, having been delayed twenty-four hours by engine failure. Westphal describes the meeting with the Commander-in-Chief, South, and Rommel's bitter accusation as he pointed in high emotion towards the visitor, crying "he has done us all an ill-turn"—presumably on the incorrect assumption that it was Kesselring who had persuaded Hitler to send the damaging signal. Annoyed, but keeping control of himself, Kesselring made a decision: taking full responsibility for reversing the Führer's

Below:
*A British 13-ton
Stuart tank
(37mm gun) races
by the dismem-
bered carcass
of a Pz Kpfw IV.
(Imperial
War Museum)*

order, he told Rommel (in an intervention unrecorded by the latter) to recommence the withdrawal at once. Within a few hours came Hitler's concurrence, subject to the saving of the unmotorized troops as well. Kesselring was "our rescuing angel", says Westphal. "Due to him . . . we escaped destruction in the nick of time." He spoke for himself, of course. The destruction of the vast majority of the Italian unmotorized infantry formations and Ramcke's Brigade, which had been told to hold its ground in the south, had been all but assured by the ill-timed exhortations of the Duce and the Führer who, in Rommel's justifiable opinion, had mixed political propaganda with the function of military command. What little chance these troops had of escaping on the 3rd had almost vanished on the 4th, as the British forces poured westward in an uncontrollable flood.

The bulk of the mechanized troops fared little better. For example, the 130 or more Italian tanks that still remained on the morning of the 4th, as the retreat got into its stride,

were brought to action by the 7th Armoured Division and annihilated as the day went by. Already, the Trieste and Littorio Divisions had ceased to exist except on paper, and soon the infantry formations, abandoned in the desert for lack of vehicles, would be rounded up with hardly a shot fired. The Afrika Korps was lucky to escape to Fuka, taking only thirty-six tanks with it (soon reduced to twelve) and but a handful of guns. As a fighting force it was worth little more than a battalion, even when added to the remnants of

the 90th and 164th Divisions. In battle-worthy terms, Rommel had little more than a brigade with which to fight an Eighth Army that was in full-cry, its morale at a peak. Somewhere in the desert to the south, Parachute Brigade 'Ramcke' was making its own arrangements to find a way back, taking transport from whoever it could – British or Italians – until it finally emerged, largely intact, at the next stopping place. For this Luftwaffe formation, Rommel had no praise, however; when Kesselring suggested the Pour le Mérite for the determined and brave Ramcke, Rommel ungenerously refused. One who did not return to the fold was von Thoma: he was yet another Afrika Korps commander to disappear, in his case as a prisoner, when his tank was knocked out of action on the 4th. And Rommel, too, was once more displaying signs of physical collapse, duly recorded by Westphal and put to use by Kesselring who signalled OKW: "Rommel and Westphal both overstrained to the highest degree and troublesome. Both require a strong boost." He was hoping, no doubt, that this blow to Rommel's prestige might quickly bring about his recall and replacement by a commander more orthodox and, therefore, amenable to Kesselring's way of thinking. But there was a long road to travel before that would be accomplished.

159

11

The Long Retreat

Rommel in retreat was not so very different in behaviour from Rommel on the advance. Either way, he was opportunist, his performance explosive, the distances he covered long, the objectives boundless. In his temperament there appeared the usual, sharp variations between ebullient optimism and abject depression, swings in outlook that sharply reflected the true image of his innermost feelings. In the days of his great successes, Hitler had fostered his ambition (without necessarily satisfying his most exorbitant demands), but in the days of his decline the Führer was to prove somewhat less accommodating. With the receipt of the astonishing signal of 3 November, Rommel's disenchantment with Hitler began. From that moment, he was to be on his guard, sensitively poised to find ways of circumventing obstructions set by those in authority over him (although he was not nearly as hostile to Hitler as has sometimes been suggested). In the meantime, his whole aim was bent upon escape from the crisis situation his Army was in. It was not so much a fighting retreat he carried out, but what some Panzerarmee officers described as "more or less a route-march under slight enemy pressure". Preoccupied as he was with holding off his masters and allies, the forthcoming round of negotiations with his superiors would test his capacity as a 'Great Captain' even more severely than the tactical problems.

He was fortunate that Montgomery was unable to press his pursuit with enough vigour to bring about the annihilation of the Panzerarmee. The British failure to destroy the 4,000 surviving fighting troops with their motley collection of eleven tanks, twenty-four '88s, twenty-five anti-tank guns and forty pieces of field artillery, is a well worn subject for debate, and only affects this account in that a combination of caution (founded upon respect for Rommel), adverse weather and administrative shortcomings on the British part conspired to give Rommel another lucky break. In any case, it is extremely hard to catch an opponent who hardly waits to fight, but motors as fast as he can for safety through terrain that he has had ample opportunity to prepare for local delaying actions.

A threat from the rear

By 10 November, however, the strategic situation had radically changed. On the night of 7/8 November, an entirely new dimension had been added to the North African theatre of war, as the Allies began extensive landings – codenamed 'Torch' – in Morocco and Algeria, with the obvious intention of seizing Tunisia at the earliest moment. The whole Axis position in Libya was threatened with extinction within a few months, if not weeks.

Prior to this sudden development – for Axis intelligence, though fearful that a large and dramatic move was impending, had failed to give warning of the place and nature of the invasions – Rommel had done his best to stem Montgomery's advance at the obvious delaying positions. Until the 9th, he paid heed to Kesselring's contention that the withdrawal from El Alamein should be "based on the general strategic reasoning that North Africa was to hold as long as possible in order to keep the war away from the southern boundaries of the Reich ... and from royal Italy whose power of resistance was no longer any match for new strains". Kesselring was not far adrift when he later wrote that a prolonged defence from one delaying position to another, though not an easy task, was worthy of a Rommel, and might have been carried out "had not Rommel opposed it in his soul. He wanted to go to Tunisia and, if possible, beyond that to Italy. He subordinated the opinions and commands of his superiors to this desire of his own."

The atmosphere at Panzerarmee headquarters by 9 November was one compounded of seemingly insuperable difficulties and a sense of doom. During the six days following the enemy breakthrough, the task of welding the remnants of the Army into a cohesive rearguard had been bedevilled by the furious enemy air attacks, by the roving enemy columns endeavouring to cut off the retreating troops wherever they paused to rest, replenish or fight, and by the endemic fuel shortage. Now, the news of the landings in their rear had a totally different impact, made none the more sufferable by the manner in which Kesselring handled the matter. For, when Westphal complained about the failure to inform the Panzerarmee of the landings, the Commander-in-Chief, South, replied that "he did not want to worry us", at which Westphal remarks: "As if we did not listen to the wireless." But Kesselring at that moment had very little time to spare for consideration of Rommel's party, which, so far as he was concerned, was engaged upon a stiff rearguard action and, in any case, was not under his direct command. He was fully absorbed in the task of fixing a grip upon Tunisia, to ensure against loss of the best supply route between Europe and North Africa. While carrying on tricky negotiations with the French in North-West Africa, with the Italians, and with Hitler and OKW to stabilize the position, he had to improvise a scheme of military occupation in a situation for which absolutely no contingency plan existed. At least he had the consolation that, at the beginning of October, he had been given responsibility for the defence of all German-occupied coastal areas in the Mediterranean, with the exception of that within the boundaries of Panzerarmee Afrika; thus, he could impose his own priorities on the build-up in Tunisia, and regulate the apportionment of supplies to Rommel – although Rommel sought to get round this by having Gause appointed as his deputy in Rome, to act on his behalf outside Kesselring's control.

The ensuing arguments between Rommel and Kesselring were central to the defence of Tunisia, which, in reality, now had to take priority over all else. There was no intention upon anybody's part to hold Cyrenaica or Tripolitania indefinitely; their defence, it was hoped, would simply provide additional time to construct a strong fortress in Tunisia. This would be based, in the north, on the ring of mountains shielding the approaches to the ports of Tunis and Bizerta and, in the south, the complex of hills and marshes linked together by the French before the war in what was known as the Mareth Line. Kesselring insisted: "It is an old experience of siege warfare that the main chances of a successful defence lie in the battles in the outpost area." To him, Cyrenaica and Tripolitania were outposts of fortress Tunisia, where maximum delay must be inflicted upon the British. The German XC Corps was now on its way from Europe to defend Tunisia and Kesselring demanded of its commander, Nehring (now partially recovered from his wounds received at Alam Halfa), that it should establish defences as far west as possible in the approaches to Tunis. But Rommel, in harmony with his unilateral approach via Berndt to Hitler on 4 November, insisted that Africa ought to be given up, in order to save the men of his beloved Panzerarmee (a plea that doubtless had some basis in the emotional over-identification of a commander who treated his followers like a family). He was telling Mussolini on the 8th that he intended to fight a delaying action at Sidi Barrani, and a few hours later informing Cavallero and the Duce that, in any case, it would be impossible to hold El Agheila (350 miles distant as the crow flies), and that even Sirte (some 200 miles even farther to the west) might be indefensible if the British applied heavy pressure. The Italians resolutely declined to accept matters at face value and resorted, as of routine, to exhortation along the lines that 'no situation was serious unless the commander felt it to be so'. Rommel, taking umbrage because Cavallero had failed to visit him to discuss the matter, responded with messages explaining the appallingly weak state of his forces.

In the meantime, the British ejected Rommel from Sidi Barrani on 9 November, a day ahead of Rommel's intended schedule, but still leaving sufficient time for many lines-of-communication troops to escape. Everybody motored furiously along the good coastal road. Only a small force (the Voss Group and the 3rd Reconnaissance Battalion) did any serious fighting as rearguard, regularly supplying timely information about impending enemy advances, persistently laying ambushes, and exacting a toll of the British advanced guards before slipping away to the next line of resistance. In fear of

outflanking, they vacated the Halfaya Pass on the 11th and Tobruk on the 13th; there, 10,000 tons of stores had to be abandoned, largely because there was insufficient time and transport to lift them, and only partly because fuel supplies were barely enough to move the troops themselves along with their combat equipment. Oil tankers continued to be sunk at sea, and Luftwaffe efforts to fly-in fuel did little to satisfy the total requirement, as well as being expensive in aircraft, which were easy prey for British fighters. Rommel leaves us in no doubt that he felt deprived – really deserted. Added to resentment that neither Cavallero nor Kesselring took the time to visit him, but only bombarded him with signals, he now received a rebuff from the Führer, to whom Berndt had again been sent as a special emissary to plead the Panzerarmee's case. When Berndt returned, it was to state that Rommel was to leave Tunisia out of his calculations, because it would be held. The Führer, it was true, sent "his very special confidence", but the atmosphere of

the meeting had been tense, the promises of ample supplies voluble, and the instruction to hold fast at Mersa Brega (where some units arrived on the 13th) quite explicit.

Rommel's despondency stemmed from far wider-ranging thoughts than those stimulated by the immediate crisis in the desert. Already, the petrol shortage had become so acute that fleeing units to the north and east of Mersa Brega were stranded. Of this Montgomery was well aware; but, luckily for the Axis, the British were also temporarily stuck when heavy rain prevented further advance. Even so, the knowledge that the British were projecting their traditional short-cut across the desert from Mechili to Msus, with the intention of blocking the road at Beda Fomm, gave Rommel several days of trepidation for the safety of his best fighting troops. The remnants of the 15th and 21st Panzer Divisions held last-ditch positions along the road to the south of Benghazi, while the 90th Light Division struggled through the port. Fortunately for them all, the 33rd Reconnais-sance Battalion at Sceleidima and the Italian Centauro Division (newly arrived from Italy) at Antelat purchased by their resolution the necessary time to complete the retreat without great loss.

To the future of Germany Rommel also turned his agitated consideration, with thoughts that were reflected in a letter to Lu on 14 November: "What will become of the war if we lose North Africa? [Perhaps he had not totally abandoned hope of holding it.] How will it finish. I wish I could be free of these terrible thoughts." In a conversation with Hans von Luck, commander of a rear-guard unit, he gave it as his opinion that Germany had lost the war, that an awful threat loomed over Europe from Russia, adding: "Winston Churchill is the one man who can save Europe." Indeed, to Westphal he gloomily foretold civil war in January, as there had been in 1919. From these grim projections, with their implied loss of faith in Hitler, he would recover. But the seeds of disenchantment were sown and would grow.

Below:
Axis light forces provide the screen by which Rommel and his men manage to escape at break-neck speed to the west. (Image Press)

Moreover, he was made more gloomy by his recurrent health problems. The 'cure' had been incomplete, and he often collapsed in the evenings.

The withdrawal into Tunisia

Meanwhile, there came a pause as the Panzerarmee drew into the familiar Mersa Brega position and British pressure relaxed. The enemy found themselves at the end of supply lines inadequate to support the major attack that would supposedly be needed to dislodge the Axis from so strong a position. There was, therefore, time for Rommel to seek ways out of his predicament (the exchange of signals and Berndt's ambassadorial mission having failed), while a long-delayed meeting with Cavallero and Kesselring on 24 November gave him little encouragement.

Deep resentment of Kesselring is the essence of Rommel's account of the negotiations he was to have with the Luftwaffe Field Marshal in the ensuing weeks, *The Rommel Papers* throw much blame on Kesselring and accuse him of over-optimism (the common charge made by so many Germans against him), of looking "at everything from the standpoint of the Luftwaffe" and of thinking "principally of the consequences which the move [back from Mersa Brega] would have on the strategic air situation in Tunisia". Ignorant of Kesselring's real accomplishments (which were remarkable in that, within a fortnight, he had fastened a firm grip on the Tunisian bridgehead, with minimal forces), Rommel was probably just searching for a scapegoat. On the 16th, Kesselring had sternly prevented Gause from acting as Rommel's private supply agent in Rome and, instead, had put Gause to work regulating supply to the entire Axis force in Tunisia, with priority allocated to the XC Corps in the north. This, of course, angered Rommel. Of the 18,000 men, 159 tanks and 127 guns that had arrived in North Africa by the end of November, Kesselring had sent the majority to Nehring, whose rôle was to be far more important than Rommel's, and who had no room in which to manoeuvre against an invasion from Algeria as it drew closer to Tunis.

Rommel, who had been working all along to persuade Bastico and the subordinate Italian generals to accept his plans, was engaged in bargaining for more supplies as the price for trying harder to hold fast at Mersa Brega (which, as he knew only too well, could be outflanked with ease). But Germany's dwindling resources were increasingly in demand on other fronts. He cannot have been unaware of the fearful events then being unfolded in Russia, when, on 19 November, an irresistible Russian counter-offensive had opened. This had already led to the total isolation of Sixth Army at Stalingrad, and had put the entire German southern salient in imminent peril. In Kesselring, meanwhile, he found an adversary who was not only his master in diplomacy and intrigue, but also a more senior officer whose roots of power were strongly planted. Kesselring also had the Führer's ear, and the support of Goering too. The Führer had laid down that it was more important to hold Tunisia than Mersa Brega, although Panzerarmee Afrika must make Montgomery's Eighth Army pay dearly for every mile it

Right:
The British columns advance, virtually unchecked, over the familiar ground of their past ephemeral victories and defeats. In the foreground a 6pr anti-tank gun. (Imperial War Museum)

advanced. Kesselring now asserted positive control over Rommel's conduct of the battle. In agreement with Cavallero, he gave Bastico authority to decide whether or not Rommel should be allowed to retreat. It was this final indignity that provoked Rommel to go to Berlin on 28 November, to have it out with Hitler.

It would seem that Rommel failed to expound his case fully or convincingly to the Führer, for his description of their meeting in *The Rommel Papers* is ambivalent to say the least. Rommel was no more able than the other German field marshals to stand up to the Supreme Commander when in his presence. And there can be little doubt that he was the target of Hitler's fury – he simply did not want to listen to pessimistic notions. Rommel

left Berlin with nothing more than promises that could not be honoured, and reiterated instructions to defend the Mersa Brega defile. Furthermore, he was sent with Goering to Rome to take part in discussions with Kesselring and the Italians with a view to putting the operational and administrative arrangements for the Mediterranean theatre of war on a firmer footing.

In his account of dealings with the Reichmarschall, Rommel says that he made Berndt, "a man with a very persuasive tongue", present his plan for holding the Gabes Gap, rather than Mareth, while he himself declined to speak out, "which would have finished any chances I might have had". Though Rommel rails against the posturing

Left:
As the Allies invade North West Africa and the sea blockade becomes increasingly effective, Ju 52 transport aircraft are used en masse to supply the Axis forces in Africa. (Image Press)

Below, left and right:
Weary Germans in retreat snatch a few moments for a snack and to clean weapons. To the right, a man uses a rangefinder to observe the distant horizon. (Bundesarchiv)

of Goering among his sycophants, it becomes apparent that the Reichsmarshall, who was no fool, saw through Rommel and treated him with scant respect. The Axis plans (which Goering had previously arranged with Kesselring, in accordance with a political deal already concluded between Hitler and Mussolini) were now revealed. On the basis of an agreement that Tripolitania would have to be abandoned, Italy was to be given Tunisia (colonial territory she had long coveted). The Mareth position was to be the main line of resistance in southern Tunisia – Kesselring had, in fact, outmanoeuvred Rommel by obtaining agreement that Mersa Brega could be relinquished when Montgomery felt ready to advance again. At the same time, he arranged for Nehring to be relieved in the north and replaced by Jurgen von Arnim, an officer in whom he had more confidence. Furthermore, Nehring's XC Corps was to be superseded by a newly-created Fifth Army under von Arnim's command. All this was but the prelude to an entirely new command structure in North Africa: in due course, some form of Army Group headquarters would be

needed to co-ordinate the complex joint-service and multi-national operations to be undertaken as the Axis holdings were compressed into Tunisia. Kesselring was indeed the man of the moment. And Rommel found himself shackled. As others have noticed, he was inadequately equipped for political infighting. Westphal says that Rommel returned from the conferences "a broken man". He also returned to a troubled atmosphere in his own headquarters, where Colonel von Bonin was about to take over from Westphal (who was to command the 164th Division) and Bayerlein was to become chief of staff. But, Westphal writes, "Serious differences had arisen between Rommel and Bayerlein during the retreat, and Rommel therefore tried for the third time to make me chief. It required great exertions on my part to reconcile both gentlemen, who were pretty obstinate."

Over the German abandonment of Tripolitania to Eighth Army much ink has been spilt, and the impression has sometimes been given that a tense struggle took place. But the British Official History comes closest to the

mark when it states that the Axis leaders, "whose policy shifted like a weathercock, decided not to fight hard at Agheila or Tripoli or at an intermediate position loosely named the Buerat line", while "General Montgomery made Tripoli his goal and was determined that Rommel should not rebound ... Therefore he prepared for deliberate battles at the Agheila position and the Buerat Line." The opposing commanders seemed almost in league, dovetailing their plans neatly, without the slightest chance of a decision being reached. Rommel was determined to fall back, and Montgomery was reluctant to stampede him. Indeed, one occasionally receives the impression that Montgomery preferred to abstain from provoking Rommel, in case this dangerous enemy might lash out when cornered. He need hardly have worried. Rommel, at the first sign of an outflanking movement at Mersa Brega on 11 December, issued orders for retreat. He had no intention of obeying instructions that told him to hold at Buerat "indefinitely", and nor was he going to be embarrassed, as at El Alamein, by a mass of immobile troops in the forward zones. When it became evident on 5 December that a British attack was impending, the Italians were sent to the rear – to the accompaniment, according to Rommel, of an atrocious din, vehicles driving through the night with headlights blazing. Most galling of all, however, was Rommel's inability, due to fuel shortage, to commit his mobile troops to a counterattack upon the British outflanking force. Therefore, in the days to come it was his main concern to break cleanly from each delaying position – a skill at which he and all his men became expert. Rarely were the covering forces caught dangerously at a disadvantage; never were their losses severe; and several times they ambushed their pursuers. This is all the more creditable when it is remembered that Axis air reconnaissance was seriously hampered by fuel shortage, and that sometimes none was possible at all. It was irritating, therefore, when Goering and Kesselring argued the necessity of holding Tripoli to retain the use of the airfields thereabouts. The running battle of recrimination between the Army and the Luftwaffe was, indeed, as vitriolic as ever, each accusing the other of wasting precious fuel supplies, and neither seeming able to make the best of their resources for the common cause. Inevitably, one draws the conclusion that Rommel could have done more to prevent this sort of dispute; equally, one comes to see that he helped inspire it in order to find scapegoats.

The new command structure

There is sometimes exaggeration by Rommel of his disagreements with the Italians. Although Westphal recalls an occasion early in December when his commander nearly came to blows with Bastico, and Rommel makes out that the Italian was against surrendering the Buerat Line, the documents show that Bastico fully understood the impossibility of holding it, and merely made reservations as to the method of implementing each withdrawal. In fact, it mattered not that Rommel was pulling back, or that Berndt was busily writing letters to Goebbels making valid excuses for Panzerarmee Afrika's performance. Hitler and Kesselring were in charge and, between 18 and 22 December, during a series of talks at Rastenberg in which the Italians were involved, they had reached certain fundamental conclusions. Hitler, having failed to persuade Mussolini to accept Kesselring as Commander-in-Chief over the combined German and Italian forces, managed to push through a devious arrangement that gave Kesselring a far greater measure of control than before (albeit subject more and more to restrictions on the supply of men and equipment imposed by the situation at Stalingrad). Promises of help that may have been made in good faith by Hitler in November were impossible to fulfil in December. Things were getting progressively worse everywhere. Although the Rastenberg conference looked ahead realistically, and formulated the command structure that was to come into being as the Panzerarmee Afrika backed into Tunisia, it solved nothing in the longer term. The German–Italian Panzer Army (eventually called First Italian Army) would come under the command of an Italian, General Giovanni Messe, who would succeed Rommel. Bayerlein would remain its chief of staff, one of his tasks being to ensure that German influence in what was (on paper) a joint force, should be predominant. But the plan was withheld temporarily from Rommel while more details were worked out and the establishment of a new headquarters, called Army Group Africa, were arranged. This formation would come directly under the Italian Comando Supremo in Rome instead of Kesselring, as Hitler had originally intended it should do.

At no time was there a clear enunciation by anybody on the Axis side of the organization that was intended. In part, this was because nobody had had time to really think it through in detail. The organization would have to evolve, as the political negotiations

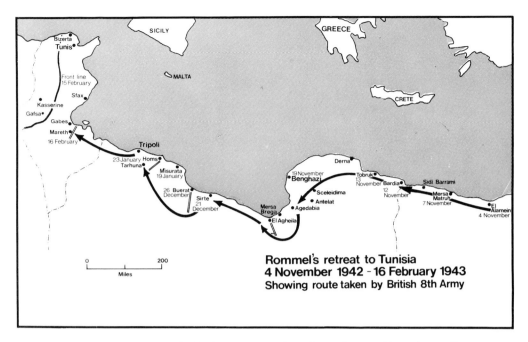

Rommel's retreat to Tunisia
4 November 1942 - 16 February 1943
Showing route taken by British 8th Army

Making use of natural features, which alone provide shelter for an army that is short of fuel and deprived of a strong mobile arm, Rommel runs for Tunisia, hardly pausing at all except at Mersa Brega, from 23 November until 11 December, and at Buerat from 26 December to 15 January, on those occasions when Montgomery chooses to call a halt.

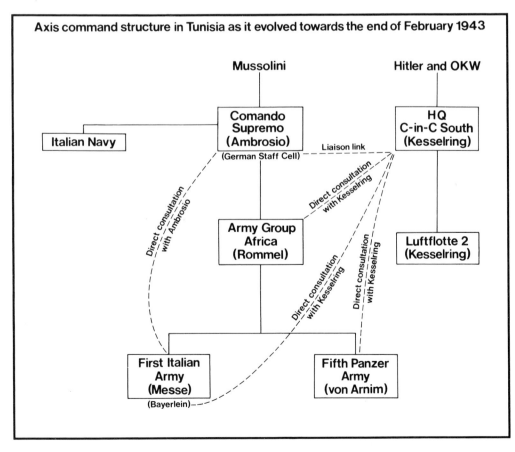

Axis command structure in Tunisia as it evolved towards the end of February 1943

Right:
A Luftwaffe officer makes the best of it in retreat. (Bundes-archiv)
Below:
In Tunisia, a 50mm anti-tank gun is unlim-bered for action. (Bundesarchiv)

progressed. Thus, Bastico was given authority on 31 December to allow Rommel to withdraw from Buerat when it was seriously threatened – a permission both he and Rommel welcomed with relief. Not until 6 January did Cavallero tell them that Tripolitania was to be abandoned, although already (on the 2nd) Bastico had been instructed to make the retreat to Tunisia last six weeks! The thinning-out of the Italians had already begun, since this was now the accepted rule, and the process was extended by Cavallero when he accepted Rommel's offer of a mobile division – the 21st Panzer Division – which was sent to Sfax as a reserve against an anticipated American thrust to the coast from Central Tunisia. In fact, Rommel gave little away: all of the Division's tanks, not unreasonably, remained with the Afrika Korps (which still had only thirty-six), leaving it to von Arnim to provide fresh tanks once it came under his command. The two combat zones were now

rapidly merging. As they did so, Kesselring's influence became more direct as, insidiously and with relentless intent, he infiltrated Comando Supremo with a preponderance of German staff officers.

From the operational standpoint, two matters needed urgent resolution. First, there was the question of who would command a new Panzer Army Group when it was activated – the initial expedient of putting in von Arnim being only tentative. Second, there was the conduct of operations in the weeks to come. For Rommel, the debates that surrounded these matters were almost equally paramount. Once more, his ambitions seem to have been stimulated, but he nevertheless realized that there was very little more glory to be gathered in Africa. He did not like the Mareth position which Kesselring insisted he should hold, and adhered to his opinion that Gabes was better. He still believed that static positions were preferable to mobile warfare in face of the enemy air superiority. Plagued all along by 'political' signals from Comando Supremo telling him to hold, when to do so would invite destruction, Rommel decided on 19 January to destroy what he could of the port at Tripoli and retire – an operation that was completed on the 22nd with exemplary efficiency behind a screen provided by the Afrika Korps. Hurt though he was by Italian accusations that he had given up Tripoli prematurely (for they too needed a scapegoat), it is scarcely to be doubted that, at that moment, he regretted that he was to be relieved of his command by Messe once the German–Italian Panzer Army reached the Mareth Line, even though the date was to be left to Rommel. "I had little desire to go on any longer playing the scapegoat for a pack of incompetents," he wrote on the day Kesselring became his superior officer.

The official reason given for his relief was his state of health, which was as unstable as ever. But the reluctance with which he actually relinquished command had nothing to do with that, for, although the last troops of the Panzerarmee backed into the Mareth Line on or about 1 February as Messe arrived, Rommel did not go at once. Already, on 22 January, it had been decided to defer his departure by a month, until his Army was firmly established. By then, however, the operational picture would have assumed a rosier hue, and both Kesselring and he had concluded that the maximum advantage should be taken of it. Again, Rommel's flexibility of mind leapt at the opportunity to win a local victory.

Below:
*Rommel
gives words of
encouragement in
which he may
have had little
belief. (Image
Press)*

12

Battles against the grain

The situation in which the Axis armies in North Africa found themselves in the middle of February 1943 was just about as bad as could be expected of forces that, paradoxically, were on the verge of scoring a series of startling tactical victories. After a long retreat, Kesselring's forces were still full of fight, but outnumbered. They could strike back and make the enemy pause, but the final collapse was imminent unless a massive reinforcement or change in political circumstances took place – as Kesselring himself realized, even though he declined to declare his underlying conclusions. An essential difference between Kesselring and his two subordinates, Rommel and von Arnim, was that, while seeing the hopelessness of the situation, he avoided giving vent to his doubts before subordinates.

As Rommel's Panzerarmee retreated at the beginning of the year, von Arnim established a stiffly-held front in the mountains of northern Tunisia, and pushed his covering forces southwards to counter the anticipated American attack towards Sfax. This deployment was extended on 18 January when elements of the newly-arrived 10th Panzer Division struck and routed the ill-equipped French, whose front extended southward from Pont du Fahs. It was this local victory and von Arnim's conviction, underwritten by Kesselring, that similar spoiling attacks aimed at seizing the passes through the Western Dorsal from Ousseltia in the north to Kasserine and Feriana in the south were worthwhile, which instigated the battles that led Kesselring, with OKW and Comando Supremo's agreement, to postpone the recall of Rommel. Yet, although the circumstances called for joint action by Fifth Panzerarmee and First Italian Army, and demanded implementation of the new 'Army Group Africa', they are not wholly convincing as the reasons for Kesselring changing his mind and

giving the Group to Rommel instead of to von Arnim. He was to write: "I believed this promotion would increase his ambition and efficiency ... After the nerve-wracking retreat, an opportunity was to be given Rommel to conclude the damaging period of retreats by a successful series of offensives." In fact, the decision was Hitler's, to whom the propaganda value of Rommel remained high. For the time being, however, Rommel had to remain with his own Army while Kesselring, using Comando Supremo as a 'front' or instrument, spasmodically performed the duties of Army Group commander. Indeed, his responsibilities at this time were truly formidable, including as they did the duties mentioned above, the representation of Hitler's operational wishes to Mussolini, control of German Air Force and Navy operations in the central Mediterranean, as well as responsibility for the supply of German forces in the region. There were to be moments when he found the urgent need to be in more than one place at a time, and this produced troubles for all concerned. The operations that now evolved – one can hardly call them 'planned' in the accepted sense – were the outcome of individual suggestions by Rommel and von Arnim, co-ordinated by Kesselring, through Comando Supremo.

On interior lines

In Russia, Stalingrad fell on 2 February, with the surrender of Paulus's Sixth Army. Now more than ever did Hitler look for a victory to relieve the gloom. On 4 February, Rommel proposed to Comando Supremo, with the tacit support of Kesselring, that he could strike at Gafsa, using mobile troops extracted from von Arnim, while his own Army recuperated at Mareth, where there seemed no likelihood of further British offensive action within the next fortnight. Von Arnim, for his part, persisted with a plan to attack at Faid, in

the direction of Sidi bou Zid. These conflicting plans came before a new Italian chief of staff, Vittorio Ambrosio, who took over from Cavallero on the 4th. While content to encourage the Germans to undertake offensive operations in Tunisia, Ambrosio began to resist German usurpation of Comando Supremo's authority: between Kesselring and Ambrosio there developed a struggle for power, with Ambrosio ever-willing to let Kesselring go to Tunisia (since that took him away from Rome) but anxious that he should not function de facto as Commander-in-Chief. This internal struggle delayed the whole process of decision-making. It was 9 February before it was at last agreed, at a meeting between Kesselring (Commander-in-Chief, South), von Arnim (Fifth Panzer Army), Rommel (Panzerarmee Afrika) and Messe (Panzerarmee Afrika designate), that von Arnim should be given precedence in order to actuate the Sidi bou Zid offensive, using the 201 tanks of the 10th and 21st Panzer Divisions (the latter still understrength), reinforced by the newly-arrived Italian Superga Division, and backed-up by a dozen of the heavily armed and armoured German Tiger tanks. Not until the 11th was Rommel's part, in what was to grow into a joint attack by the two Panzer Armies, defined. A so-called Afrika Korps detachment, consisting of fifty-three German tanks from the 15th Panzer Division and seventeen Italian tanks from the Centauro Division, was to move northward on Feriana, via Gafsa, in phase with von Arnim's attack. Both advances were to commence on the 13th.

Rommel's attitude to the venture was one of frequent change. Over and over again, he and von Arnim (and, to a less voluble extent, Kesselring) had drawn the attention of Hitler and OKW to the parlous state of supply in fuel, transport and ammunition in Tunisia. They all knew that defensive, let alone offensive, operations hung by a thread, and that their days in North Africa were numbered. Once again, on the eve of battle, Rommel reminded Lu of his failing health, but also of his determination to lead his Army to the best of his ability. He also wrote to her of Germany's plight and the desperate necessity for every effort on his country's behalf. Yet, the oscillations in Rommel's strategy indicate a fluctuating intellectual process, which falls below the standards demanded of a truly 'Great Captain'. Kesselring was right when, after the war, he drew attention to Rommel's primary intention of saving his army regardless of the overriding demands of OKW

policy and national survival; he was also right when he expressed his conviction that Rommel regarded Italy as a secondary theatre of war and that, therefore, its outer defences could be abandoned stage by stage, right back to the Alps. Having reached Mareth, claimed Kesselring, Rommel would argue that it could not be held, and that a retreat to Enfidaville (just south of Tunis) was imperative; once at Enfidaville, he would have announced a further crisis to Hitler and demand a withdrawal to Sicily – and so on. "His aim", wrote Kesselring, "was the defence of the Alps, as a result of which – I am fully aware of the significance of my words – the whole war would have ended in later 1943 or early 1944." Central to the argument was the delay factor; whether or not, in prolonging the war, Hitler could find a satisfactory solution for Germany, Rommel may have overlooked. There is no evidence that he considered it at this stage.

Sidi bou Zid

In February 1943, however, with the prospect of attacking an 'inferior' enemy – the Americans – once more presented, Rommel was eager to exploit local advantages to their fullest extent, even if he might have been pessimistic as to the long-term result. All thought of retreat was cast aside when he strove to prise troops away from von Arnim prior to launching his thrust towards Gafsa. But he was placated only by the proviso that the 21st Panzer Division would be transferred back to him once its task at Sidi bou Zid was complete. It soon was: on the 14th, while Rommel advanced gingerly in the direction of Gafsa, Fifth Panzerarmee won its greatest victory, and routed the outnumbered elements of the inexperienced American II Corps at Sidi bou Zid. Rommel also had a good day, opposed as he was by only the lightest of French and American forces. These, on instructions from above, gave way before him, an Allied withdrawal becoming essential in the light of the débâcle at Sidi bou Zid, and especially after an American counterattack had been smashed on the 15th. Expecting a tough battle for Gafsa, and demanding the 21st Panzer Division for the purpose, the Afrika Korps detachment found itself in possession of the town with a useful haul of war material on the evening of the 15th, without having to fight. All around lay the familiar evidence of an army in disruption. Instinctively, Rommel was stimulated to further action. News that the enemy was burning stores at Tebessa, a base depot 80 miles to the north-west, led him to thrust onwards to Feriana, and inspired his request to Kesselring that a far more ambitious plan should be adopted. His gaze fastened far ahead on the territory beyond Tebessa. A substantial victory looked in the offing if only this distant objective could be reached with all three Panzer Divisions united.

But Kesselring was on a visit to Berlin when the request arrived, and von Arnim had already decided, with Kesselring's earlier blessing, upon a more limited advance to Sbeitla, with the prospect then of a northward hook to Sbiba. Furthermore, von Arnim was distrustful of Rommel's motives and grandiose scheme. In any case, he had already planned another more limited stroke in the north, so he now saw no need to release the 21st Panzer Division to Rommel, and the Axis forces failed to pursue on the 16th and 17th with all the strength of which they were capable. Instead, von Arnim 'thought small', while Rommel exceeded his orders and tried to maintain a bluff pursuit with inadequate forces, endeavouring meanwhile to persuade Kesselring to place the whole mobile force under his command for the lunge towards Tebessa and beyond, with the aim of forcing the enemy to withdraw totally into Algeria. But so lukewarm was the response from on high that, on the 17th, Rommel actually began to send a part of his reserve back to Mareth, though signalling Kesselring and Comando Supremo in the hope of inspiring their optimism into granting his real desire. In the meantime, his advance towards Tebessa on the 17th had overrun American airfields, catching many aircraft on the ground and producing a decline in air attacks upon his column. It all took time, when time was mighty short, but Kesselring did not disappoint him. He too preferred the Tebessa route. However, the Italians, by stipulating that Rommel moved closer to the existing battlefront in the north by attacking towards Le Kef instead of swinging wider to the west, inhibited the project (and satisfied von Arnim, since it suited his narrower concepts). Because a genuinely unified Army Group still did not exist, command was conducted by committee, with Rommel, on the 19th, running out of patience (or perhaps, as Kesselring suggests, forbearing to press von Arnim) and deciding that he must instantly make do with whatever forces were on the spot. Since the 21st Panzer Division had been retained at Sbeitla by von Arnim, who was about to despatch the 10th Panzer Division northward for a quite separate spoiling

attack, Rommel tried in desperation to demonstrate the potential of his plan by throwing the Afrika Korps detachment against the Kasserine Pass. In addition, he ordered the 21st Panzer Division to move towards Sbiba, in the mistaken belief that this complied with Kesselring's intention to make Le Kef the main objective.

Kasserine

Although Rommel had stipulated that his more grandiose thrust must be dependent upon adequate supplies, he was again biting off more than he could chew. He might fear and complain that in making for Le Kef he was liable to confront the mass of the enemy reserves, but his original concept of driving via Tebessa would, in the slightly longer run, have been extremely risky. The Allied might was considerable and, in sending almost the entirety of the Axis mobile forces towards the west and north, he was leaving his rear at Mareth almost completely exposed, besides over-stretching his logistic strength. It was fortunate for him that the British measured approach to Mareth from Tripoli was ponderous, and anything but the rescue operation that Montgomery later claimed it to be. Kesselring (this time on Rommel's side) was angry when he discovered that von Arnim had procrastinated and withheld full support, and disappointed that Rommel had misinterpreted Comando Supremo's directive by thinking the narrow Le Kef hook, instead of the wide Tebessa sweep, had been his intention. He insisted upon the 10th Panzer Division being returned to Sbeitla.

The time wasted in promulgating Rommel's assumption of unified command (formally actuated at 0600 hours on the 20th) gave the Allies ample opportunity to bring reinforcements down from the north to block the Kasserine Pass and hold the gap at Sbiba. On the 19th, Rommel pinned his main hope upon a breakthrough at Sbiba, but held back the 10th Panzer Division until a hole in the Anglo-American defences had been made. He merely probed the Kasserine Pass, although he was there in person as the Afrika Korps went into action. At once, his mountaineer's training came to the fore, and he was quick to notice why the initial Afrika Korps attack had been held by the Americans. By advancing along the valley floor instead of seizing the rugged peaks on either side, his men were overlooked. Forcibly, he told his local commanders to put desert tactics behind them and concentrate on another kind of warfare. The desired results began to be achieved as, throughout the 19th, the peaks fell gradually under German control, exposing the enemy positions below and to the north to German observation and fire. At Sbiba, the 21st Panzer Division could not budge the defenders, and the attack stalled with the loss of about ten tanks. This, too, Rommel saw for himself: indeed it was he who helped to make it so by sending in tanks instead of infantry. At the conclusion of a distinctly unprofitable day, he realized that if he was to break through anywhere it would be at Kasserine. There, too, his units were suffering heavy losses, but they at least were making progress, and a report came in of Americans retreating towards Tebessa. Here, he sensed, results might be obtained, and to this front he called forward the 10th Panzer Division early on the 20th.

By then, it was apparent that he was 'reinforcing success' in the classical manner. In the light of dawn, the Americans holding the

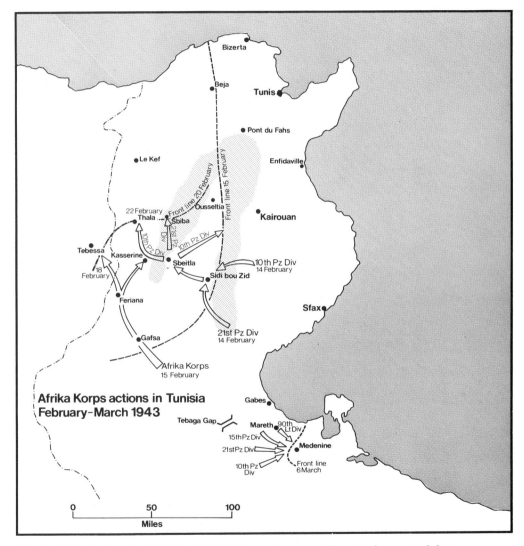

Afrika Korps actions in Tunisia February–March 1943

Von Arnim's attack against Sidi bou Zid shatters the American defenders of the Eastern Dorsal, while Rommel joins in with the weak Afrika Korps group from Mareth through Gafsa in the direction of Kasserine and Tebessa. The Germans pause for reconsideration on 17/18 February, but eventually strike northward on the 19th to meet, and be stopped by, the oncoming Allied reserves at Sbiba, Thala, and in the valley to the east of Tebessa. In pursuit of his intention to make a heavy spoiling attack upon Eighth Army, Rommel throws all three German Panzer divisions against the British at Medenine on 6 March. With the mass of his infantry (Italian and German) in the north and centre, he brings the Panzers through the hills to launch converging blows in the centre and along the southern flank. Hardly any progress is made: the Axis armour is repulsed with the loss of one-third of its strength, while the British losses are very small.

Above left:
The last German triumphs in North Africa, led by strongly-reinforced Panzer divisions. The vehicles, from left to right, are a Pz Kpfw II, an SPW half-track and a Pz Kpfw IV. (Bundesarchiv)
Above right:
Pz Kpfw IV crews unload spent shell cases. (Bundesarchiv)
Left:
A British prisoner of the German parachute troops. (Bundesarchiv)
Right:
A German spearhead stalled in the foothills. (Bundesarchiv)

On the 21st, and for the last time, Rommel rode with victorious Panzers in pursuit of a defeated enemy, sweeping northward with the 10th Panzer Division towards Thala (while the Afrika Korps moved more warily in the direction of Tebessa), sharing the dangers with men who looked upon him as Victory personified. He exulted in the piles of high-quality booty that dropped into his hands (but groaned at the ultimate meaning of so much good equipment being at the disposal of the enemy – an opponent who still

Above:
General Sir Harold Alexander with (right) General Dwight D. Eisenhower, under whose command the Allied armies in Tunisia defeated the Axis forces. (MacClancy Press)
Right:
Tunisian mud. A German supply column in difficulties. (Bundesarchiv)

Kasserine Pass began to collapse. In fact, the Americans fought well initially, relieved to some extent by the tardy build-up of a combined German–Italian assault consisting of elements of the 15th Panzer and Centauro Divisions. Rommel complains bitterly in *The Rommel Papers* about the delayed deployment of the 10th Panzer Division's elements as they arrived from Sbeitla. He castigated its leaders for being too far from the front, and insisted upon altering the plans that its commander had already made (in other words, subjecting them to the sort of treatment to which the officers of Panzerarmee Afrika had grown accustomed). But he did not complain unduly to Kesselring when, at midday, they met in the mouth of the Pass. They quickly agreed that a breakout must take place that day or not at all and, within a matter of hours, they had their demands satisfied by the dauntless troops. The Americans broke, and the 10th Panzer Division crashed through, falling upon a small Anglo-American rearguard that had just arrived from the north.

Kesselring, meanwhile, had taken the final plunge to place Rommel in full charge on this front. After upbraiding von Arnim for withholding troops from Rommel, he submitted (with Hitler's approval) a recommendation to Comando Supremo that Rommel be given charge of those units of Fifth Panzerarmee designated for diversionary operations near Pont du Fahs in the north, thus making it harder for von Arnim to follow his own bent in the days to come. At the same time, he finally resolved to arrange for Rommel to become Army Group commander when the time was ripe.

had much to learn in terms of tactical skill, but who was rapidly catching up with the Germans in the art of war). It did not matter now when news came in of a further rebuff at Sbiba; the failure of this right-hand hook of his offensive could be dismissed as a diversion as he concentrated upon the left-hand 'punch' from Kasserine.

To Rommel's advantage, the weather was so bad that it hampered Allied air attacks; he cared less that the Luftwaffe was also unable to help. But the concept of the operation was a gamble, made additionally hazardous by the dispersion of effort caused, inevitably, by Rommel's hope that by "deploying troops at several danger spots I hoped to split the enemy forces far more than my own". This, the rejection of the principle of concentration that had, everywhere and always, provided the cornerstone of successful German practice, was a fatal error. The fact that the enemy was well aware of Rommel's movements and content to let him extend himself against their light, highly-mobile rearguards, which

gave ground steadily throughout the day, picking off as many opponents as they could at a series of delaying positions, merely compounded his mistake. Everywhere, defences sprang up that were strong enough to shake his dispersed spearheads. As a result, Rommel's men were progressively slowed down at a time when a rapid rate of progress was mandatory to forestall the deployment of enemy reinforcements.

This race he could not win, even though that night the 10th Panzer Division overran a British battalion to the south of Thala. Thereafter, it could get no farther against a superior opponent. Next day, its leading troops were hammered by deadly Allied artillery concentrations under highly-skilled British direction; it became obvious that an undisclosed force of British armour lay in wait close by, and more was seen arriving from the north. With tank losses high, Rommel lost heart. Despite the availability of

enough fuel to carry him forward another 150 miles, and an adequate ammunition supply, he despondently (and perhaps correctly) repudiated the 10th Panzer Division's chances. Similarly, he put little value on the attenuated Afrika Korps' continued, though retarded, advance towards Tebessa, At midday, the weather began to clear, and with it came the certainty of strafing from the air, and a downpour of enemy bombs. Kesselring arrived with Westphal and Hans Seidemann, the Luftwaffe commander, to discover that a truculent Rommel had already passed to the defensive. Later, Kesselring said that he felt Rommel might have been inclined to exaggerate the threat then slowly making its appearance at Mareth, but the contemporary documents show that it was the local situation to the north of Kasserine that dominated Rommel's thoughts. After an hour's assessment, interrupted by frequent telephone calls, they agreed to pull back. Kesselring

Below:
Pz Kpfw IVs awaiting the next call to action. (Bundesarchiv)

took the view that it was futile to insist upon a depressed Rommel carrying out an operation in which he had lost confidence; under these circumstances, he would very likely find a way to disobey anyway. Instead, they examined together alternative offensive schemes, and agreed to Rommel's proposal to switch the mobile formations to a pre-emptive strike at Eighth Army, where it was forming up opposite the Mareth Line.

One more important decision was also made at Kasserine, twenty-four hours before Army Group Africa was at last formally activated on the 23rd. It was put to Rommel by Kesselring that he, not von Arnim, should take command of the Group. But Rommel was unenthusiastic, giving ill health as his reason for declining the command. In fact, he saw no future or joy in such an appointment. In his *Papers*, written in 1944, he lists his reasons, most of which are valid in the light of his appraisal of the situation in February 1943.

Knowing that von Arnim had already been earmarked for the job was one reason; his distaste for working under Comando Supremo, the Luftwaffe and Kesselring another. Above all, he saw no hope either of holding out or of imposing his will upon a group of men who were unanimously opposed to his methods. In effect, the offer was made for prestige reasons and at the Führer's insistence; except for a few doting members of his staff (such as Berndt), Rommel was actually regarded with suspicion and mistrust by those both above and below him in the chain of command.

The incongruous arrangement that permitted Rommel to remain for as long as he cared, prior to handing over to von Arnim, is expressive of the relationships existing. He was treated as a figurehead, even though the idea of a spoiling attack against Eighth Army at Medenine (to be commanded by Messe) was his, and von Arnim's forthcoming attack

Right:
Italian officers, with Germans in the background, waiting to see what Montgomery might do next. (Image Press)

Right:
Weary German infantry prepare to face the Eighth Army again. (Bundesarchiv)

towards Beja, in the north, was ostensibly his responsibility. The latter attack, for example, was arranged in discussions between von Arnim and Kesselring and presented to Rommel as a fait accompli by Westphal, who was chosen for the task because he was persona grata with Rommel. Naturally, Rommel exploded, realizing that this diversion would delay and jeopardize the Medenine attack; for the same reason, he rejected as impracticable von Arnim's suggestion that the 10th Panzer Division should hang on near Kasserine in the hope that its presence would make the enemy defer returning reserves to the north.

Rommel spent the next few days in an attempt to rationalize Axis strategy, by consolidating the individual assessments of the two Armies under his command in a detailed appreciation of the worsening situation. He concluded (in complete agreement with von Arnim) that the enemy superiority in numbers, equipment and supplies left the only course open to the Axis an immediate withdrawal of the formations in the south to the Enfidaville position. In the document summarizing his conclusions, which was presented to Kesselring on 1 March, Rommel asked OKW and Comando Supremo for their long-term plans for the campaign in Tunisia. He also stated, unequivocally, that delivery of 140,000 tons of supplies per month was essential – a figure more than 100,000 tons above what was then being received. In effect, he and von Arnim were advocating a total withdrawal, to which neither Hitler nor Mussolini could possibly agree. And, although Kesselring concurred that the front should be shortened, he denied the necessity of doing so until enemy pressure made it unavoidable, and emphasized (somewhat unrealistically) the need to retain as many airfields as possible in Tunisia. For the moment, it was hoped that the impending attacks in the north and at Medenine would purchase a few more weeks' grace. There was nothing Rommel could do but shrug his shoulders at being overruled and complain about Kesselring's rosy optimism and ignorance of the true state of affairs.

The Medenine attack

There is conflict between the American and British Official Histories with regard to Rommel's attitude and rôle in the attack (Operation 'Capri') against the British at Medenine. The former, without producing evidence, says he was "eager"; the latter, implying that Rommel acted as a sort of chairman in a debate starting on 28 February

between his commanders and staff officers, suggests that he did not impose his customary personal control, but permitted "a scrappy plan", "took no interest in the details", and contented himself with giving a 'pep' talk to the divisional commanders on the day before the battle. In *The Rommel Papers*, Rommel claims full responsibility for the attack, makes no bones about it having been difficult (because there was little chance of surprising the enemy), and admits that the whole enterprise depended upon striking before Montgomery's Eighth Army was ready. The final plan, a three-pronged converging advance by the trio of Panzer Divisions debouching from the Matmata Hills to the eastward, he ascribes to Messe. His own proposal to send in two of the Panzer Divisions close to the coast was not welcomed by his subordinates because the terrain was considered too difficult; in this sector, they preferred to let the Italian infantry make a diversionary effort. Rommel had no grounds to overrule Messe, who was responsible for the attack in any case.

On the day of the assault, there was little chance of anybody – even Rommel at the height of his powers – making much impression on Montgomery's masterly deployment. To begin with, radio intercept, 'Ultra' decoded messages and air and ground reconnaissance had told Montgomery the exact date and place of the attack. He had been able to reinforce Medenine heavily and to deploy vastly stronger forces than those in the assault. Furthermore, the defensive layout gave priority to well-concealed anti-tank guns sited to destroy enemy tanks rather than (as in the past) purely to defend the infantry: the newly-arrived 17pr anti-tank guns, with their ability to reach out and penetrate even the most heavily-armoured German tanks at battle ranges, made this possible. British tanks, on the other hand, were not to be committed unless a breach of the front was made. They were to be conserved for later offensive operations, just as they had been, to a lesser extent, at Alam Halfa.

Command of the Axis forces was not all it might have been on the 6th. While Rommel watched the gathering of his troops and their advance to contact from a distance, Messe seems to have stayed away altogether, leaving the work to his chief of staff, Bayerlein, and to Hans Cramer, now in command of the Afrika Korps, which contained all three Panzer Divisions, plus elements of the 90th Light Division and the Italian Spezia Division, with a total of 160 tanks and 200

guns. From the outset, they foresaw trouble. The columns were bombed on the approach march, and the troops were heavily shelled and shaken in the forming-up areas. The British anti-tank gunners (hardly disturbed by inaccurate German fire), watching the phalanx of enemy tanks closing upon them through rising mist, could hardly believe their luck. Carelessly crossing a ridge, the tanks of the 21st Panzer Division were badly mauled at 400-yards' range, and never reached the British lines; those of the 15th Panzer Division, having closed, were easily repulsed. All had difficulties with mines. Neither the 10th Panzer Division nor the 90th Light Division did any better, so the assault was soon halted while the commanders conferred. Cramer, urged on by Rommel, managed to start moving again in the afternoon, this time with dive-bomber assistance, but by then there was less chance than ever of making progress, and the tank losses swelled as the Divisions lost direction as well as losing heart. In the evening, Messe proposed calling off the attack, and Rommel, who had come forward and saw that he was beaten, concurred. To one of his column commanders, Theodor von Sponeck, he explained that to punch a way through would cause losses which would jeopardize the subsequent defence of southern Tunisia. Upon that they must now concentrate; it was back to static warfare. As it was, fifty-two German tanks were left behind on the battlefield and nearly 700 casualties had been suffered by the Axis. The British had not lost a single tank and had suffered minimal casualties despite German claims to the contrary.

Most worrying of all for Rommel was the uncomfortable realization that, as his forces withdrew, the Afrika Korps could muster only eighty-five German and twenty-four Italian tanks – a dangerously low figure. He cannot have been aware of this during the night, for, upon receipt of a false report that the 10th Panzer Division had reached a key position in the enemy lines, he briefly reconsidered resuscitating the attack. Failure, however, was absolute. There were no more laurels to be won in Africa, and now was the time for him to return home, to write his report and recommence the 'cure' at Semmering that had been interrupted by Montgomery at El Alamein. Bruised in mind and body though he might be, he could at least reflect that there was no stain upon his shield as a fighting man. It remained to be seen how he would fight for his career and for Germany in the future.

Above left:
Italian infantry with flame-throwers struggle forward in their last attack on Rommel's behalf. (Image Press)
Left:
Destruction of the German armour. A Pz Kpfw IV in ruins and a crewman pulped. (Imperial War Museum)
Above:
The last commander of Panzergruppe Afrika, General von Arnim, is taken into captivity. (MacClancy Press)

BATTLES AGAINST THE GRAIN   187

13

In Search of Employment

In some respects, it appears that at the conclusion of Operation 'Capri' Rommel posed something of a dilemma to Hitler – an embarrassment almost. For one thing, Hitler was beset by two factions representing opposite intentions. There was the military faction, led by Goering and Kesselring, tacitly aided and abetted by the Army General Staff, who were only too pleased to have Rommel out of their sight; the excuse provided by Rommel's variable health was entirely convenient to them, and von Arnim's appointment as commander of Army Group Africa a relief. (Rommel, indeed, was angered by the almost indecent haste with which Kesselring called von Arnim and von Vaerst – who took over Fifth Panzerarmee from von Arnim – to a conference in Rome as soon as 'Capri' was over.) The other faction was led by Goebbels, who, anxious to enhance Rommel's propaganda value, seems also to have acquired a quite different understanding of Rommel's standing with Hitler than the Führer gave Rommel to believe.

On 6 March 1943, Hitler had sent Rommel a sharp rejoinder to his appreciation of the 1st, a rebuttal in which he angrily reminded Rommel that he had promised there would be no more crises once Mareth was reached. (Nowhere do *The Rommel Papers* refer to this rebuke or to any promise about all being well at Mareth, but it is interesting to compare Hitler's recognition of Rommel's 'thin-end-of-the-wedge' tactics with a similar assertion by Kesselring referred to on page 175.)

There are two versions of Rommel's meeting with Hitler on 10 March. There is Rommel's, in which he complains miserably of Hitler's unwillingness to come to terms with the situation as he saw it in Tunisia, and in which the Führer refused point-blank to allow him to return to lead the Army Group, while fobbing him off with ludicrous talk of a future command for an expedition to retake

Casablanca. There is also Goebbels' version, in which the Propaganda Minister rhapsodizes happily upon Rommel's report to Hitler, "which pleased the Führer tremendously. Rommel again holds all the trump cards. His talk with the Führer went off wonderfully ... The Führer spontaneously awarded Rommel the diamonds to his Oak-Leaf Cluster decoration after their talk." It must be borne in mind that this meeting took place at a moment of desperation in Hitler's conduct of the war. Several people noticed that he lacked his previous confidence, and was prepared, temporarily, to seek and accept the advice of tried General Staff officers, such as Erich von Manstein, who would at last bring a halt to the Russian advance near Kharkov. The Army everywhere was in bad shape, especially in Russia; low industrial production at home was being hampered by poor organization, and the increasingly-damaging air bombardment, which had reduced tank output to the extent that the Panzer divisions in Russia, for example, had only an average of twenty-seven tanks each. Civil discontent was also evident. Goering, who was present at the meeting, was castigated for allowing the Luftwaffe to fall to such a low ebb in numbers and technical efficiency. From the record, it seems unlikely that the exchange of military information between Goebbels and Hitler was very extensive. The fact remains that, for the next few weeks only, Hitler's treatment of Rommel was cool and reserved, while Goebbels, anxious to exploit every possible morale-booster, used his favourite Army officer to the maximum, regardless of what had actually gone wrong in North Africa. In this, he was influenced by Berndt, who had extolled Rommel on every occasion to the extent, it seems, of helping smooth the way to his becoming Army Group commander in February for sectional reasons. For, on 26 February he had written to Frau Rommel:

"Right in the middle of our successful operations we received the decision – Army Group 'Rommel' with both Armies under command. It was a further great confirmation of the Führer's and Duce's confidence. I brought this about in order to renew his belief that he still enjoyed the fullest confidence, even after the retreat. He was always persuading himself to the contrary." Seen in the light of a flattering letter Berndt wrote to Goebbels at this time, in which he gave the impression of affairs in Tunisia being "in relatively good shape", Goebbels' optimistic view of conditions in Africa, as well as of Rommel's ability, becomes understandable.

Despite the adulation, Rommel was out of a job. He had suggested to Hitler on 10 March that he be given command of his old troops to defend Italy from an Allied invasion – guaranteeing success if he had his wish. But Hitler promised nothing, and Rommel retired to Semmering again. Meanwhile, Berndt kept Goebbels supplied with tit-bits of information denigrating those who had been in command in North Africa (almost everybody, that is, with the exception of Rommel), and Goebbels, for his part, canvassed for a fresh job for his protégé. The possible reconstruction of Sixth Army (destroyed at Stalingrad) was one idea. "That, of course," he wrote, "would be a task worthy of Rommel's great talents and ambition" – although it is none too apparent how the offer of an Army could compensate for loss of command of an Army Group. By 11 April, the need for remedial action on Rommel's behalf had become more urgent as the enemy press began to revile him. "That is too bad," complained Goebbels, "especially since he has had nothing whatever to do with Tunisia recently. The Führer is keeping him in reserve for a greater task."

The surrender in North Africa posed Goebbels with the problem of explaining to the world in general, and the German people in particular, the embarrassing matter of Rommel's non-involvement in the defeat. Previous reports had spoken of his being in command. Now, his absence of over two months had to be explained – and at a time when the people were showing signs of disbelieving the German news media. In his diary on 11 May, Goebbels wrote of Hitler's total distrust and dislike of his generals: "All generals lie, he says. All generals are disloyal. All generals are opposed to National Socialism. He just can't stand them." In the same entry, he refers in detail to another talk Hitler had with Rommel, in which he went to great lengths to issue a communiqué absolving Rommel from responsibility for failing in North Africa. Rommel, he correctly stated, was to be kept on the Führer's personal staff ready for "the first difficult task that may arise". Hitler even went so far as to say that one reason for the collapse in North Africa was because Mussolini pushed Rommel out. And so it went on...

However, despite Hitler's reservations (which Goebbels failed to detect), Rommel was to be given another chance. The bulk of the blame for the collapse in Africa was adroitly shifted to the Italians, to Goering and to Kesselring – although the latter retained command, and was charged with the hard task of building up the defences of Sicily, Sardinia, Corsica and Italy. Against a background of OKW mistrust of Kesselring (who was considered by Keitel and Jodl at OKW as far too optimistic and a blatant Italophile), it was easy for Rommel to make headway in what amounted to a vendetta against the Luftwaffe Field Marshal. Although Rommel, in a much-quoted passage, was in 1944 to revise his opinion of Kesselring, in 1943 he bore him a grudge for having, as he saw it, let him down at El Alamein and thereafter – the *Papers* and his letters leave no doubt as to that. He held a series of conversations throughout May with Kurt Zeitzler (Halder's successor as Chief of Staff since September 1942), beginning on the 15th, at which he carefully outlined his next task. By the 18th, enough progress had been made to allow him to assemble staff from those officers of his former headquarters who had not been left behind in Africa. But still no task was allocated, despite a meeting with Hitler and the principal members of OKW on the 20th, at which Rommel asked for command in Italy and pronounced the need for energetic action to prevent the Italians closing the Brenner Pass and defecting to the Allies. In the latter event, Hitler told Keitel, Rommel seemed to be the right man to handle the situation (quite regardless, it seems, of the fact that this would again upset the existing command arrangements). But, when Rommel wrote to Lu on the 24th, saying he had arrived again at Rastenberg safely and "I am confidently hoping we'll pull it off", he was on the verge of a decision. For it was not, as Manfred Rommel believed (in the absence of other evidence), "the war as a whole" that was the subject for discussion, but the allocation of the task he had been angling for – the leadership of a new Army Group (called 'B') which, with formations withdrawn from Russia, would eventually comprise 13 or 14 divisions to carry out the occupation of Italy (Plan 'Alarich'). Once more, Rommel was driving German strategy off-course, for Hitler originally intended those divisions to launch an important offensive in Russia.

Informed through Luftwaffe channels of Rommel's manoeuvres, from which he had deliberately been excluded, Kesselring quietly negotiated with the Italians in a determined attempt to retain their loyalty, and to station sufficient troops at the most threatened spots (notably Sicily) before the Allies could strike. By 10 July, just prior to the invasion of Sicily, he had succeeded in persuading the Italians to accept seven German divisions on their soil, five of which were already there, the others in transit. By then, too, Hitler had abandoned 'Alarich', because Kesselring had brought things so well under control, and also because he had finally decided to use the divisions saved for the last great offensive in Russia at Kursk, starting on 5 July. So Kesselring remained the most powerful, though by no means unchallenged, German in Italy, and Rommel was once more outmanoeuvred. He might well say to Lu (as reported by Manfred) that he had frank discussions with Hitler in which the Führer admitted that the war was lost but that he

Right:
A cheerful meeting between Rommel and Goebbels, while Berndt, Rommel's eminence grise, looks on with unconcealed approval. (Bundesarchiv)

intended to fight to the bitter end. He could also (according to Bayerlein) in July, after the failure at Kursk, recognize that Germany had lost the initiative, but state that the vast arsenal of new weapons coming from the German factories would make it possible to contain the Russians and beat off invasions by the Western Allies. Probably, he was deluded by the flood of optimistic promises Hitler poured out for the benefit of despondent followers. And, undoubtedly, he was impressed by details of the secret weapons to come, because he frequently referred to them. The fact remained that, at bottom, Rommel continued to believe in the Führer and, if not in the possibility of final victory, certainly in the chance of achieving a satisfactory peace providing defensive successes could be won in the field. There was neither original thought nor rebellion in his political stance. Nor is it compulsory to believe everything he wrote about his private conversations with Hitler.

That Rommel was out of touch, unwilling or unable to understand Hitler's basic intentions of unyielding defence, became apparent when he told Bayerlein that he felt a withdrawal in Russia, to economize in forces, was desirable – from his own experience, he can hardly have expected that of Hitler. But he adopted a truly Hitlerian, and, incidentally, infantry-oriented opinion when he pronounced that it only required a mass of anti-tank guns posted behind thick minefields to halt the Russians. He had forsaken the tank as Germany's essential decisive weapon because he felt there was "not the slightest hope of our keeping pace with the enemy in the production of tanks" – an opinion which indicates that he did not appreciate the defensive capabilities of even a few good tanks. So he tacitly approved Kesselring's arrangements in Sicily, where the defences were laid out with the intention of meeting the invasion on the beaches and throwing it back in the sea before the relatively weak Axis mobile troops could be overcome by a mass of enemy tanks. These would be the tactics he would later copy in another much larger context.

Unhappily for the Germans, the Allied invasion of Sicily was not stopped on the beaches, and the steady, though stoutly resisted, advance of the enemy towards the toe of Italy caused stresses that bore heavily upon those who were responsible for defence. At the same time it raised Rommel's hopes for action. On 13 July, Jodl, who among the OKW staff was perhaps the most doubtful of Kesselring's abilities, concluded that the continued defence of the island was impossible, if only because the Italians were giving up too easily and there were insufficient Germans to fill the gaps. In collaboration with Rommel, he wrote proposing a joint German–Italian command in the Mediterranean under Rommel, with unified command of the air forces under the Luftwaffe's Wolfram von Richthofen who, at that moment, was leading Luftflotte 2. This would effectively eliminate Kesselring, whose position they were already undermining by forcing upon him, as commanders and staff, officers who were pro-Rommel. Two days later, Hitler agreed that Sicily would have to be evacuated, but came to no conclusions as to unified command or the person for the job. Then came a setback, angrily recorded by Rommel on the 18th: "I hear the Führer has been advised not to give me command in Italy as I am adversely disposed to the Italians [a not unreasonable conclusion on all counts, it may be thought, but not entirely for the reason Rommel supposed] I imagine the Luftwaffe is behind this." Naturally the Italians had a say, and Hitler was in no position to impose Rommel upon them. Within the week, in fact, he removed Rommel from command of Army Group B and sent him to Greece, where deliberately misleading injections of Allied intelligence had suggested the invasion would actually come. But, within minutes of his arrival there on 25 July, he was on his way back again. Suddenly, everything had become focused upon Italy, where, as a complete surprise to the Germans, Mussolini had been deposed in Rome. Rommel was at once to initiate the preliminary state of Plan 'Alarich'. As the Führer's head 'fireman', the demands upon his flexibility of mind can hardly have been less exacting, but what this sort of thing did to his constitution is unrecorded, his published diary notes for this period being remarkably uninformative.

The difference between Rommel's and Kesselring's reactions to Mussolini's deposition is revealing of their relative calibres. In this delicate situation, Kesselring, a diplomat to the finger-tips, skilfully played for time and gradually, without fuss, bloodshed or loss of prestige, stabilized the situation. (Even Rommel, on the 30th, was compelled to admit that things in the south looked clearer.) Rommel, on the other hand, was all for precipitate action, and thus in tune with the hysterical debates then being conducted by Hitler; but, while Hitler demanded instant political action (such as kidnapping the

Italian king), Rommel was among those who counselled caution in this sphere and, for his part, made bold military proposals. He argued that Kesselring should evacuate Sicily (where he thought an attempted withdrawal under heavy air attack would be a disaster), surrender Sardinia and southern Italy while the going was good, and fall back to a line in the Apennines guarding the Plain of Lombardy. There, the divisions withdrawn from the south would merge with his; he would take overall charge and Kesselring could be dismissed (to Norway — as far away as possible). After long discussions with the Führer, he felt confident, as he wrote to Lu on 3 August, that Kesselring would be "played out in Italy sooner or later", but a directive giving him the job he desired hung fire. Kesselring, using the subtle methods that were foreign to Rommel, held things together, his job made easier by Hitler's refusal to allow Rommel to enter Italy (for fear of upsetting the Italians). For the time being, Rommel's men, as yet few in number, had to be content with occupying a few key points, such as the passes in the north.

Hitler must have found it hard to choose between Rommel, who had caught his imagination with his rough charisma and past achievements, and the charming, polished Kesselring, who, by depth of experience and with an ironic sense of humour, was getting results. Although Hitler once said that Kesselring should not have the command in Italy "because he has not got the reputation. We'll publish it [the appointment of Rommel] once we move in", it did not yet come to that. By a supreme effort in overcoming both his subordinates' objections and enemy pressure, Kesselring had, on 17 August, completed a brilliant evacuation from Sicily at low cost. As a result, his appointment was extended. Once more, Rommel was in suspense — having been proved totally wrong in his forecast that a successful evacuation from Sicily was impossible.

A conference at Bologna between the Italians, Jodl, Rommel and Kesselring on 15 August achieved nothing of value for the Germans, except a row caused by Kesselring handing in and then withdrawing his resignation because he was originally excluded by Jodl. An ill-disguised attempt to impose Rommel as superior commander to the Italians was deflected; instead he was made subordinate to Ambrosio. Plans for defending Italy were discussed, but neither side trusted the other, since the Germans suspected that the Italians were seeking peace with the Allies, and the Italians, who were doing just that, were fearful of being found out. But, on the 17th, as Rommel moved his headquarters from Munich to the Lake Garda area in Italy, it was decided to create a new Tenth Army under Heinrich von Vietinghoff, with its operational area in central and southern Italy, and directly responsible to Kesselring. As tension mounted, the Germans took tighter control without ever guessing what really was in store for them. On the 22nd, Tenth Army was activated and at once made ready to withdraw its covering forces from the south, in preparation for making its principal stand in the vicinity of Naples and Salerno. Indeed, as Rommel tightened his grip on the north by means of an infiltrated occupation, and the British Eighth Army invaded Calabria on 3 September, only central Italy, including Rome, was not firmly in the German grasp. Therefore, when the armistice between Italy and the Allies was dramatically announced on the 8th, it was the simplest thing in the world for von Vietinghoff and Rommel to play their parts in Plan 'Achse' (the new scheme to take over Italy), leaving Kesselring to sort out the most awkward and dangerous situation in Rome.

Unhindered by enemy landings, and with ruthless efficiency, Rommel pounced on the Italian formations and units within his boundaries. The rounding-up, disarming and swift transportation of these units led to friction that sowed the seeds of future partisan resistance. In many places, arms were hidden away in secret caches, and Kesselring was later to point out that it was in the area of Army Group B that a large proportion of the coming guerrilla war would occur. Von Vietinghoff, on the other hand, even as he fought off an invasion, managed to persuade the Italians in the south to surrender passively and disperse, while Kesselring, after narrowly escaping death from bombing, and enduring many hours of acute worry, gained control of Rome and its environs by subterfuge. But his compromise, whereby the Italians disarmed themselves and dispersed to their homes, drew recriminations from Rommel, who sent an insulting signal deprecating the decision not to take the Italians prisoner. As Westphal complained, it was "as if to say he, Kesselring, had grossly failed in his duty". This signal, unjust as it was, indicates something more than Rommel's lack of appreciation of the fine arts of diplomacy and power-politics. It reflects in his behaviour a confirmed belief that it was only a matter of days before he would be Commander-in-Chief, the final version of Plan 'Achse' having laid down on 30 August that Kesselring would withdraw to the Rome area and then conduct operations in accordance with Rommel's instructions.

Unfortunately for Rommel's ambition, the enemy once more gave Kesselring an opportunity to demonstrate his masterly ability as a commander in the field. When the Allies landed at Salerno on 9 September, he and von Vietinghoff collaborated to contain the invaders and, by the 14th, had nearly succeeded in persuading them to re-embark. And, although they failed when the Allies recovered their nerve, it mattered little to Hitler, who had already given permission on the 12th to withdraw to a safer line a little farther north. In the upper hierarchy, only Goebbels felt hurt, complaining that his premature claim of a German victory, prompted by Kesselring's optimistic forecast, had been made to appear ridiculous. A few days later, however, he was to discover that Hitler regarded Kesselring well, a changing state of opinion that he might have comprehended earlier when Hitler back-pedalled on his previous inclinations and, in a fresh directive issued on the 12th, separated Kesselring's command from that of Rommel. Compelled to watch his chances slipping, Rommel was temporarily removed from contention on the

Right:
The latest German tanks roll forward into Italy as the war creeps up the peninsular and Rommel is denied the top job in command. The Panther tank: weight 44 tons, armour (max) 110mm, gun 75mm, speed 28mph, crew 5. In the foreground stands a Sonderschlepper B IV, a non-expendable, radio-controlled vehicle capable of depositing a large explosive charge on enemy emplacements or pill-boxes. (Bundesarchiv)

17th by appendicitis. By the end of the month, when he returned, he was both weak and out of touch with the fast-evolving strategic debate.

Kesselring, as assiduous in his attention to Hitler as was Rommel, and doubly convincing now that he had demonstrated the feasibility of holding the enemy in the mountainous Italian countryside, had dextrously amplified his argument that a prolonged stand could be made south of Rome. Rommel's argument that this risked outflanking by amphibious landings was valid, but conflicted with Hitler's natural inclination to hold on to everything he had, and to keep the enemy at arm's length, as far from the German frontiers as possible. On 4 October, he enjoined Kesselring to prove his strategy by attempting to save Rome – which Rommel had intended to give up as he swiftly retired to the Apennines. In a series of exchanges with Hitler during October, Kesselring strengthened his reputation by subtle argu-

ments and local successes in the field, while Rommel, in enforced inaction, frittered his away. On the 17th, Hitler asked Rommel point-blank: "Would he be prepared to execute the strategy of limited and prolonged withdrawal from river line to river line such as Kesselring proposed?" Rommel could so easily have prevaricated and later had his way; instead, he returned a straightforward "no" because he could not assume the responsibility (which is stronger than his excuse to Lu that he had "aroused no great hopes"). Justifiably, Hitler paused.

Over the next few days, in reply to repeated questions from Rommel's chief of staff, there was reticence on OKW's part, with Jodl remarking on the 19th: "It is possible that the Führer's view . . . has undergone a fundamental change." Jodl, in fact, was partly instrumental in this. He retained some confidence in Rommel, but he had also come to recognize Kesselring's manifest soldierly virtues. On the 25th, Hitler finally confirmed Kesselring as Commander-in-Chief in Italy as from 6 November – the interval between decision and promulgation imposed, no doubt, by the need to find something else for Rommel and the staff of Army Group B, who were thus made redundant. On the 28th, the very sort of 'troubleshooting' job the Führer had in mind presented itself. A report on the 25th from the Western Theatre of war by its commander-in-chief, Field Marshal Gerd von Rundstedt, had underlined the dangers of imminent invasion there, and the inadequacy of defences to prevent it. On 6 November, Rommel received an appointment after all – one that looked as authoritative as the one he had lost. With a reduced staff, he would go to the west and, independent of von Rundstedt while reporting direct to Hitler and OKW, become commander of Army Group for Special Employment, with the task of inspecting the western defences prior to taking up an, as yet undefined, operational task in that theatre.

Influential it looked and important it was; but to a few acute observers in the shadows of Germany, it also smacked of a snub, a setback to the career of an ambitious man whose advancement until then had been rapid and continuous. To men such as these, many of whom had been hurt by Hitler and his supporters in an attempt to make radical changes in Germany's political direction, Rommel all at once seemed to take his place among the disenchanted. Towards the end of the year, as Rommel prepared to move west, he began to receive visitors whose missions were sinister.

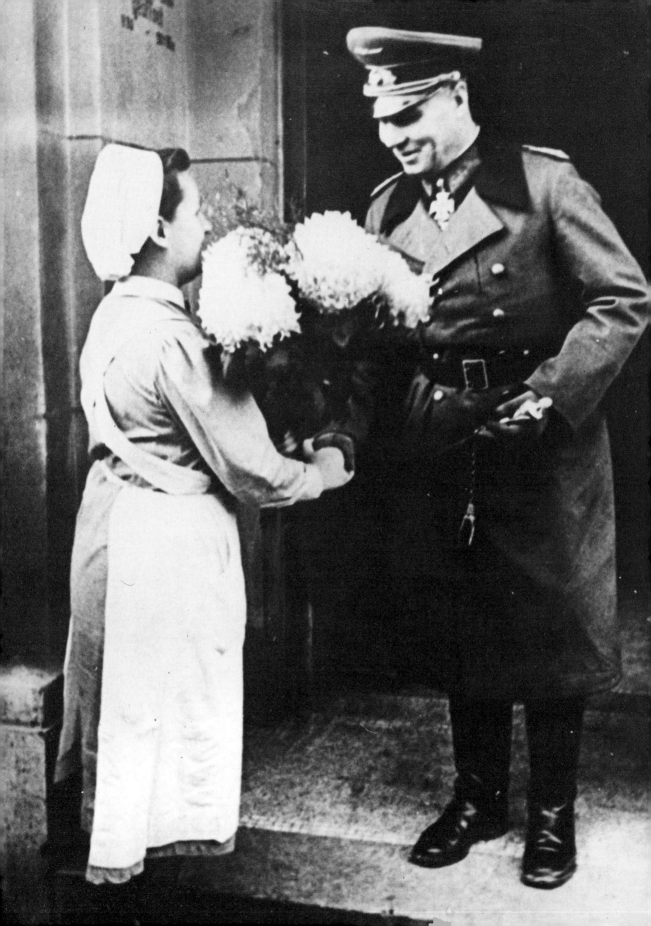

14

The Crash

Left:
A demonstration of the faith that ordinary people still had in Rommel. (Image Press)

Not once in Rommel's career can it be said with conviction that he decided upon outright political opposition to Hitler and the Nazi régime. That disillusionment set in at El Alamein in November 1942, and gradually rose to a peak in July 1944 is beyond doubt – but so it was with most of the German generals. An accumulation of adverse events and searing experiences at Hitler's hand showed them that Germany was in peril of destruction, and that the Führer was incapable of working a miracle. But the extent of Rommel's disenchantment may not be so grand as some have suggested.

Nevertheless, the immediate aftermath of his rejection as Commander-in-Chief, South, marked a crucial point in his education; coincidently, he seems to have come into possession of information concerning the genocide of the Jews, and also to have received the first advances from those who were clandestinely bent upon eliminating Hitler. A great many serving German generals with reputations superior to Rommel's had already been sounded out by the plotters. Guderian, von Kluge and von Manstein were among them, but they sat on the fence, fearing the consequences of unconstitutional political activities and feeling bound by their oath of loyalty to Hitler. Anybody in close contact with Hitler's entourage could also have been aware of the mass killings of Jews, and even those on the periphery of his circle probably knew more than, for reasons of conscience, they would ever admit. The fact remained that nearly everyone in harness (including Rommel) went on doing his best in securing Germany's defence. Their patriotism and ingrained sense of duty forbade any course of action that would lead to Germany's defeat. The most senior and celebrated officers who became deeply involved in the plot against Hitler prior to 1944 were those who previously had been sacked – men such as Ludwig

Beck, Erich Höppner and Erwin von Witzleben – soldiers of past importance, whose reputations meant nothing to the public and the bulk of the Wehrmacht, and therefore were unlikely to win a strong following.

By a curious set of coincidences over a period of time, Rommel was to be contacted by fellow Swabians among the plotters: Karl Strölin, the Bürgermeister of Stüttgart; Konstantin von Neurath, a former Foreign Minister; and an intellectual of some merit, Hans Speidel, who, in April 1944, was to become his chief of staff at Army Group B in France. Furthermore, Rommel was to find as his subordinates the Military Governors of Belgium and France, Alexander von Falkenhausen and Karl-Heinrich von Stülpnagel, both of whom in pre-war days had been his friends and superior officers, and both of whom were in touch with the inner circle of plotters. Their most brilliant co-ordinator was Klaus von Stauffenberg, who, until seriously wounded, had served with distinction under Rommel in Africa.

Strölin, a very old friend of Rommel's, who had served with him on the staff of LXIV Corps in 1918, made the initial approach via Lu, in November 1943. During an interview in February 1944, Rommel is said to have expressed his willingness to join an attempt to seize Hitler and compel his abdication, and this consent was said to have been transmitted to Karl Gördeler at the centre of the conspiracy. But there is no real evidence of this.

From that moment, the trail of conspiracy moved steadily to its climax in July. Strölin and Gördeler intended Rommel to be a figurehead capable of winning the confidence of the Army, as well as the people, and thus preventing civil war. They would make him either Head of State or Commander-in-Chief – a thoroughly sensible political concept, in that Rommel received fan-mail from innumerable people who saw him as the nation's potential saviour. But the conspirators recognized Rommel's limitations, and left his manipulation chiefly to Speidel and the others, partly for reasons of security, and partly, to quote Sir John Wheeler-Bennett, "because he had neither the mental equipment nor the personal inclination to take part in a political discussion". It was Speidel who ran the plot in Army Group B, keeping Rommel in the background because his commanding officer could not spare time for such pursuits and, in any case, was anathema to most of the inner circle of plotters as well as to the many senior serving officers whom he had offended by his past behaviour. Placed in prominence at their head, he might well have proved divisive. Probably, Rommel became aware of the proposal to make him Head of State or Commander-in-Chief, and saw himself in that rôle. Without doubt, he knew of the assassination plan and, like Guderian and Kesselring, rejected it, insisting upon Hitler's arrest and trial as the only judicious way of cloaking their activities in legality. It would be cynical to suggest that Rommel, because of his Nazi leanings, could not be a man of 20 July 1944; but he was certainly not in the mainstream of the plot.

Command in the West
For the most part, Rommel was absorbed in his new job of making a preliminary inspection of the Western Theatre from Denmark to Brittany. This he carried out with typical dash and dynamic zeal, hoping perhaps to find a ray of hope to relieve the gloom of Germany's difficulties elsewhere. The U-boat offensive had been defeated; the Allies had complete air superiority, and were pounding German industry by day and night; the Eastern Front was contracting remorselessly towards the Reich, as successive Russian offensives proved too strong to hold. Only in Italy had the Wehrmacht managed to put a brake upon the enemy's land forces, and there Kesselring was deftly proving the validity of his claims that he could hold Rome for at least six months. Everywhere, to a lesser or greater extent, the occupied countries manifested dissidence and resistance. Pressures from all directions dictated the forces that could be made available to defend the West, where massive concrete fortifications had been built, or were under construction, for the protection of ports and vital points. But the number and quality of the formations to man them waxed and waned in response to the demands of the other fronts.

Von Rundstedt's command was weak because it was the repository of ailing divisions sent west to recuperate from the hammerings they had received elsewhere. Only on 3 November did Hitler and OKW, recognizing that the time for a genuine and generous reinforcement of the West had come, give him priority of resources over other theatres. But it is apparent that, although Hitler acknowledged von Rundstedt as the doyen of the Army leaders, according him the same respect as did the officers and men, he possessed clear reservations about an elderly Field Marshal whose triumphs dated from 1940, and whose personality was immersed in the traditions of the Great General Staff that Hitler so distrusted. Von Rundstedt was the antithesis of those charismatic leaders like Guderian, Dietrich and Rommel whom Hitler preferred; he conducted campaigns and battles from the remoteness of an office, at the end of a telephone while consulting maps. And he did not go out of his way to inspire his men with flashes of dynamic, personal leadership at the front.

Rommel found little that was to his liking, as his report to OKW dated 31 December 1943 showed. The coastal defences were not sufficiently deep or adequately manned, nor were the mobile reserves large enough or positioned 'correctly', close to the coast. Having rejected mobile warfare as a viable strategy in the face of overwhelming air power such as the Allies possessed, he was wedded more closely than ever (as was Hitler) to the need for static defences founded upon concrete fortifications. He wanted infantry localities strongly wired and mined-in, with armoured forces located near at hand, to intervene swiftly and smash enemy penetrations early. He seems to have overlooked the poor quality of the infantry divisions available, and to have underestimated the armoured formations. The policies of von Rundstedt and of Geyr (the commander of Panzer Group West, which was to comprise the mass of Panzer divisions stationed in the west) he rejected as being outmoded. Neither of these officers, as he pointed out, had experienced warfare under the circumstances ruling in the West. Arguable though this was, he found himself in agreement with the generally-held opinion that the enemy was sure to launch the main invasion against the Pas de Calais. Although he was to demand the strengthening of the defences in Normandy (where the invasion would actually come), he was to reject on 5 May a proposal

Right:
*Rommel and
Gerd von
Rundstedt (right).
(Bundesarchiv)*

for a massive reinforcement of that area, and never conceded, until long after the attack had taken place, that Normandy would be other than one of several subsidiary battle zones. Maybe he was deluded by false leads, and even by German conspirators. The fact remains that he was outwitted. Once more, he had failed to calculate the logistic implications of his proposals, and to realize that neither labour nor materials were available in sufficient quantity to satisfy his demands.

The recommendations he made in his report concentrated principally upon the need for vast labour- and material-consuming constructional work, a programme that also occupied the infantry, whose training suffered in consequence. He asked, for example, for 50–100,000,000 mines for the whole western front, a ludicrous demand when only about 1,700,000 were immediately available. And he objected to Ernst Sauckel (Director for the Allocation of Labour) deporting a million French workers to Germany, because this would be ruinous to France and his own plans. When all was said and done, his plan was an enormously upscaled version of standard German defensive practice and not, as Bayerlein has claimed, in "independence of orthodox doctrine and systems". Von Rundstedt approved the con-

cept of trying to hold the enemy on the beaches, but knew that penetrations were bound to be made. He realized the impossibility of accomplishing Rommel's grandiose construction schemes, and appreciated that only a mobile reserve could preserve stability. If Rommel had put as much effort into devising a logistic plan to ensure mobility despite enemy air attack, he might have achieved better results. As it was, his only accomplishment lay in the improvisations carried out (many of them to the credit of subordinates), and the colossal drive he put into ensuring that things got done his way, which contributed to a rise in the soldiers' morale and a renewed belief in the possibility of victory.

On the surface, and apart from matters of detail, Rommel and von Rundstedt appeared in accord. But beneath the surface there was a struggle for supremacy, as Rommel, characteristically, sought to supersede his superior officer, and von Rundstedt (to whom non-General Staff generals such as Rommel were barely persona grata and sometimes referred to as "these people") spasmodically held his own. A primary cause for disagreement was that Hitler, after reading and largely concurring with Rommel's report in January 1944, continued to hold Rommel responsible

Right:
Hans Speidel (centre), Rommel's new chief of staff in replacement of Gause, works with his master. On the left is Generalmajor Feuchtinger, whose 21st Panzer Division was the only one to counterattack on 6 June, 1944. (Bundesarchiv)

directly to OKW. Rommel regarded this as unworkable. While welcoming OKW's intention to treat his Army Group as one for 'special employment', and exercising to the full his privilege as a Field Marshal of direct access to Hitler, he realized too that von Rundstedt as Commander-in-Chief, West, would cramp his style in the same way as had Kesselring. The fact that von Rundstedt appears to have allowed him considerable scope – either out of bored resignation or because it allowed Rommel to expend his immense energy to useful purpose – was not enough. Kesselring would not have permitted it, and von Rundstedt might become difficult over vital issues.

There was, indeed, strong disagreement already between them over the stationing of the central mobile reserve in the region of Paris, despite their agreement over the desirability of defeating the invasion at sea or in the vicinity of the beaches, in order to avoid the need to commit that reserve. This was fundamental in that it brought to a head the whole question as to who really did command in the West, and gave Rommel a pretext to act. He demanded command of First and Fifteenth Armies as well as the GHQ Artillery units and, above all, Panzer Group West. In February, while von Rundstedt was on leave,

he prepared the way for these changes, in conjunction with Jodl. Then, in March, at a conference at which Hitler and von Rundstedt were present, he sprang his surprise and was granted his wish. Von Rundstedt was plainly astonished, and only afterwards submitted a reasoned, written protest to have the decision modified into a typical OKW compromise. Rommel was given control of three of the available Panzer divisions for employment close to the coast, leaving Geyr with four mobile divisions (three of them Panzer) for allocation by von Rundstedt. This effectively reduced von Rundstedt (who was no Kesselring in his determination to retain control) to that of a paternal overseer, stripped of an operational rôle and forbidden to commit reserves without Hitler's permission – left without much power, but still with responsibility for the theatre as a whole, a convenient Army scapegoat if required by the OKW, which still passed orders to Rommel through von Rundstedt.

The results of the differences of policy enunciated by Rommel and von Rundstedt, though distracting, were not as harmful as has sometimes been suggested. Far more damaging was the shortage of resources – which led, for example, to an appalling deficiency of combat formations in the West at

Right:
Mines, concrete and wire – the fibre of static defence upon which Rommel pinned his hopes. (Bundesarchiv)

Above: *Rommel prepares the Atlantic Wall—inspecting his troops and a gun emplacement. (Bundesarchiv)*

Below: German work parties caught by the camera of an Allied aircraft over the beaches. (MacClancy Press)

one period of the early spring. There was a lack of transport; a general inferiority in numbers at almost any time; a crippling inferiority in the air; and, perhaps worst of all, a lack of reliable intelligence about the enemy in almost every department, which reduced the forecasting of hostile intentions to the realms of guesswork. To make matters worse, the enemy, who held the initiative in every respect, was well apprised from a plethora of sources of German deployment, policies and strategy, and could dovetail his deception measures perfectly to suit his own carefully arranged plans. The German chances of success were minimal from the outset, but Rommel could not see it or would not admit it.

As the invasion season drew closer, Rommel's forces were allowed to grow, and he was to be found expressing confidence in the outcome, possibly, of course, because he had finally learnt that to say the opposite was to invite dismissal. His letters to Lu were filled with hope without playing down the threat; even in January he felt the assault could be beaten off and, in May, was rejoicing in a cheering conversation with the Führer. At the end of May, he could count on the services of seven Panzer and thirty-five infantry divisions, with a call upon more from the rest of Europe. But their arrival would be dependent upon the demands of the Italian Front, which cracked open towards the end of May, and of future eventualities in Russia,

Right:
Erwin, Lu and Manfred Rommel at Herrlingen, celebrating her birthday on the eve of the Allied invasion of Normandy. (Popperfoto)

where the usual late-spring pause due to bad weather was in progress. Against him, the Western Allies could be expected to commit a far larger force, but one whose arrival at the front would be conditioned by the rate at which it could be brought in by sea and air — as opposed to rail and road in the German case. In other words, the key to the concentration of forces in the battle area would be transportation and the extent to which movement could be interrupted. These things Rommel allowed to let slide. Although the German air and naval forces were almost incapable of destroying or disrupting enemy transport, and quite powerless to protect their own, a way of moving men and supplies efficiently under the cover of night had not been

fully examined. True, few among those on the higher staffs fully appreciated the danger, but Rommel seems to have done nothing to drive them into seeking a solution, probably because the intricacies of logistics eluded him. As usual, there was divergence of effort within the German forces, brought about by inter-service priorities and prejudices. For example, Goering declined Rommel's request to concentrate the anti-aircraft guns of III Flak Corps to strengthen the anti-tank defences of the coastal areas between the rivers Orne and Vire, because its primary anti-aircraft duties demanded dispersion (and also, no doubt, because Goering disliked Rommel as much as Rommel still disliked anything to do with the Luftwaffe).

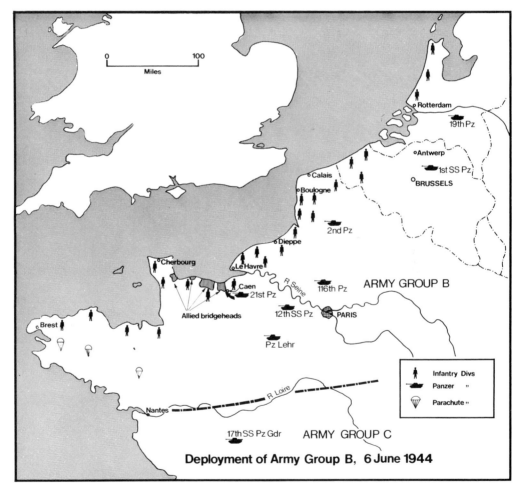

Deployment of Army Group B, 6 June 1944

The deployment of formations within Army Group B on 6 June 1944 shows the alignment of infantry divisions (including parachute units) close to the coasts – the preponderance of numbers in the Pas de Calais – and the location of the Panzer divisions, those belonging to Panzer Group West being 1st SS, 12th SS, 17th

SS Panzer Grenadier (located with Army Group C) and Panzer Lehr. No sooner has the invasion begun than the mobile formations within reach of the expanding beachheads are put into motion, but only the 21st Panzer Division makes a counterattack on the 6th. By the evening of the 7th, three large bridgeheads have become established.

The invasion

By the end of May, only a proportion (sixty-eight per cent in Fifteenth Army, eighteen per cent in Seventh Army) of the measures Rommel had instituted, and tried to urge to completion by untiring visits and conferences, were finished or even in train. None of these measures was sufficient to achieve the purpose. In all too many places, there was no depth; in others work had hardly begun. By that time, too, Speidel, Falkenhausen and Stülpnagel were well advanced in their plans to bring about an armistice in the West when the time was ripe and, by 28 May, had worked out their proposed terms, of which Rommel was cognizant. They hoped (according to Speidel) to put it into action before the invasion began; but in that respect, as in so many others, they were too late. Misled by an incorrect belief that an invasion was not immediately in prospect, because the tides were wrong, Rommel left on 5 June, intending to spend the night with his family at Herrlingen near Ulm and then to see Hitler at Obersalzberg. It is implied by Speidel that Rommel went with the intention of speaking about both the military and political situation prior to the invasion. But Speidel, who for post-war reasons burnished Rommel's reputation, rather overdoes his attempt at painting Rommel as the 'knight above reproach', and is not corroborated by a diary kept by one of Rommel's staff, on his behalf, in which it says that he went to argue the case for a substantial reinforcement of troops, and to underline the manpower and material inferiority of his forces. There was every reason why the political undertones should have been omitted; if he had spoken out, it might well have been the first time ever, and possibly the last. But the meeting was doomed to cancellation. The Allies struck first, beginning their invasion in Normandy (which Hitler alone had guessed as the venue) while Rommel was still at home.

Rommel once wrote that, "It is a mistake to assume that every local commander will make as much of a situation as there is to be made out of it", and that therefore subordinates "must always have to reckon with his (the Commander-in-Chief's) appearance in personal control". It was singularly unfortunate for him that he did not arrive back at his headquarters at La Roche Guyon until 1700 hours, and that his presence at the front was delayed until the next day: by then, any chance he had of making the local commanders implement his intention of destroying the Allied invasion on the beaches had vanished. Naturally, the battle drills detailing the 21st Panzer Division, the nearest mobile element to the invasion area, to intervene, had automatically been put into operation. News of enemy parachute landings had come in at 0100 hours. At 0500 hours, Speidel had authorized the Division to counterattack immediately, and this was repeated by telephone to Rommel at Herrlingen. But the approach of the Division to its attack position was bedevilled by communication delays and conflicting orders, so that when it did at last strike at 1600 hours (and distinguish itself as mounting the only German counterattack of the day), its strength was dispersed, and its purpose foiled by a rapidly-expanding enemy bridgehead. Likewise, after von Rundstedt, at 0400 hours, had ordered the 12th SS Panzer and Panzer Lehr Division towards the parachute landings (two hours before the sea landings began), his orders were countermanded at 0730 hours by Jodl at OKW because Hitler, who was still abed and not to be disturbed, had not given approval. And von Rundstedt, instead of demanding instant connection with Hitler, let it go at that.

If the conspirators are to be believed, the main purpose motivating the defence of the West in the coming weeks was founded upon the need to maintain a demonstrably viable battle front as the essential basis for negotiating credibly with the Western Allies. If that is so, Rommel's every decision and many of his acts must be judged in that light. If he could throw the enemy back into the sea with a co-ordinated counterattack on the 7th, that would be best of all; but, already that day, the British, employing armoured vehicles in the leading waves of the assault (very much in Rommel's style), had seized an area that reached almost as far as Caen. The Americans, in the west of the invasion area, were making progress to link up their initial bridgeheads, after gaining only rather tenuous footholds in the first twenty-four hours because they were short of armour in the assault. Neither on the 7th, while the 21st Panzer Division remained on the defensive and two more Panzer divisions converged on Normandy, nor on the 8th, when Panzer Group West was put in charge of the intended massed counter-stroke, was Rommel's influence strongly to be felt.

Seventh Army, within whose sector the blow had fallen, was indecisive in its reactions, and Rommel, though he was racing from place to place holding discussions, failed to impose any plan of his own upon

anybody. Indeed, although he appreciated that the British would attempt a breakout in the vicinity of Caen, he became far more concerned on the 7th with the security of the Cotentin Peninsula, and it was here that he directed much of his reserves. Totally deprived of the slightest insight into British plans, although fully aware from captured papers of the American intention to capture St. Lô and Cherbourg, he allowed himself to be distracted from concentration upon the stated aim of his pre-invasion strategy – the immediate counterattack on enemy penetrations. As so often in the past, he failed to detect the central strategic issue, and became immersed in tactics. From the outset, he became committed to roping-off the enemy lodgements, and was transfixed by each local threat. Not until the 10th did he and Geyr achieve a state of concentration sufficient to counterattack north of Caen, and even then the three Panzer divisions available were below half strength. The remainder were scattered and pinned down in defensive fighting. But at least Geyr insisted upon attacking, while Rommel wavered and showed preference for a new plan, which would have delayed a start. Yet no attack materialized, because von Geyr's headquarters was heavily bombed from the air that

evening, his operations staff wiped out, he himself wounded, and central control eliminated – just at the time when fresh enemy attacks made it imperative to switch the assault troops to defensive tasks. This they accomplished with deadly and economic efficiency, giving little ground. But the decisive moment was past.

The long report Rommel sent to his superiors on 10 June was on the lines of the exculpatory papers he had written before, comprising a review of events, an outline of the action he hoped to take and an extensive dissertation upon the reasons for failure in implementing what had originally been intended. As usual, he attributed the enemy success to their overwhelming air and material superiority, a conclusion that could not be denied. But his latest scheme for attacking the Americans was vetoed by Hitler, who demanded he tackle the British. They were fully in agreement that troops should not yet be taken from the Pas de Calais, contrary to Speidel's inference in his post-war book that Army Group B thought it unlikely that the enemy would land to the north of the River Seine. The absence of a German counterattack had handed the initiative to General Montgomery, whose task it was to co-ordinate the Allied battle under

Above:
*Germans
surrendering on
Utah beach, as
the American
landing gains a
firm foothold.
(MacClancy
Press)*

Eisenhower, rather as it was Rommel's to co-ordinate the German effort under von Rundstedt. But, whereas Hitler persisted in bombarding his commanders with a barrage of orders and exhortations, Montgomery was given a free rein to orchestrate strategy his way. From now on, he dictated the terms of battle, and Rommel danced to his tune again, while making not the slightest headway in convincing Hitler of the coming disaster. Keitel and Jodl, however, were beginning to appreciate what was in train, even though they were remote from the front. At last, on the 16th, they were able to persuade Hitler to go to France to hear von Rundstedt and Rommel, hoping to achieve a revision of German policy to the extent of persuading Hitler to allow a radical thinning-out of troops in all other sectors (except Fifteenth Army) in order to concentrate everything upon throwing the enemy out of Normandy.

The temper of the meeting in the command bunker at Margival on 17 June is perhaps exaggerated by Speidel (who was there) to give an impression that Rommel led the opposition to Hitler and that von Rundstedt merely lent support. Speidel, indeed, is suspect in much that he claimed, post-war, to have done. His testimony was composed to satisfy the post-war political needs of his country and, in this, he put expediency before history. Von Rundstedt, on the other hand, has written that he made concrete proposals of his own. It is much more likely, in the light of events and the record of that meeting, that Hitler allowed little room for discussion, and merely treated them to a characteristic call for loyalty based upon the promised power of secret weapons to come (following the first V–1 flying bombs, which had been launched from the Pas de Calais on the 12th). He imposed an implacable demand that ground should not be given up anywhere. Maybe Rommel did protest, but to his subordinates he displayed an absolutely immovable determination to obey the Führer's command, as did Speidel in backing up Rommel's orders. As Chester Wilmot puts it so well in The Struggle for Europe, "In despair, or subservience, Rommel insisted upon literal compliance and gave no quarter to those who demurred" – a judgement that certainly falls in line with the man's attested character. On the 17th, they came away empty-handed and, on the 18th, Hitler returned in haste to Germany after a wayward V–1 landed close to his refuge. That day, too, Rommel described the conference to Lu, implying that it was the officers of OKW who were in need of education, putting the blame

Left:
*Camouflaged
Panther tanks on
their way to
counterattack
after the invasion
has achieved its
first lodgement.
(Bundesarchiv)*
Below left:
*Young German
infantrymen
crowd the engine
deck of a Panther
on the way to the
attack. Their
efforts, however,
would be
fruitless.
(Bundesarchiv)*
Below right:
*Knocked out US
M3 tank-
destroyers at St.
Lo. (Mac-
Clancy Press)*

on others and ending (inexplicably, were he honest): "We've got a lot of stuff coming up. The Führer was very cordial and in a good humour. He realizes the gravity of the situation ..." Yet both Speidel and Günther Blumentritt, who was also present, recall that Rommel had tried to raise the issue of the war's continuance, and Hitler had told him to mind his own business.

In this strange twilight mood of simulated and contradictory attitudes not one of which, in retrospect, seems reliable, most of the participants were unable to cope with a situation that shifted relentlessly towards the point of uncontrollability. On the 20th, Rommel expressed satisfaction with the state of affairs, but the campaign was moving towards collapse. Cherbourg fell on 30 June and, in the interim period, the British deepened their sector of the bridgehead to the west of Caen. Even if the German defences did exact a heavy toll and restrict enemy penetrations, this only postponed the inevitable disaster. When, on the 28th, Rommel and his senior commanders congratulated themselves upon a defensive success and looked forward next day to the large Panzer offensive for which they had yearned and upon which the fate of the enemy bridgehead now hinged, they failed to create the meticulously-

planned assault needed. The elements of eight Panzer divisions, three of them severely reduced in strength from the previous fighting, the others, newly arrived and by no means complete, had been drawn against the British incursion and wended their way into battle as the result of a series of improvised actions brought about in response to the need to relieve further British pressure. In the absence of von Rundstedt and Rommel, who were en route on the 28th to see Hitler in Berchtesgaden, and of the commander of Seventh Army (Friedrich Dollmann) who committed suicide just prior to the attack, there was failure. As with Operation 'Capri' at Medenine, the Panzer divisions stumbled against British defences that had been forewarned. They met their fate before a wall of gunfire. As at Medenine, they hardly managed to reach the ranks of guns and tanks drawn up in the hedgerows by Sir Richard O'Connor, the British Corps commander involved (whom Rommel had rounded up in April 1941, and who had escaped to torment his captor).

The Berchtesgaden meeting, called at short notice by Hitler for the 29th at the request of the two Field Marshals, may have had its origin, to some extent, in a decision of 25 June by the conspirators to hasten the execution of

their plans – though this is unlikely. Rommel was inflexibly against assassination of the Führer, but he did not dissuade the conspirators (even though he may have been given the impression that he did), because he was not in control. He preferred that the scheme to remove Hitler from his post should coincide with an armistice in the West; he wanted to give Hitler one more chance to face the facts and intended, according to Speidel, to deliver an ultimatum. There is no evidence, and certainly no written record, to say that he ever actually mustered up courage to take this line direct to Hitler's face, although there is plausibility in his realization that there was nothing more to be gained by submissiveness to Hitler. He claims that he deliberately went forward on a collision course, but there is no evidence of a real collision. That there was disagreement in the meeting is likely, but it was only von Rundstedt who made this apparent in the aftermath; outright vituperation there obviously was not. There was even a concession by Hitler, who, having insisted that ground must not be surrendered to the enemy, seemingly abandoned future offensive operations in the West. Far more important was the move made by Rommel after his return to France, when he read the latest assessments by Paul Hausser (the new commander of Seventh Army) and Geyr, who was back at duty after a rapid recovery from his wound. They recommended withdrawal from Caen, where the British pressure was becoming intolerable. Rommel's headquarters assented to this, and sent a copy of Geyr's report to von Rundstedt, who endorsed it. Rommel may or may not have concurred – that was not stated – but the responsibility was his, even though the matter seems to have been presented to OKW in such a way as to make it appear to have come only from Geyr and von Rundstedt, not from Rommel. Indeed, Guderian, who as Inspector General of Panzer Troops (and later Chief of Staff[*]) saw much of Hitler and was closely conversant with the debate over employment of armour in Normandy, makes it clear that Rommel remained persona grata from a military point of view with Hitler until the end, and that it was only over Rommel's involvement with non-military matters that he fell out of favour.

Such outright disobedience to Hitler usually received its own reward, as must surely have been expected on this occasion.

---

[*] Albert Speer has recorded that not until Guderian became Chief of Staff in July were there outbursts against Hitler – and not seriously until January 1945.

At 1740 hours on 1 July came Hitler's signal confirming that no withdrawal was permissible; a few hours later von Rundstedt was dismissed, and Günther von Kluge nominated to replace him. But, although everybody expected Rommel to be sacked as well, strangely, the dismissal did not come: that may have been, as so often before, too hot a political 'potato' to handle, but it also indicated that Rommel was probably still in Hitler's favour and that he had not protested strongly. Now, von Kluge arrived and told Rommel (as in 1941 he had told Guderian in Russia, just prior, with Hitler's concurrence, to sacking the latter) that "he would have to become accustomed to obeying orders". Von Kluge was another of those officers who, in the past, had shown unfaltering loyalty to, and belief in, the Führer, despite his professed dislike for the man and his long involvement with the conspirators. But when Caen fell on the 9th (after a truly massive and unprecedented bombardment by 467 RAF heavy bombers dropping 2,560 tons of bombs), and the situation at the front deteriorated, von Kluge was to change in his mind. On the 3rd, Rommel had sent Hitler another exculpatory letter setting out the reasons for failure in Normandy, but without making proposals or recommendations, and on the 15th he prepared a stronger memorandum (later endorsed by von Kluge, who had now come to agree with Rommel's assessment of the situation) in which he pointed out that "the unequal struggle is approaching its end. It is urgently necessary for the proper [political] conclusion to be drawn from this situation." Speidel says that the word "political" was originally drafted by Rommel but deleted, since it would drive Hitler into a rage and prevent his "sensible reflection". He adds, too, that Rommel remarked, "I have given him his last chance. If he does not take it we will act." The fact remains that this oft-quoted letter was only one of a series of pessimistic military documents produced at this time, and it was not sent to Hitler at once. There is no doubt that Rommel did now intend to act eccentrically, as was his habit in moments of despondency, and that even if his interest in the plotters' schemes was initially minimal, it now grew. But the measure of his determination in this direction is impossible to gauge.

Contact with the main conspirators had been made again on the 9th through Caesar von Hofacker, a fellow Württemberger acting on von Stülpnagel's instructions, and Rommel had told him that the front in the West would only hold for another three weeks – a most accurate estimate. At that, the conspirators decided to go ahead. In the meantime, Rommel took the opportunity to sound out as many officers as possible, and to test their reactions if he called for a local cessation of the fighting. According to Speidel, Rommel even took Sepp Dietrich of the Waffen SS into his confidence, and received a reply that satisfied him that this redoubtable Nazi-sponsored officer would not make difficulties. But the evidence in favour of this is unreliable.

Throughout the 13th, 14th and 15th, Rommel was constantly at the battle front, a period in which the British and Americans were engaged in preparations for their culminating breakout attempt. They maintained pressure at all points in well-rewarded endeavours to prevent the Germans from relieving the Panzer divisions that had been drawn into the front line, and they succeeded in preventing the shift of those divisions from the Caen area to south of St. Lô, where the Americans were destined to make their big effort. Meanwhile, in Germany, the conspirators advanced anxiously with their scheme. If fate had been kind to them it would have been activated on the 11th: von Stauffenberg took his bomb to a conference, but neither Goering nor Himmler were present, and this decided him against the attempt, since he needed them dead as well as Hitler. Again he tried on the 15th, but this time Hitler left before the bomb could be set off.

By the time von Stauffenberg found himself presented with the opportunity to detonate the bomb in Hitler's presence on 20 July (even though Goering and Himmler were not present), Rommel had been struck off the list of participants. Forewarned by air reconnaissance of a large build-up of British armour to the east of Caen on the night of the 16th/17th, he had spent the morning of the 17th in that sector, checking defensive arrangements. In the afternoon, on his way from the headquarters of Panzer Group West, his car was attacked by British fighters and its driver killed. He was thrown out in the ensuing crash and was severely concussed and lacerated. He would take no part in the heavy fighting that would check the British initial attempt at Caen on the 18th; nor would he be in command to meet the all-enveloping Allied attacks on the 25th, which would lead to the collapse he had foretold. For Rommel, the fighting soldier, the battles were over. The final reckoning would not be long delayed.

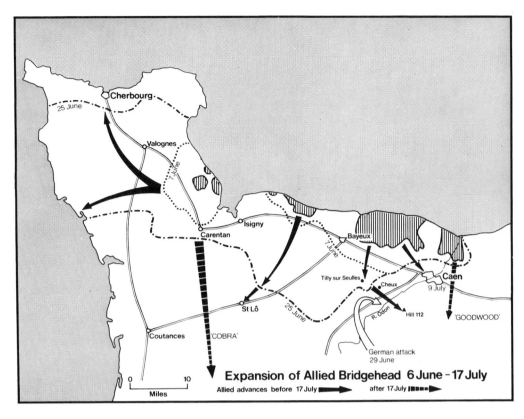

The expansion of the Allied incursion is shown by stages, from the final linking-up of all three bridgeheads on 11 June, to the sealing off (by 18 June), the capture of the Cotentin Peninsula by 26 June, and the gradual envelopment of Caen leading up to its fall on 9 July. Against this is to be set the arrival of Panzer divisions, their solitary ill-coordinated 'massed' offensive to the west of Caen on 29 June, and their steady committal to holding the line (where the weakened infantry divisions are failing) instead of being extricated for use in a more mobile rôle. Also shown are the Allied offensives planned to begin after Rommel's accident on 17 July.

Right:
Rommel with Sepp Dietrich of the SS. As commander of I SS Panzer Corps, Dietrich was loyalty and determination personified; as a supporter of Rommel's defections, his part is insufficiently documented for credibility. (Bundesarchiv)

15

The Martyr

The story of Rommel's battles and campaigns ends on 17 July 1944. He had but three months to live, struggling for life in hospital, and then making a remarkable recovery that spoke highly of a wiry constitution strengthened by abstemious living. Part of his convalescence he spent writing up his memoirs and, by October, he was nursing hopes that he might again be employed. But the train of events that had been set in motion by his involvement with the bomb plotters, whose attempt had misfired on 20 July, moved inexorably to settle his fate. Von Stülpnagel, thoroughly implicated as a conspirator, tried, but failed, to commit suicide; in a delirium from his self-inflicted injuries, he cried out the name "Rommel". While under torture, von Hofacker, it was said, mentioned Rommel's complicity in addition to that of von Kluge and Speidel. Von Kluge committed suicide in August, while Speidel cleverly convinced his accusers of an innocence that was anything but complete, in the process seeming to implicate Rommel. The dossier was passed to Keitel, who showed it to Hitler. No longer had Rommel a friend at Court. It was ironic that he, who in the past had been adept at shifting responsibility upon others, was now to be the victim of the same practice – and fatally so. And yet, while Hitler was convinced of Rommel's guilt, and no more inclined to spare him than he had the other plotters, he saved him from the punishment inflicted upon the others, who died in the most horrific manner. The idol of the people and the Army could not be vilified and degraded as were the other officers who had been brought before the special tribunal and condemned to barbarous deaths. It was Rommel's unhappy destiny to be asked to commit suicide by poison, to simulate an honourable death as the result of his wounds. At an elaborate State funeral, von Rundstedt, on Hitler's behalf, read the oration.

Thus was the legend of Rommel preserved, until the arrival of peace brought an end to censorship, and the German people and the rest of the world came to hear as fact what, until then, had been but rumour. The shock effect of these revelations, coming as they did when the war was over, were, in the first instance, of only passing interest to most people. For the time being, people dearly wished to forget about the war, and concentrate upon peace and reconstruction. It was not until the threat of war reappeared towards 1949 that there was a sudden large-scale reawakening of interest in the history of the previous struggle – and, with it, a revival of the Rommel legend.

The need to resurrect Rommel was largely linked to the demands of Western defence. Once more, a German Army was needed as a vital element in helping to make Western Europe safe against a possible Soviet invasion. But the prospect of reviving German militarism was abhorrent to the mass of people (Germans among them) who could not forget past horrors. To permit the political acceptance of new German armed forces, many safeguards had to be erected, and not least among these was the creation of an officer corps that would be kept well under civilian control, and which would be inspired by what came to be known as 'emblematic figures'. The Germans looked around for inspirational figureheads from the past who would be regarded by most people – the Germans and their allies – as symbolic of everything chivalrous, and who could be regarded as the antithesis of Nazi-tainted generals. Had the opinion of General Heinrich von Vietinghoff been known and accepted, it might have been different: for, asked which of the German commanders of the Second World War he would most like to see filling the rôle of a Hindenburg, he emphatically replied, "None, I trust." As it was, expediency ruled, and Rommel was chosen—suitably cleansed of his blemishes, and polished so as to be politically presentable. To the future Bundeswehr, as well as to the world, he was displayed as a shining example of what the modern German officer should be. Hans Speidel, who was to be the Army's Commander-in-Chief when it was reformed in 1955, published a book in 1949 that spoke only of the best in Rommel, and cast him as a convinced anti-Nazi who, in the end, repudiated Hitler. Authors in many lands took up the theme with articles and biographies that were favourable to Rommel's reputation, and which played down or ignored the unattractive side of his character and performance. His *Papers*, carefully edited by his son and Captain Basil Liddell Hart, were published and extremely well received. Old comrades joined in by extolling his triumphs and playing-down his errors, Kesselring standing almost alone in his criticism of the Württemberger. In German barracks, portraits of Rommel were prominently displayed. Films were made about him, and British, French and American audiences flocked to watch images of the man who had so often defeated them. Only a hero's clear complexion was shown; the 'warts' were charmed away.

It is therefore disappointing (and, to some, a shock) to discover the blotches on Rommel's character, and to be forced to face up to the difficulty of portraying the disagreeable aspects of a man who has been built into a paragon. The political implications alone are daunting, for there are those in Germany who, while admitting to the truth of Rommel's failings in private, would die rather than say so in public. So what now of the soldier and the man?

The points to his credit are plainly visible. He was a fine tactician and a splendid leader of men. His feats in the First World War would have won acclaim even if he had not gone to so much trouble in acquiring his Pour le Mérite and subsequently publicizing his exploits. The lower ranks followed him out of admiration, but scarcely lovingly, well knowing the perils into which he could lead them. To them, he was just "Rommel"—he never acquired an affectionate nickname. They responded to his immense courage and rough ways, seeming to sympathize with him in his determination to overcome the barriers placed in his way by the enemy and, at times, his own side. Perhaps the rank and file identified themselves with him because he stood apart from the old, upper caste of officers, and was therefore more closely in accord with the revolutionary Nazis in whom so many of them believed. This way, indeed, he could be rated as a good soldier, because he complied with the dictates of the elected government.

Undeniably, he possessed a fine sensitivity for detecting an opponent's weaknesses, and rarely was this better demonstrated than during the 1940 campaign, when he instantly recognized signs of a fatal uncertainty among the French. Easy as it is to criticize the risks he took while commanding the 7th Panzer Division, it must be admitted that they were justified by the enemy's apparent ineptitude. Similarly, he spotted the British weakness at the beginning of his first desert campaign in 1941, during the riposte to Gazala in January 1942, and at Kasserine in February 1943. But, even in connection with these battles, and certainly when discussing many of the later ones, one must have reservations about his qualities as a commander of larger formations. From the moment he rose to Corps commander, the limitations in his make-up—above all the intellectual deficiencies—became more noticeable.

When assessing Rommel as a higher-level commander, it is as important to evaluate the quality of his enemy as it is to ponder the

contribution made by his close colleagues – while never forgetting the excel-
lence of the troops and equipment provided
for his use. Until he was stopped by Auchinleck at El Alamein in July 1942, he had been
extremely fortunate in being confronted, for
the most part, by a badly-generalled enemy.
Incompetent handling of British forces in
April and June 1941, and the initial errors by
the commander of Eighth Army during Operation 'Crusader' in November 1941 were in no
way caused by pressure on Rommel's part.
The primary British setbacks were almost
invariably the products of faulty battle plans,
which were all the more disastrously exposed
because of Rommel's talent for spotting

weaknesses and exploiting them to the
full – except, that is, during Operation
'Crusader', the battle in which, through obstinacy, he refused to recognize the threat to
his Army and, through miscalculation, threw
away a tactical victory that had been won by
the excellent handling of his troops by subordinate officers with a grasp of the situation
superior to his own. Repeatedly, it was
Crüwell, and on one celebrated occasion
Westphal, who made the vital decisions,
while Rommel was pursuing an incorrect
strategic line. Ironically, it was their judicious handling of tactics that further enhanced
Rommel's reputation, as he gathered glory by
a series of flamboyant exercises that were, for

the most part, irrelevant to the battle and certainly no rôle demanded of a corps commander, let alone the commander of an allied army. Paradoxically, it was this same reputation that impressed his opponents to the extent that, for many battles to come, the British (and later the Americans) would miss their opportunities for fear of what Rommel might do. Vitally important, therefore, was Goebbels' part in fostering the charismatic aura of this heroic figure; to him and his scriptwriters, unwittingly aided and abetted by their opposite numbers in the Allied camp, goes much credit for winning the desert victories.

But charisma, which enhances the powers of leadership in battle, does not in itself win campaigns; nor does it compensate for lack of outstanding intellect or logistic insight when it comes to the formulation of strategy. Rommel's deficiencies in these spheres are too obvious to demand further elucidation, but their presence is sufficient to relegate him to a place in the lists of great commanders below those such as Guderian, Kesselring, Manstein and Montgomery. Nevertheless, it was that very charisma that carried him to the top in Goebbels' and Hitler's estimation. Indeed, without their wholehearted support, it is very unlikely that Rommel would have risen to command a regiment, let alone an army group – for the orthodox Army hierarchy (and with some justice) was set against him from the beginning, and continued to object to his elevation to the bitter end.

It is not only as a soldier, therefore, that Rommel must be regarded, but also as a political figurehead. To the Nazis, he was a valuable symbol of the Army's association with the Party, one general who appeared, at least, to be a willing tool of theirs. In fairness to Rommel, it must be stated that he probably fell into collaboration with the Nazis because of his political naivety. Very likely, he was duped, as were most of his contemporaries. On the other hand, there is nothing to suggest that he strenuously resisted Goebbels' blandishments, or to deny the assertion that, but for the Propaganda Minister's intervention in 1934, Rommel's career would never have 'taken off'. It was almost as of routine thereafter that Goebbels eulogized his hero; that in 1940 he pushed him to the heights of national adulation; and that he saved him in 1942 and twice more in 1943 when the Führer's patronage was in doubt. It was merely a strange irony that, in the final dénouement, when Goebbels was bound to desert Rommel for his ostensible disloyalty to Hitler, the Field Marshal was, to all intents and purposes, innocent of serious intrigue against Hitler's life.

What is to be said of a soldier who seems to have been obsessed by his career to the almost total exclusion of other interests? Dedication is, of course, a virtue that the profession of arms thrives upon. At all levels, a high degree of commitment, besides competence, loyalty and self-sacrifice, is demanded of an officer. These attributes Rommel had. And yet, on a disquieting number of occasions, he seems to have put personal ambition first and to have laid claims to achievements that belonged to others or should have been shared with them. Too often, he ill-treated or abused close colleagues and subordinates; too frequently, he conspired against his superiors; and, on too many occasions, he sought to find scapegoats rather than shoulder the blame himself. Kesselring's disapproval of Rommel, motivated by personal distaste though it may have been, was not without cause: the Field Marshal from Württemberg was, to use an old-fashioned term, something of a 'cad'.

But, it will be asked, are not ruthlessness and guile attributes with which the successful commander must be fully equipped? The emphatic answer is "Yes" – providing that they are not used to excess, and that he is also in possession of all-round technical competence, sound judgement and the ability to acquire and retain the co-operation of his peers. Leadership is a finely balanced art, which embodies insight into human nature and the ability to get on well with all kinds of people. Its implementation at the rarefied levels of command calls for these qualities in large measure – and it is because Rommel fell short in these requirements that he was eventually ruined. It is not too much to suggest that, if it had not been widely known that Rommel had the Führer's ear, he would have been disposed of far sooner than was the case (probably no later than the summer of 1941, when Halder was feeling thoroughly disenchanted with Rommel's handling of the Afrika Korps). By the time the stakes were at their highest, in the summer of 1944, there was nobody left on his side, however. By then, his behaviour had made him too many enemies, and not even Goebbels could come to his aid. In the end, he who had prospered from the favour granted by patrons might well have repeated the biblical quotation of a famous British soldier, the Earl of Strafford, when his fate was announced: "Put not your trust in princes, nor in the son of man, in whom there is no help."

Select Bibliography

Blumenson, M. *Salerno to Cassino*.
Department of Army, Washington DC,
1969
*The U.S. Army in World War II: break out
and pursuit*. Department of Army,
Washington DC, 1961

Bradford, G. R. *Armour Camouflage and
Markings: North Africa, 1940–1943*. Arms
& Armour Press, London, 1974; G. R.
Bradford, Ontario, Canada, 1971

Brown, A. Cave *Bodyguard of Lies*. W. H.
Allen, London, 1976; Harper Row, New
York, 1975

Chamberlain, P., Doyle, H. and Jentz, T. L.
*Encyclopedia of German Tanks of World
War Two*. Arms & Armour Press, 1978;
Arco, New York, 1978

Chamberlain, P. and Ellis, C. *British and
American Tanks of World War II*. Arms
and Armour Press, London, 1969; Arco,
New York, 1969

Churchill, Sir W. *The Second World War*. 6
vols. Cassell, London, 1948–54;
Houghton Mifflin Co., Boston, 1948–53

Ciano, G. *Ciano Diaries, 1939–43*.
Heinemann, London, 1946; Doubleday,
New York, 1946

Dönitz, K. *Memoirs: 10 years and 20 days*.
Weidenfeld & Nicholson, London, 1959;
The World Publishing Co., New York,
1959

Douglas-Home, C. *Rommel*. Weidenfeld &
Nicholson, London, 1973; Saturday
Review Press, 1973

Ellis, L. F. *Victory in the West*, Vol. 1.
HMSO, London, 1962
*The War in France and Flanders,
1939–1940*. HMSO, London. 1953

Garland, A., and Smyth, H. *Sicily and the
Surrender of Italy*. Department of Army,
Washington DC, 1965

Goebbels, J. F. *Diaries*. Edited by L. P.
Lochner. Hamish Hamilton, London,
1948; Doubleday, New York, 1948

Guderian, H. *Panzer Leader*. Joseph,
London, 1952

Halder, F. *The Halder Diaries*. 7 vols.
Infantry Journal Press, Washington DC,
1950
Kriegstagebuch. 3 vols. Kohlhammer,
Stuttgart, 1962–64

Harrison, G. A. *Cross-Channel Attack*.
Department of Army, Washington DC,
1951

Hogg, I. V. *British & American Artillery of
World War 2*. Arms & Armour Press,
London, 1978; Hippocrene, New York,
1978

Howe, G. F. *Northwest Africa: seizing the
initiative in the West*. Department of
Army, Washington DC, 1957

Irving, D. *The Trail of the Fox*. Weidenfeld
& Nicholson, London, 1977. US edition:
*The Trail of the Fox: The Search for the
True Field Marshal Rommel*. Dutton, New
York, 1977

Kahn, D. *The Codebreakers: the story of
secret writing*. Weidenfeld & Nicholson,
London, 1968; Macmillan, New York,
1967

Kesselring, A. *Memoirs*. Kimber, London,
1963. US edition: *Kesselring: a soldier's
record*. Morrow, New York, 1954

Lewin, R. *Rommel as Military Commander*.
Batsford, London, 1968

Macdonald, C. *The Mighty Endeavour:
American Armed Forces in the European
Theater in World War II*. Oxford
University Press, New York, 1969

Macksey, K. *The Crucible of Power*.
Hutchinson, London, 1969
Guderian, Panzer General. Macdonald,
London, 1975. US edition: *Guderian:
Creator of the Blitzkrieg*. Stein & Day,
New York, 1976
Kesselring, The Making of the Luftwaffe.
Batsford, London, 1978; David McKay,
New York, 1978

Manteuffel, H. von *7 Panzer Division Im Zweiten Veltkrieg*. Traditionverband, 1965

Mellenthin, F. W. von *Panzer Battles, 1939–1945: a study of the employment of armour in the Second World War*. Cassell, London, 1955; University of Oklahoma, 1956

Playfair, I. S. O. *The Mediterranean and Middle East*. 5 vols. HMSO, London, 1954–73

Purnell's History of the Second World War. Edited by B. Pitt. Purnell, London, 1966

Rommel, E. *Infanterie Greift an*. Translated by G. Kiddle. US Infantry Journal, 1944 *The Rommel Papers*. Edited by B. H. Liddell Hart; translated by P. Findlay. Collins, London, 1953; Harcourt Brace, New York, 1953

Schmidt, H. W. *With Rommel in the Desert*. Harrap, London, 1951

Speidel, H. *We Defended Normandy*. Jenkins, London, 1951. US edition: *Invasion 1944: Rommel and the Normandy Campaign*. Translated by T. Smith. Regnery, Chicago, 1950

The Trial of the Major War Criminals Before the International Military Tribunal, Nuremberg, 14 November 1945 – 10 October 1946. 42 vols. International Military Tribunal, 1949

Warlimont, W. *Inside Hitler's Headquarters, 1939–1945*. Weidenfeld & Nicholson, London, 1964; Praeger, New York, 1964

Westphal, S. *Erinnerüngen*. Hase und Koehler, Mainz, 1975

Wheeler-Bennett, J. *The Nemesis of Power: The German Army in Politics, 1918–1945*. Macmillan, London, 1953; St. Martin's Press, New York, 1954

Wilmot, C. *The Struggle for Europe*. Collins, London, 1952; Harper, New York, 1952

Winterbotham, F. W. *The Ultra Secret*. Weidenfeld & Nicholson, London, 1974

Young, D. *Rommel*. Collins, London, 1950. US edition: *Rommel, the desert fox*. Harper, New York, 1950

Index